Close Encounters with the Cold War

Personal Battles with Evil Empires, Cold Warriors and Others

Other Books by Richard Hermann

Mother's Century: A Survivor, Her People and Her Times
(Persimmon Alley Press, 2018)

Encounters: Ten Appointments with History
(Persimmon Alley Press, 2017)

21st Century Legal Career Series (sponsored by the National Association for Law Placement). 18 booklets (2017-2018).

The Hidden Legal Job Market: Law Jobs Aren't Always Where You Think They Are (DecisionBooks [an imprint of Lawyer Avenue Press], 2016)

Manufacturing Business and the Law
(American Bar Association, 2015)

Practicing Law in Small-Town America
(American Bar Association, 2013)

From Lemons to Lemonade in the New Legal Job Market: Winning Job Search Strategies for Entry-Level Attorneys
(DecisionBooks [an imprint of Lawyer Avenue Press], 2012)

Landing a Federal Legal Job: Solving the U.S. Government Job Market (American Bar Association, 2011)

Managing Your Legal Career: Best Practices for Creating the Career You Want - Runner-up, Benjamin Franklin Award for the best career book of 2010 by the Independent Book Publishers Association. (American Bar Association, 2010).

The Lawyer's Guide to Job Security: How to Keep Your Job – and Make the Most of It – in Good Times and Bad
(Kaplan Publishing & Simon and Schuster, 2010)

The Lawyer's Guide to Finding Success in Any Job Market
(Kaplan Publishing and Simon and Schuster, 2009)

JD Preferred! 600-Plus Things You Can Do With a Law Degree (Other Than Practice Law)
(Federal Reports, Inc., 1993, 1994, 1996)

The ALJ Handbook: The Insider's Guide to Becoming a Federal Administrative Law Judge
(Federal Reports, Inc., 1993, 1994)

The 110 Biggest Mistakes Job Hunters Make (And How to Avoid Them)
(Federal Reports Inc., 1993, 1996)

Close Encounters with the Cold War

Personal Battles with Evil Empires, Cold Warriors and Others

Richard L. Hermann

Persimmon Alley Press
Arlington, VA

www.persimmonalleypress.com

Copyright © 2020 by Richard L. Hermann

All rights reserved. No part of this book may be reproduced in any form or by any electronic or mechanical means, including information storage and retrieval systems, without written permission from the author, except in the case of a reviewer, who may quote brief passages embodied in critical articles or in a review.

Published by Persimmon Alley Press
Cover design by David E. Manuel

All images and cover photographs are public domain, author-owned or fair use.

Library of Congress Control Number: 2020936723

ISBN: 978-0-9991366-4-5

To Anne, who has been a captive audience for these tales

for almost as long as the first Cold War endured.

Contents

	Page
Introduction	1
Chapter 1. Dodging the Big One	5
Chapter 2. Plane Spotting	16
Chapter 3. Gimme Shelter	26
Chapter 4. An Enormity of Warheads	36
Chapter 5. The Wrong Direction	43
Chapter 6. Spasiba (Спутник), Sputnik	49
Chapter 7. American Apogee	60
Chapter 8. Channeling Vienna	62
Chapter 9. G.I. Joe College	84
Chapter 10. Just the Basics	94
Chapter 11. Boomer Bomber	119
Chapter 12. Czeching In	141
Chapter 13. Back in the World	148
Chapter 14. Puzzled at the Palace . . . and Beyond	160
Chapter 15. Task Force Tasks	197
Chapter 16. Health Effects	203
Chapter 17. The Spy in the 'Hood	238
Epilogue. Takeaways	243
Appendix A. Chilling with the Coldest Warriors	271
Appendix B. Measuring Radiation Exposure	297
Acknowledgements	299
Bibliography	301
About the Author	311

Images

	Page
VE-Day Celebration in Toronto, Canada (Public Domain)	5
Life in an Iron Lung (U.S. Centers for Disease Control and Prevention)	9
1950s School Children Ducking and Covering (Library of Congress)	10
Bert and the Monkey (youtube.com)	11
HBomb: The Mother of All Mushroom Clouds (Public Domain)	13
On the Lookout (Old Orange County Courthouse Museum)	16
Ground Observer Corps Recruiting Poster (Public Domain)	17
Ground Observer Corps volunteer, 1956 (US Air Force)	18
GOC Recruiting Billboard (Public Domain)	19
Soviet Tu95 "Bear" Bomber (National Archives)	20
Ground Observer Corps Pin (Public Domain)	21
America's First Three Lines of Defense (National Defence of Canada)	21
Canandaigua, NY High School Track (Author's Collection)	22
Track Runners at Philadelphia's Franklin Field (yalebulldogs.com)	25
KaBOOM! (Public Domain)	26
Scene from Dr. Strangelove, 1964	27
A HighEnd Fallout Shelter (Wikipedia)	28
Danger: Radiation Symbol (Public Domain)	29
Main Street USA (Canandaigua, NY) (Public Domain)	30
The Ubiquity of Fallout -Map (Public Domain)	32
Encouraging Boy Scouts to Self-Destruct (Boy's Life Magazine)	33
Seneca Army Depot Igloo (Public Domain)	36
Seneca Army Depot Bunkers (Public Domain)	38
The Soviet "Tsar Bomba" detonation (Wikipedia)	39
The Spectacular Seneca White Deer (Public Domain)	42
The Brandenburg Gate, Berlin (Public Domain)	45
Canandaigua VA Medical Center (Public Domain)	47
Mao Tse-tung, Josef Stalin, Walter Ulbricht (TheWilson Center)	48
Sputnik: The Dawn of the Space Age (Public Domain)	50
Laika, the First Dog in Space (Hungarian Stamp—Author's Collection)	51
The NASA Logo (Public Domain)	53
Official Havana Sugar Kings Logo (Twitter.com)	55
Fidel at the Exhibition Game (Wikipedia)	55
The Unisphere at the New YorkWorld's Fair (Wikipedia)	61

Images (cont.)

	Page
Khrushchev Misreads Kennedy in Vienna (Public Domain)	62
Schönbrunn Palace (Wikimedia Commons)	63
Khrushchev and Nixon (Wikipedia)	64
White House State Dinner (Wikipedia)	65
The U2 Spy Plane (History.com - Public Domain)	67
The SR71 "Blackbird" (Wikipedia)	68
Castro and Che Guevara Enter Havana, January 1, 1959 (Wikipedia)	69
First Presidential Debate, September 26, 1960 (tutorialspoint.com)	70
The Bay of Pigs, Cuba (History.com)	70
Khrushchev and Kennedy (researchgate.net)	75
Divided Vietnam (alphahistory.com)	77
Destroying a Country in Order to Save It (Wikipedia)	80
The Freshmen Arrive on the Old Campus (Yale University)	84
Bust of Yale Track Coach Bob Giegengack (Author Collection)	86
Tamara and Irina Press (genderverificationinsports.com)	87
First Lady Lady Bird Johnson (National Park Service – Public Domain)	89
Gene McCarthy and Bobby Kennedy, 1968 (Wikipedia—Public Domain)	91
White House Cabinet Room Meeting, Feb. 9, 1968 (Wikipedia)	93
Army Recruiting Poster (Library of Congress – Public Domain)	94
Echo (The Author's) Company at Fort Dix, January 1969 (U.S. Army)	96
Former Main Entrance to Fort Dix (U.S. Army – Public Domain)	98
Mike and Me (US Department of Defense – Public Domain)	103
The Rifle Range (U.S. Army – Public Domain)	105
LearnWhile You Earn (A Pittance) (U.S. Army – Public Domain)	106
Trainees Duking It Out with Pugil Sticks (U.S. Army – Public Domain)	110
The SADM, America's "Backpack" AtomicWeapon (U.S. Army)	119
MADM Component Parts (Public Domain)	120
Boris and Natasha (Wikipedia)	122
Oberammergau (Wikimedia)	124
Warner Barracks (U.S. Army)	132
Map of West Germany (Wikimedia Commons)	134
Alexander Dubcek (Austrian National Library)	141
The Crushing of Prague Spring (The Central Intelligence Agency)	143
Charles Bridge (Author Collection and Sergey Ashmarin, Wikimedia)	147
Ruins of the SovietWar Memorial Column (Author's Collection)	147

Images (cont.)

	Page
The New School for Social Research (Wikimedia)	149
Irmgard Möller - German Wanted Poster (Public Domain)	153
The DD214 (Anonymous Example) (Department of Defense)	154
The Pentagon (Department of Defense)	160
A U.S. Senate Hearing (U.S. Coast Guard – Public Domain)	169
Calling Mr. Bear (USDA National Agricultural Library)	171
The Not-So-Good Book (Photograph of Cover – Origin Unknown)	173
AFRTS Program Guide – April 17, 1967 (Department of Defense)	175
The Navy Annex (U.S. Navy)	178
2019 Discretionary Budget Request (Nationalpriorities.org)	179
The DIVAD (Wikimedia)	180
The Bradley Fighting Vehicle (U.S. Army)	181
The Amphibious Bradley (Wikimedia Commons)	182
It's a Gusher! (SMU Central University Libraries)	184
A Geothermal Power Plant (Wikimedia)	186
Gulf Coast Salt Dome	188
Joint Task Force Bravo (U.S. Department of Defense)	197
Burn victim, Japan, circa 1945 (National Archives)	204
Three Mile Island (Centers for Disease Control and Prevention)	207
Chernobyl Reactor No. 4 (International Atomic Energy Association)	214
Ed Shomaker (Michele Shomaker Collection)	220
The "Ring of Fire" (U.S. Geological Survey – Public Domain)	222
Ishinomaki, Japan after the Tohoku Earthquake (U.S. Marine Corps)	223
The Castle Bravo HBomb Test (Pexel.com – Public Domain)	225
Daigo Fukuryū Maru (Japanese book "ASAHI CHRONICLE")	226
U.S. Army Troops Close to an Exploding Atomic Bomb (Wikipedia)	228
The Tsar Bomba Fireball (nationalinterest.org)	230
Cleaning Up Rocky Flats (U.S. Environmental Protection Agency)	232
U.S. Nuclear Weapons and Reactor Waste Sites (Dept. of Energy)	232
Nuclear Waste at Hanford (NOAA)	233
The Yucca Flats Test Site (National Nuclear Security Administration)	234
A PlutoniumPowered Pacemaker (Los Alamos National Laboratory)	235
Aldrich Ames (Federal Bureau of Investigation)	237
The Ames Arrest (Federal Bureau of Investigation)	239
The Ames "Manse" (Author's Collection)	241

Images (cont.)

	Page
Robert Hanssen Mug Shot (Federal Bureau of Investigation)	242
Marie Curie (Wikimedia)	244
Radium Baths, Will Rogers Hotel, Claremore, Oklahoma (Wikipedia)	245
Lise Meitner around 1906 in Vienna (Wikipedia)	246
Albert Einstein (Wikipedia)	247
The Most Important Letter EverWritten (Wikimedia Commons)	248-249
August 15, 1945. Japan Surrenders (U.S. National Archives)	250
Atoms for Peace Postage Stamp (U.S. Postal Service)	252
The Sorcerer's Apprentice (Wikimedia)	253
The Runit Dome (U.S. Department of Defense)	256
The Big Piney River of the Missouri Ozarks (rollanet.org)	274
268' wide by 53' deep SADM Crater (U.S. Army)	276
Preparing a Shape Charge for Detonation (Buckley Air Force Base)	283
Rosinante's Sister (Wikimedia - MartinHansV - Public Domain)	289
Peter Principle (Wikimedia)	295

Introduction

The Cold War was the most protracted and unconventional conflict of the twentieth century.
   –Lee Edwards and Elizabeth Edwards Spalding,
      from *A Brief History of the Cold War*

Here's my strategy on the Cold War: we win, they lose.
   –Ronald Reagan

I do not know with what weapons World War III will be fought, but World War IV will be fought with sticks and stones!
   –Albert Einstein

From the moment as a child I first ducked and covered, I have been fascinated, nay *obsessed*, with the Cold War. I grew up with the epic confrontation over which economic and societal system—Capitalism or Communism—would prevail in the long run and whether anyone on the planet would be alive to know who actually won the competition.

It's been thirty years now since the putative end of the Cold War, but neither I nor our planet can seem to get beyond it. Maybe because it informed so much of Baby Boomer lives. Or, perhaps because it never really ended, but just took a breather for a decade and change until Vladimir Putin emerged as the Czar of the New Russia and decided to resume the epic competition. His obsession with bringing back the vaunted days of Soviet yore is manifested in the 1,600 strategic thermonuclear warheads atop intercontinental ballistic missiles he keeps aimed at the U.S. This is in addition to Russia's 2016—and beyond—all-out cyber war on U.S. democracy that Donald Trump denies is happening and refuses to defend us against.

In other words, welcome to Cold War II. Sadly, this go-round the U.S. is vigorously waving the white flag of surrender. My god, what have we come to?

As an adolescent and young adult, I read all the books about the Cold War I could get my hands on and watched all the movies about the confrontation—*Dr. Strangelove, On the Beach, Ice Station Zebra, Fail-Safe, Seven Days in May*—many of them more than once. From childhood, I experienced sleepless nights worrying about nuclear holocausts, Sputnik, proxy wars, KGB spies, missile gaps, missiles in Cuba, nuclear proliferation, and all of the other angsts, anxieties, and neuroses associated with Armageddon. I fretted about B-52s losing their atomic bombs somewhere off the Spanish coast. I took it seriously when Nikita Khrushchev took off his shoe at the United Nations General Assembly, banged it on the desk and announced: "We will bury you!" I worried about the enemy's weaponry that was capable of knocking a U-2 spy plane out of the sky, and about the fate of Francis Gary Powers, the captured U-2 pilot, during his Moscow show trial. I studied the unsubtleties of the DefCon (Defense Condition) ladder that, step-by-step, takes us from peacetime to global thermonuclear war. I agonized over "two-man control." I followed the trail of Party Chairman Nikita Khrushchev as he toured the United States. I was riveted by his "kitchen debate" in Moscow with Vice President Nixon. And on and on and on.

I gobbled up all I could learn about nuclear tests. As a child, I even wrote letters to Presidents Eisenhower and Kennedy expressing my concerns and recommending rather naïve proposals for reducing East-West tensions. One of the rote responses included instructions on building fallout shelters. Later in life, I was (and am today) likely one of the only human beings neurotic enough to actually read the arcane and numbing particulars contained in the Test Ban Treaty, SALT I and II, Start I, Start II and the Intermediate Range Nuclear Forces Treaty and new START. As I write this, the INF Treaty was just abrogated by President Trump.

If it had to do with the Cold War and its potential for nuclear annihilation, I ate it up.

And then, suddenly, I found myself on the front lines of the nuclear era, dealing on a daily basis with the technology, armaments and terrifying capability that mankind had unleashed in its eagerness to destroy itself. That surreal experience is the prime, but hardly the only, motivation for this book. Some of the other motivators were direct conversations with people on the actual and theoretical front lines of the U.S.-Soviet contest and other personal interactions with the Cold War and its warriors; others were a bit more oblique.

The more I thought about the Cold War, the more I realized that, at times, I was much more than a passive observer. At various stages of my career, I was very much a participant. In those incarnations, I was actively engaged in the whole deal, battling in my own way and sometimes on my own terms against what Ronald Reagan labeled the "Evil Empire."

This book recounts these personal intersections with the biggest and most consequential preoccupation of the last half of the twentieth century. The book discusses my involvements from my earliest memories of ducking-and-covering through the junctures at which the Cold War directly affected me (and in a microscopic way, me it) to two national security task forces I headed as a government consultant and into my one-person-removed connection to two of the three most calamitous nuclear accidents of the atomic era—Three Mile Island and Chernobyl. The last chapter is an attempt to assess what happened and ends with a series of proposals designed to help the planet and its populations move beyond the existential danger into safer space. The Epilogue is a series of profiles of some of the more interesting cold warriors I encountered along the way.

The story interweaves personal stories with what was happening globally, the "micro" and the "macro." That technique has served me well in past books.

When I first began writing this story, I started with the assumption that there was a yin and yang to it, a binary good vs. evil theme that carried through from one episode to the next: we, of course, were the good guys and our superpower rival, the Soviet Union was the bad—*really bad*—guy. However, the deeper I got into the project, the more I realized that my assumption needed to be more nuanced. There was and is no "good" guy in this story. Consequently, I felt compelled to modify the subtitle from the singular "Evil Empire" to the plural "Evil Empires." No nation is innocent in our rush to kill ourselves, the rest of humanity and those billions of creatures with whom we share this marvelous orb and who we arrogantly label the "lower animals." Both Cold War antagonists were—and still are—complicit.

While there are occasional humorous occurrences sprinkled throughout this tale, don't lose sight of the deadly seriousness of this topic. The overall message is not meant to be amusing.

Chapter 1
Dodging the Big One

For 15 minutes between the end of World War II and the beginning of the Cold War, the world seemed a safer place.
— Richard Hermann

A VE-Day Celebration in Toronto, Canada
(Public Domain)

The Vanished Victory

The great global exuberance engendered by the end of World War II was short-lived. Very soon, there were a slew of other major threats to worry about. The Bomb was one obvious one. Combined with the brief tenure of the American nuclear hegemony (it was only four years until the Soviet Union, thanks to the excellent work of its spies, was able to replicate a successful atomic explosion), the Cold War escalated global tensions beyond anything ever experienced in what passed for peacetime. The stressors were not limited to nations. Individuals around the planet also became increasingly anxious about the competition between the two superpowers, both now armed with the ability to end civilization and humanity's brief run at the top of the food chain. Despite the end of hostilities, America was not yet able to exhale.

Even peace, such as it was, was not destined to last very long. The rearrangement of the map of Eastern Europe to suit the Soviet Union and its paranoid leader, Josef Stalin, escalated international tensions almost as soon as the war ended. The phrase "captive nations" captured the temper of the times very well. Berlin, a divided city surrounded on all sides by the newly-created Communist heartland, quickly became a flashpoint, culminating in a Soviet/East German blockade designed to starve the city into submission. It took an almost two-year, Herculean airlift by the West, led by the United States, to supply West Berlin's more than 2 million inhabitants with food, water, medicine and other essentials.

In 1949, Mao Tse-tung's People's Army conquered the last *Kuomintang* redoubts and assumed control of the most populous country on earth. A raging, highly politicized debate about "who lost China?" ensued in Washington, DC, which only served to increase the already heightened anxieties felt by the body politic.

The next year, more bad news: in June 1950, the Communist North Korean regime, encouraged by its Soviet and Red Chinese patrons, invaded South Korea following an ill-advised speech by U.S. Secretary of State Dean Acheson (known by his political opponents thereafter as "The Red Dean") defining the U.S. "defensive perimeter" in the Pacific as a line running through Japan, the Ryukyus, and the Philippines, thus leaving out South Korea.

Five months later, the U.S. found itself back in full military mode, reinstituting the draft and reconstituting its Army and

Marine Corps for a grim three years of inconclusive battle on the Korean Peninsula, during which we seriously considered using nuclear weapons. It was the worst of the Cold War's "hot" wars pitting the U.S. and the Soviet Union against one another and also the West's most expansive implementation of its "containment" policy that dominated American strategy for decades.

Domestic Dysfunction

Adding fuel to the already raging international fires, Congressional Republicans decided to aggravate the "Red Scare" by conducting a series of sensational hearings into Communist infiltration of both the government and entertainment industry. Bolstering this particular silliness, Freshman Senator Joseph McCarthy of Wisconsin, at a speech in Wheeling, West Virginia in February 1950, announced that he was aware of 205* card-carrying members of the Communist Party who were working at the U.S. Department of State. This speech incited an era of paranoia and frenzy marked by the coinage of summary phrases that said a lot: "HUAC" (for House Un-American Activities Committee, the principal investigative body that obsessed over Communists penetrating and threatening every facet of American society), "McCarthyism" (the smear-campaign tactics employed by the Senator of the same name), "Red Scare" (the fear that the Commies were everywhere) and "Pink Lady" (the moniker applied by California Senate candidate Richard M. Nixon to slander his opponent, Helen Gahagan Douglas, in 1950). People were lifting their bedsheets to see if a Communist might be lurking underneath.

Note: At every speech during his short-lived heyday, McCarthy cited a different number of State Department Communists.

Terror Close to Home

As if all of this international and political stürm und drang and growing public sense that we were losing the Cold War and that the Communists were closing in were not enough, there was another scare, a much more personal and intimate one that injected the fear of God into every American household that included children: the scourge of polio. The general panic that loomed over America beginning with the Great Depression, then World War II, followed by the Cold War and its threat of sudden annihilation, probably exacerbated the national angst about polio.

Polio, a.k.a. poliomyelitis or infantile paralysis, was a devastating disease quite well known to the post-war public. President Franklin D. Roosevelt was both a polio victim and a champion of polio research and the search for, if not a cure, at least therapies and a prevention strategy.

Polio is an infectious disease caused by a virus. The virus is most commonly spread from one person to another via infected fecal material that is swallowed. It may also be spread by food or water containing fecal matter or more rarely by saliva. It comes on very quickly, sometimes in only a few hours. That is what happened to President Roosevelt in 1921 when, at age 39 while on vacation on Campobello Island in the Bay of Fundy, he was suddenly struck down.

The statistics are scary. While most people fully recover after experiencing some muscle pain, 15-30 percent of adults and 2-5 percent of children die. Five percent of people are permanently disabled. Decades after recovery, some people come down with "post-polio syndrome" which mimics polio's muscle weakness. A client of mine who had polio in his youth 50 years before contracted post-polio syndrome and was confined to a wheelchair.

Polio has been around for many thousands of years, but the virus causing it was only first identified in 1908. By the 1930s, it became the childhood disease that parents feared the most. Terrifying images of children in what were called "iron lungs," assistive breathing devices for children whose chest muscles were no longer able to engage their lungs, contributed to public panic.

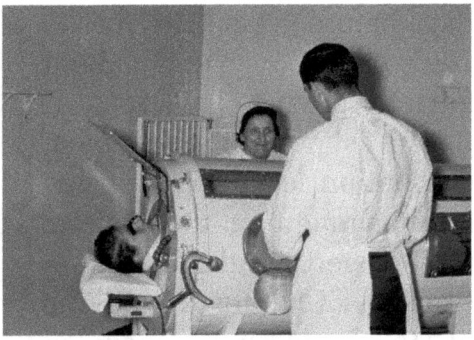

Life in an Iron Lung
(U.S. Centers for Disease Control and Prevention)

The first polio vaccine was developed in the 1950s by Dr. Jonas Salk, followed shortly thereafter by an alternative oral vaccine developed by Dr. Albert Sabin. Parents rushed to have their children vaccinated. Schools became the scene of mass vaccination efforts and soon, the public polio panic subsided. Since there was no cure, however, the kids consigned for what remained of their lives to an iron lung were soon forgotten by all except their families.

Now, all that was left for Americans to obsess about was the possibility of nuclear annihilation.

Duck-and-Cover and Other Inanities

The explosion of the first Soviet atomic bomb—code name First Lightning—in August 1949 shattered the American public's illusion that we had a monopoly on nuclear weapons and thus were safe and secure behind our vast oceanic buffer zones. The formerly exclusive nuclear club now had two members who really did not like each other. Nerves quickly frayed. Suddenly, our world did not look quite so comfortable.

The Soviet A-bomb was an exact replica of *Fat Man*, the weapon that the U.S. dropped on Nagasaki four years minus 20 days before. That tells you all you need to know about Soviet espionage.

The shock of the Soviet detonation led directly to the establishment of the Federal Civil Defense Administration (see also Chapter Two). The FCDA's mission included educating and reassuring the public that it was possible to survive a Soviet atomic attack.

1950s School Children Practicing Nuclear Annihilation Prevention
(Library of Congress)

The agency quietly commissioned a university study on how to achieve "public emotion management" given the Cold War. In other words, along with so-called practical advice, the FCDA intended to pull the wool over our eyes.

The FCDA's "don't worry, be happy" approach went down two rather bumbling parallel paths:

1. **Engagement with schools and teachers.** Teachers in selected cities were urged to conduct air raid drills where they would suddenly yell, "Drop!" at which directive students would kneel down under their desks with their hands clutched around their heads and necks. Some schools, with the FCDA's blessing, went further, distributing metal "dog tags" to students—like those worn by soldiers—so that their bodies could be identified after an attack had turned them into little ash piles. New York City distributed 2.5 million such identifiers. School officials in Milwaukee wanted identifying tattoos inscribed on students' arms. These methodologies would not, of course, have been worth much following an attack. Both tattoos and tags would have been vaporized along with the children. These deviations from the

FCDA's calming mission were not exactly reassuring to either the older students who were of an age to understand the implications of the dog tags, or to parents.

2. **Development of an "educational" film** for distribution to demonstrate to kids how to protect themselves should the Evil Empire lob a Big One on top of their community. During the preliminaries, the production company, Archer Films, put together a focus group of school administrators and teachers and obtained the endorsement of the National Education Association. A school administrator from McLean, Virginia mentioned that her school had participated in "duck and cover" drills. A light immediately went on in the producers' heads. They loved the phrase and decided to use it as the title of their film.

Duck and Cover was completed in 1952. The film included live actors and an animated turtle named Bert who showed kids how, if they saw a bright flash of light, to duck down to the ground and get under some type of cover, be it a desk or table (or, in Bert's case, a turtle shell) or, if those were not available, to huddle next to a wall. The flash would presumably be produced by an atomic blast. Left unmentioned was that the kids would be rendered blind by the flash of light from an atomic blast and would likely be vaporized by the 10,830 F temperature produced by the bomb (going by the Hiroshima numbers). There would not even be any ash residue to do the ducking and covering.

Bert and the Monkey Just Before the Firecracker Goes Off
(youtube.com)

Bert, by the way, wore a pith helmet and quickly ducked his head into his shell when a monkey in a tree outside the school set off a firecracker.

Duck and Cover's world premiere took place at a Manhattan movie theatre and was attended by educators. The screening had the aura of a gala lacking only Bert and the monkey making their way into the theater on a red carpet. It would have taken Bert too long a time to crawl down the red carpet, so that particular gimmick was not included.

After the showing, the film was distributed to schools around the country. It was also shown on television stations nationwide and was seen by tens of millions of Americans.

I first viewed the film in second grade and recall being fascinated by it. I was especially intrigued by Bert and the monkey and what must have happened to them as a result of the Soviet bomb dropping out of the sky, since they were outside and there was no place to duck and cover. It made me sad.

My beloved teacher, Ms. Connie Melito, would shout "Drop!" at unexpected times during the school day, whereupon we would dutifully crawl under our desks and protect our heads with our hands and arms. I recall that our third grade teacher took over the cause, but she was a confirmed cynic and did not put the passion into her "Drops!" that Ms. Melito did.

At some point, our school principal, a very wise man in every respect, became concerned that perhaps ducking-and-covering was not going to cut it. Instead, he instituted drills where we would process out of our classrooms and hunker down in the corridors up against the walls. He was on to something here, given that the windowless corridors were probably safer than the classrooms and had the benefit of putting more concrete, brick and cinder block between us and the bomb effects. It was like a fire drill without going outside.

When *Duck and Cover* was delivered to the FCDA in January 1952, the agency loved Bert and the monkey so much that they decided to include the film in their "Alert America

Convoy," yet another bonehead idea designed to assuage public anxiety. The convoy consisted of 10 trucks and trailers that toured the country for nine months in 1952. Each vehicle came replete with dioramas, posters, 3-D models and a film theatre playing *Duck and Cover* and a number of other "educational" movies about surviving The Bomb—the agency themed its presentations as "Beat the Bomb." More than a million people eventually saw (that is, were subjected to) the convoy's exhibits.

Assessment

The FCDA was way behind the times. Its entire program was geared to cooling public emotions about an atomic bomb attack. However, by the time *Duck and Cover* and the convoy were deployed all over the country, the United States was on to bigger (much, much bigger) and far more horrific things.

The first hydrogen bomb, "Ivy Mike," was successfully detonated in November 1952. After only a 9-month gestation period during which Russian physicists Ivan Kurchatov and Andrei Sakharov (the very same Sakharov who decades later became the global poster child for anti-Soviet agitation and nuclear non-proliferation) digested what they had learned, legitimately but also thanks to superb KGB tradecraft, the Soviet Union exploded its own H-bomb.

H-Bomb: The Mother of All Mushroom Clouds
(Public Domain)

Ivy Mike and its Soviet counterpart launched the new era of the possibility of global thermonuclear war. The H-bomb put dinky little devices like "Little Boy" (Hiroshima) and "Fat Man" (Nagasaki) to shame. They were minnows in comparison to their whale-like thermonuclear progeny. Hydrogen bombs dwarf their atomic forebears in their effects. These fusion bombs actually employ small atomic bombs as triggers. Their explosions can be more than a thousand times more powerful. Temperatures at ground zero are measured in millions instead of thousands of degrees F. Fireballs are far more extensive and blast waves carry much farther. Fallout from an H-bomb spreads over enormous areas of the earth.

The U.S. panicked when it observed that the Soviets were testing H-bombs with yields exceeding one megaton. In the four years between the USSR's first successful test of an atomic bomb and the advent of the Soviet H-bomb, the Pentagon and intelligence agencies had not been too concerned because Soviet delivery system (missile) tests typically landed off-target by an average of four miles (the "miss distance"), thus negating a lot of the potential damage that a nuclear weapon was capable of doing. However, monster bombs with huge yields could compensate for poor missile guidance systems,

In short, if duck-and-cover was largely irrelevant when it came to A-bomb survival strategy, it was rendered a really bad joke with the advent of the H-bomb.

Duck-and-cover, the movie and the school drills, terrified me. They took an abstract threat and made it immediate, perhaps because I had a vivid imagination. I was scared out of my socks and stayed that way for years.

Probably the only silver lining in the mushroom cloud was that I grew up and went to school in Western New York, 350 miles from New York City, and thus was relieved from having to wear dog-tags. The lengths to which government authorities went were ridiculous, a warning to the citizenry of absurdities to come, such as the Department of Homeland Security's recommendation during the run-up to the ill-conceived Iraq War that Americans buy duct tape and plastic sheeting to secure windows and doors in the event of a terrorist attack. The Homeland Security apple has not fallen far from the Federal Civil Defense Agency tree: *Duct-and-Cover*.

Chapter 2
Plane Spotting

Your call could save a city
—Ground Observer Corps Billboard

Origins

The Ground Observer Corps (GOC) began during World War II. It gave the non-Rosie-the-Riveters on the home front the opportunity to participate in the war effort in a non-combat role. The Army Air Force (the U.S. Air Force was then still part of the Army) enrolled 1.5 million civilian volunteers who were tasked with manning 14,000 observation posts along U.S. coasts.

Radar was still new and its range was limited. The GOC's mission was to eyeball the skies for enemy aircraft attempting to penetrate American airspace.

While there was some thin justification for this mission at the beginning of the war, the logic behind it soon dissipated. The Axis powers did not have any warplanes that could reach anywhere close to the continental United States from bases in their homelands or conquered territories. Aircraft carriers could have brought the threat closer, but the theoretical never came close to reality. Germany did not

On the Lookout for Bear Bombers
(Old Orange County Courthouse Museum)

have a single carrier. Italy had one serviceable carrier that had been converted (clumsily) from a passenger liner, but it never made it out of the Mediterranean. Japan, however, had ten carriers at the beginning of the war. They were employed effectively to surprise Pearl Harbor, but Japan's ability to project air power suffered a major collapse at the Battle of Midway, when four carriers went to the bottom of the sea. Nevertheless, the fear was that Japan still might be able to threaten Hawaii, Alaska and even the Pacific Coast with bombing raids. Consequently, plane spotters were in position in these locales.

As the war dragged on and Japan's ability to project force virtually disappeared along with its carrier force, the need for and the vigilance of plane spotters declined. With the threat disappearing, the Army Air Force shut down the GOC in 1944.

Revival

Ground Observer Corps Recruiting Poster
(Public Domain)

The Cold War between the United States and the Soviet Union—the two surviving superpowers at the end of World War II—began the minute the war against the Axis powers ended. It provided the defunct GOC with a new *raison d'être*. It took a few years, however, for the idea of exhuming the GOC to emerge.

Fast forward to February 1950 when Continental Air Command Commander General Ennis C. Whitehead proposed the formation of a 160,000 civilian volunteer GOC to operate 8,000 observation posts scattered in gaps between proposed radar network sites. By June, when the Korean War began, there was a belief among some of the more paranoid U.S. military and civilian leaders that it might be the precursor to a possible Soviet attack. This view, borne of incredibly shoddy intelligence, was widely circulated among an already angst-ridden public. Consequently, the Air Defense Command had no problem recruiting GOC volunteers. By early 1951, 210,000 GOC volunteers were manning 8,000 observation posts and 26 "filter centers" were being tested for the first time in nationwide exercises. A filter center was a GOC station that received information on aircraft sighted at observation posts and relayed it on to stations where it was evaluated for action.

These exercises indicated that it was taking much too much time for a reported sighting to make it through the filter centers to Ground Control Interception Centers. The result was an expansion of the GOC, adding even more volunteers and observation posts. The revised plan was called "Operation SKYWATCH" and was launched on July 14, 1952. Eventually it numbered more than 800,000 volunteers standing alternating shifts at 16,000 observation posts and seventy-three filter centers.

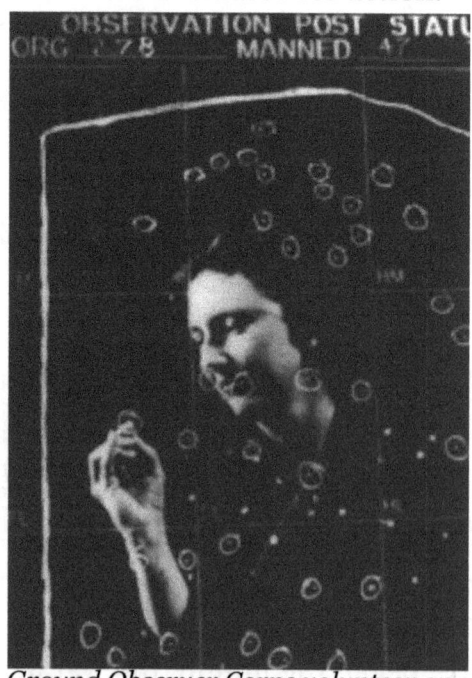

Ground Observer Corps volunteer on duty in one of the 73 Continental Air Defense Command Filter Centers, 1956
(Official US Air Force photograph – radomes.org)

The Air Force relied heavily on billboards (see below) and Public Service Announcements to recruit. A typical radio spot went like this:

> *It may not be a very cheerful thought but the Reds right now have about a thousand bombers that are quite capable of destroying at least 89 American cities in one raid . . . Won't you help protect your country, your town, your children? Call your local Civil Defense office and join the Ground Observer Corps today.*

GOC Recruiting Billboard
(Public Domain)

By the late 1950s, a new short-range radar was deployed that performed the plane-spotting function far better than humans. Dozens of these new devices were deployed, rendering the GOC obsolete. Air Defense Command disestablished the Ground Observer Corps on January 31, 1959.

GOC Cold War plane spotters underwent a few days of training, which consisted largely of identifying silhouettes of multiple Soviet bombers, fighters, attack and reconnaissance aircraft: Ilyushin-28 "Beagles," M-4 "Bisons," Tu-4 "Bulls" and the intimidating Tu-95 "Bears;" MIG-17s, 19s and 21s; SU-7s, 9s, 11s and 15s; YAK-25s and 28Ps; and a bunch of others.

It was a lot for anyone to absorb in a very short time, much less the aging volunteers, many of whom were World War *One* veterans. Remember, this was the 1950s, an era of full employment (the unemployment rate averaged 4.4 percent per year) and incredible economic growth (also averaging 4.4. percent per year, the best numbers in U.S. history then and now), thanks in part to pent-up demand during World War II. That meant very few potential volunteers of working age. Consequently, the observation posts were largely manned by old guys.

Soviet Tu-95 "Bear" Bomber
(National Archives)

The GOC and Me

Growing up in a small town in rural western New York State, I was very much aware of the local GOC plane spotters. I could see them with their binoculars on clear days staring up at the clouds, shouting out whenever they spied a plane or a contrail as I biked around town. They took their mission very seriously despite their disappointment at never spotting any Soviet bombers overhead. They also wore distinctive GOC insignia in the form of pins on their lapels. Being curious, I went up to them once during a bicycle circuit of my small town and asked what they were all about. They could not have been friendlier.

I was, however, skeptical of their utility, given that we were more than 3,000 miles south of the Distant Early Warning (DEW) Line, the system of radar stations that stretched from the Alaskan Arctic coast and Aleutian Islands across extreme northern Canada to the Faroe Islands, Greenland, and Iceland. Moreover, there were two additional radar arrays farther south that blanketed Canada and the northern U.S. border that would have probably picked up any Soviet air incursions in the unlikely event the DEW Line missed them.

Ground Observer Corps Pin
(Public Domain)

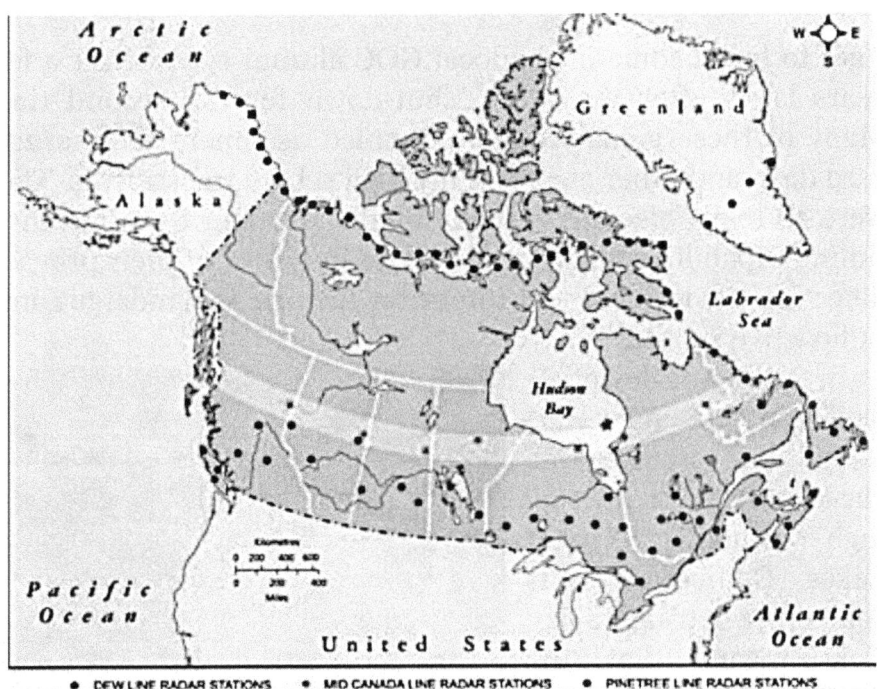

America's First Three Lines of Defense (DEW Line at the Top)
(National Defence of Canada)

I also thought it highly unlikely that (1) U.S. interceptors would have completely failed to counter any Soviet aircraft, especially slow-moving bombers intent on inflicting nuclear holocaust, before they reached our borders, and (2) the Soviets' malevolent intentions targeted little, out-of-the-way, not exactly strategic or threatening Canandaigua, New York (my home town).

In addition, the local plane spotters were all pretty old and suffering from many of the maladies associated with old age. Several of them even had trouble holding their binoculars up to their eyes and peering skyward for more than a few seconds at a time. While they looked down and collected themselves, a whole squadron of Soviet bombers might have slipped by.

Off to the Races

I got to know some of the local GOC alumni even better a few years later, after the Corps shut-down for the second time. Many of these genial codgers doubled as timers for the 220-yard dash and other events at my high school track meets. They were all really nice guys—many by then in their 80s—but their timing capabilities likely provided an indicator of their prowess detecting Soviet bombers intent on turning Canandaigua into radioactive rubble.

In a major deviation from the customary half-a-lap race around one curve, the 220 in my high school's Finger Lakes Conference was run on a straightaway. That meant that the timers were manning their stopwatches a full eighth of a mile distant

The 220-yard dash timers would have been at the far end of the track by the far fence
(Author's Collection)

from where the runners began the race. Here is where I learned much more about the relative speeds of light and sound than in Physics class. Being octogenarians, the timers had no hope of seeing the smoke ejected by the starter's gun when it went off, which is how the starts of all track races back then alerted the timers to press the button triggering their stop watches in order to begin timing the race. Today, of course, technology has taken over and races at almost every competitive level are timed electronically.

Hand-timing geared to visual sighting of the smoke from the starter's pistol provided pretty accurate times, given that light waves covered the distance between the starting line and the timers in about a ten-thousandth of a second.

The old guys, however, had to rely on *sound*. That is, the sound generated by the starter's gunshot. Since sound only travels at a speed of 1,112 feet per second at 800 feet above sea level (Canandaigua's elevation), that translated to approximately a .6 second delay at best before the sound reached the timers' ears. That had two consequences:

1. Given their age-affected reflexes, it's a certainty that the timers lost at least an additional half-second before their brains were able to send a signal down fragile nerve paths to their hands, at which herald they needed to press the stopwatch start button to begin timing the race.
2. Some of the "old timers" had suffered hearing loss sufficient to make it impossible for them to hear the starter's pistol go off. They compensated by looking down at the stopwatches of their non-hearing-impaired colleagues and starting their stop watches when they saw their colleagues press their start buttons. That meant an additional delay.

And that was not the end of it. At the finish line, despite being virtually on top of the racers, it took them several tenths of a second to react to the winner breaking the tape.

These delays, though, meant my 220 times were pretty impressive for high school. I was certain I would be running the 220 even faster once I got to college.

College and Consequences

Unfortunately, I discovered just how unimpressive my high school times were when I arrived at college and participated in my first 220 time trial a couple of months into my Freshman year. While college 220s were run around the curve, placing the much younger timers much closer to the staggered starting lines, it was still a shock to find myself a full second and a couple of tenths slower than in high school. I was so slow that I never got to run the race at all that year.

It took me more than a year of training and adding thirty pounds of muscle, plus superior track shoes, to approach my high school 220 times. When I finally got to run, I ran slightly faster than in high school but not enough to be consistently selected to compete (instead I had to content myself with the long jump and an occasional, inhumanly painful 440, a race likely devised by the Inquisition).

I should add that my home surface in college was, like my high school track, what was known then as a cinder track. When we ran at away meets at schools such as Rutgers and Princeton with high-tech, rubberized-asphalt surfaces, our times dropped dramatically. Running on cinder tracks probably made at least a one-second difference, if not more, in a 220.

Today, high school 220s are run on the curve and track surfaces are state-of-the-art technology. They are lightning fast. The plane spotters are long gone to their just reward (where, hopefully, they no longer must gaze upwards), and the timers are now either all electronic devices or come from the ranks of younger, track team parents.

*My Successors Running the 220 on the Curve
at Philadelphia's Franklin Field*
(yalebulldogs.com)

Timing Is Everything

The Cold War was all-consuming, drilling down to affect even such mundane activities as running an eighth of a mile on a track. Despite all that and the disappointment of not being a sprint star, I owe the plane spotters a debt of gratitude for making me feel like one for a few brief shining moments . . . moments that lasted longer than they should have.

In the almost decade that the GOC operated, not a single enemy plane was spotted.

Chapter 3
Gimme Shelter

Oh, a storm is threat'ning
My very life today
If I don't get some shelter
Oh yeah, I'm gonna fade away
　　　　　　--The Rolling Stones (*Gimme Shelter*)

Ka-BOOM!
(Public Domain)

High Anxiety

Plane spotting was just one of Canandaigua's efforts at protecting itself from a Soviet nuclear attack. The other major activity involved the construction of fallout shelters.

It is impossible to explain to contemporary Americans under a certain age what the 1950s and 1960s anxiety about nuclear obliteration was like. It was manna from heaven for certain government quarters such as the Department of Defense and the intelligence establishment (both of which grew like weeds) and also for the news media. A nightly news show did not go by on any of the three (and only three) broadcast networks that did not feed the general public angst, replete with images of mushroom clouds, imploding buildings and fried-to-a-crisp human dummies (sometimes the mother dummy was at the kitchen sink wearing an apron when the bomb went off). Books like Nevil Shute's *On the Beach* about post-apocalyptic Australia, Ian Fleming's *James Bond* series, and John Le Carré's Cold War spy novels became instant best-sellers. Movies like *The Manchurian Candidate*, *Torn Curtain* and *The Third Man* were widely viewed and did nothing to tamp down the collective panic. Cold War memories still resonate so strongly today, almost 30 years after the collapse of the Soviet Union, that contemporary novelists and film makers can still make a good living writing about an atomic holocaust.

B-52 Pilot Major T.J. "King" Kong Riding the Bomb Into Armageddon
(from the film, *Dr. Strangelove*, 1964)

It was as if a Sword of Damocles hovered over the nation, held up by a thin, unraveling thread. Armageddon seemed to many Americans to be just around the corner.

Sheltering In Place

That was true no matter where you lived in the vast expanse of the United States. You could be residing adjacent to an Intercontinental Ballistic Missile (ICBM) silo in North Dakota, where you might have good reason for concern, or in "Tornado Alley" in central Oklahoma, remote from anything of strategic importance. Or, you could be living in Canandaigua, New York.

No matter where you lived, you were likely to encounter more than a handful of people who struck you as otherwise sane, stable, grounded and reasonably well-adjusted and educated, but who nevertheless invested thousands of their hard-earned dollars in building bomb/fallout shelters in their back yards. The urge to shelter was not limited, however, to individual homeowners who were fortunate enough to have a back yard. During the early days of the Cold War, bomb and fallout shelters could be found in public and commercial buildings as well, including school basements and beneath large apartment complexes and government buildings. Institutional shelters were indicated by the symbol that came to exemplify the nuclear age (see p. 29).

A High-End Fallout Shelter
(Wikipedia)

What prompted this?

On June 14, 1954, millions of Americans in the largest U.S. cities participated in the first-ever nationwide civil defense drill. The drill was organized and later evaluated by the FCDA. It took place in 54 U.S. cities (including nearby Rochester, New York) and Canada. The scenario was that North America was under massive nuclear attack from both aircraft and submarines (both the U.S. and the Soviet Union at that time lacked ICBMs, the third leg of the nuclear triad) and that most major urban areas had been targeted. At 10:00 AM that morning, sirens sounded in the selected cities, at which time all citizens were supposed to clear the streets, seek shelter and prepare for the attack. Prior to the drill, every citizen had received information about the location of the nearest fallout shelter. *Note: While the notice used the term "fallout shelter," this was a bit of a misnomer. In the eyes of both the builders and potential occupants, these were supposed to be bomb shelters.*

Danger: Radiation Symbol
(Public Domain)

Shelters included the basements of government buildings and schools, subway tunnels, and even some private shelters. President Eisenhower and members of the cabinet and Congress were whisked away to underground bunkers in Washington, DC.

The entire drill lasted only about 10 minutes, at which time an all-clear signal was broadcast and people emerged, cicada-like, from below ground and went back to their daily tasks. Life returned to what passed for normal in those high-anxiety days.

The FCDA estimated that New York City would suffer the most loss of life, losing over 2 million people. Overall, it was estimated that more than 12 million Americans would die in an attack.

Things went pretty smoothly for the most part. One New York City woman, however, created a massive traffic jam in mid-town Manhattan when she stopped her car in the middle of the street, jumped out and ran for cover. There were no signs of panic or criminal behavior such as looting. Left unsaid was that the Soviet Union's recent successful test of a hydrogen bomb rendered any such drill irrelevant. The H-bomb would have likely incinerated any of the existing shelters.

The drill was extensively covered by the media. It only worsened the widespread concerns about living under a nuclear threat. Following it, digging in suburban and rural backyards increased despite the fact that the vast majority of the country was an unlikely target of Soviet malevolence. However, those areas marked by backyards and open country were the most conducive to shelter construction.

The Locals Go Ballistic

Main Street USA (Canandaigua, NY) Back in the Day
(Public Domain)

I turned eight years old the week of the drill. Since we always watched the *NBC Nightly News* anchored by John Cameron Swayze while we ate dinner, I was acutely aware of the whole national "to-do." My reaction was to lobby my parents incessantly to build a shelter in our backyard, convinced as I was that Kremlin targeting officials were surely aiming several megatons at Canandaigua. My father essentially told me I was nuts and that we were not going to waste money on something so pointless. He never had much of a filter when it came to speaking to kids, so he went on to explain that, in the highly unlikely event that our obscure, remote, unpronounceable and unspellable little town was attacked with nuclear weapons, a shelter would be no protection at all. "We'll all be vaporized."

I didn't understand what "vaporized" meant, but it did not sound like fun. My mother was angry at my father for speaking, as she put it, "so bluntly."

Years later it occurred to me that there was another very good reason why my father was loath to build a shelter: we were Jewish. One of our tribal deficiencies (Israelis excepted) is an inability to do anything requiring handyman skills. We can perform magic when dealing with complex, high-dollar transactions, but break down when it comes to using a screwdriver.

I don't know how many Canandaiguans actually constructed shelters, but I ran across a few in my wanderings around town. I even got a tour of one from a man who lived a few streets away from my house and who was either a surveyor or a civil engineer (I don't remember which). He had dug up his back yard and constructed the *Taj Mahal* of fallout shelters. It had cinder block sides and a very heavy lead roof on hinges.

His construction was intended as a true fallout shelter as opposed to a bomb shelter. He was, in fact, the first person who explained the difference to me. "A pure bomb shelter might—or might not—protect you from the immediate blast. A fallout shelter," he explained, "protects you from the dangerous, radioactive ash and other stuff falling from the skies in the months after the blast." The only problem was that his fallout shelter probably would not have prevented fallout from insinuating itself into the shelter. Instead of dying instantly before they knew what hit them, he and his family would have died weeks or months later after suffering the agonies of acute radiation poisoning.

A Brief Primer on Fallout

A nuclear explosion vaporizes matter. The fireball created by the blast absorbs neutrons from the explosion and becomes highly radioactive. The lighter-than-air vaporous residue from the fireball rises into the atmosphere and eventually condenses in rain, forming dust and light sandy, pumice-like material. The radioactive fallout that rains down emits alpha and beta particles, as well as gamma rays. This irradiates anything it lands on, people included. And it can penetrate virtually anything. The consequence is disease and often death.

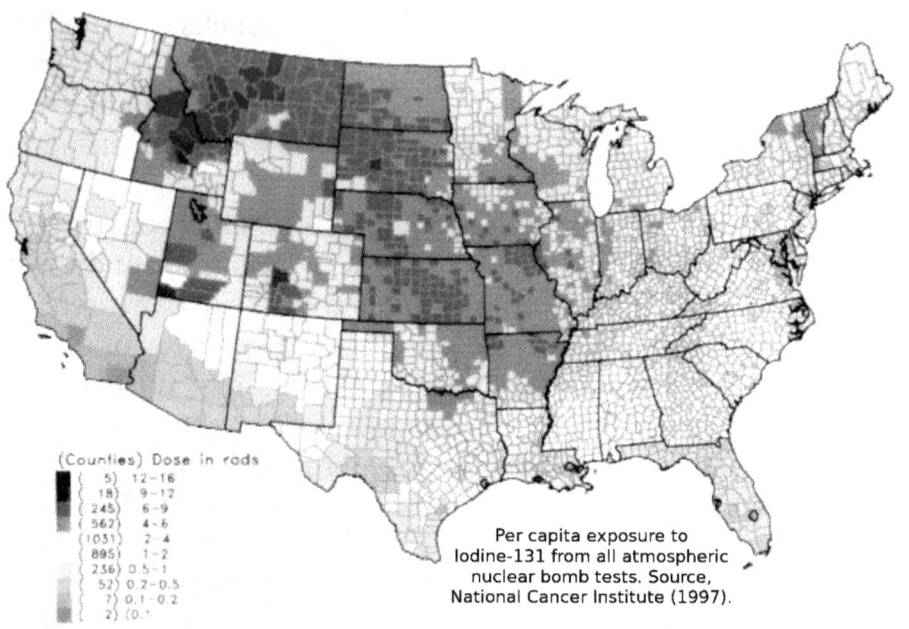

The Ubiquity of Fallout
(Public Domain)

Back to the Taj

This particular shelter was incredibly well-stocked with food and drink, all neatly organized on shelves. It also featured a gas-operated generator, lights, a working toilet and even a TV set and radio, although he said he doubted that they would work after a nuclear explosion and something called an "electromagnetic pulse." The capstone was a well-appointed bedroom sleeping four (he had a wife and two children). I was in awe and very envious.

The cost of this underground palace? $1,750 in late 1950s currency. That would be just over $15,300 today before furniture and food stocks.

Contrarians

While the majority of Americans were worrying about a nuclear holocaust, a number of enterprising fellow citizens were viewing the Cold War competition as just another get-rich-quick opportunity. By the mid-1950s, they realized, the U.S. was going to need a boatload of uranium if it was going to keep up with Soviet bomb production. By this time, the CIA and Department of Defense, like any worthy bureaucracies, discovered that it made good survival and appropriations sense to hype the Soviet threat to the max. They also quickly found that they had a receptive audience in the easily gulled politicians holding the purse strings. All of this created a perfect storm for the flood of uranium prospectors that suddenly abandoned their day jobs and headed west to replicate the nineteenth century California gold rush.

Encouraging Boy Scouts to Self-Destruct
(Boy's Life Magazine)

This proved a lucrative venture for some. The government paid out millions of dollars for uranium discoveries. The Atomic Energy Commission analyzed uranium samples for free. No license or any certifications were needed to dig for uranium. Magazine covers from *Boy's Life* to *Popular Science* fueled the excitement. None of the media said anything about the dangers of handling something as dangerously radioactive as uranium.

It was the Wild West all over again, but wilder.

Post-Cold-War Coda

As I advanced through my teen years, I increasingly looked down my nose at the folks who thought that a fallout shelter would save them or was necessary given our town's remoteness and twentieth century "irrelevancy." I purposely use this term because, during a chunk of the nineteenth century, Canandaigua was, in contrast, highly relevant to the national conversation:

- It was the most important settlement in Western New York State, the county seat of the entire region.
- It presented the nation with four cabinet members.
- It gave rise to the Anti-Masonic political party, which morphed into the Whig Party and elected several presidents. After two decades at the top of the political heap, the Whigs in turn evolved into the Republican Party and elected Abraham Lincoln president.
- It was home to an almost-President. Francis Granger was William Henry Harrison's Vice Presidential running mate in 1836 when he lost to Martin Van Buren. No single candidate received enough electoral votes to win the Vice Presidency so, per the Constitution, the U.S. Senate had to decide the winner (the only time in our history that happened). It selected Daniel Johnson over Granger. In 1840, Harrison ran again and won. This time, Granger refused the VP nod, burned by his disappointment four years earlier. Harrison then selected John Tyler to run with him. When Harrison died 30 days after he was inaugurated, Tyler became President.
- Canandaiguan John Canfield Spencer hosted Alexis de Tocqueville during his U.S. visit and then became the American publisher of his *magnum opus*, *Democracy in America*.

- It was where the idea for the Erie Canal originated. While in prison here, a debtor wrote a series of articles and letters to New York Governor DeWitt Clinton advocating such a ditch.
- It gave rise to the U.S. Naval Academy. John Spencer's son, Philip, was the only person ever charged with mutiny in the U.S. Navy. After he was hung from the yardarm of a naval vessel without benefit of much of a trial, the Navy decided it needed to better train its new officers, so it launched the U.S. Naval Academy in Annapolis, Maryland.
- It was briefly the home town of Stephen A. Douglas, Lincoln's 1860 presidential rival.
- Three religions began in the neighborhood: Mormonism, Spiritualism, and Millenarianism.
- Susan B. Anthony was tried and convicted here for illegally voting in the 1872 election.
- And much more.

If Canandaigua had maintained that prominence into the late twentieth century, it might well have worked its way into Soviet consciousness and become a prime target.

To everyone's amazement, Canandaigua, it turned out, while not a direct target, was decidedly vulnerable to a nuclear attack. It was less its proximity to Rochester, New York, the home of the U.S. optics industry, than its uncomfortable nearness to a place very much on the minds of the targeters milling around the Kremlin map room. The next chapter tells the story.

Chapter 4
The Nuclear Mother-Lode

The professed function of the nuclear weapons on each side is to prevent the other side from using their nuclear weapons. If that's all it is, then we've gotta ask: how many nuclear weapons do you need to do that?

–Carl Sagan

One of the 155 Seneca Army Depot Igloos in Which Nuclear Warheads Were Stored
(Public Domain)

If you ask where was the location of the highest concentration of death-dealing devices ever assembled during the Cold War, it is unlikely that you would anticipate the answer to be a remote, rural region of Western New York State in the heart of Finger Lakes wine country. At times during the U.S.-U.S.S.R. standoff, more than *8,000* nuclear warheads were stored in 155 concrete bunkers (a.k.a. "igloos") on 10,587 acres at a place called Seneca Army Depot in the barren hills high above Seneca Lake, approximately half-way between Seneca and neighboring Cayuga Lake.

A Rich Military History

The Depot began operating as the Army Ordnance Depot in 1941, just as war clouds were beginning to assemble over the United States. That was just the beginning.

In 1942, construction began nearby on a second military installation in rural, sparsely-populated Seneca County, just down the slopes from the Depot on the east shore of Seneca Lake. This was an improbable location for a huge U.S. Navy facility, situated more than 300 miles inland from the Atlantic coast. Yet Sampson Naval Training Base eventually encompassed 2,535 acres on the lake's east shore, taking up four-and-a-half miles of lakefront.

From groundbreaking to completion took only 270 days and cost approximately $56 million ($1.4 billion in 2019 dollars). Around 5,000 Navy personnel operated and maintained the base and a total of 411,429 sailors were trained there during its three-and-one-half years of operation. At war's end, Sampson became a separation center for discharging sailors. In spring 1946 the base closed down.

Sampson was improbable, but not completely illogical. Seneca Lake is a very large body of water, 38 miles long and five miles across at its widest point. It is also very deep at 618 feet, which makes it deeper than two Great Lakes. The Navy found it ideal for submarine testing and training.

That takes care of the Army and Navy. The Air Force presence in the area was also not to be denied. Sampson Air Force Base, up the hill from the Naval base and adjacent to the Depot, was employed as a training center from 1942 to 1956. After it closed down, the Depot used its jet runway to ferry nuclear warheads in and out of its facility.

But wait, that was not all. The U.S. Coast Guard opened a transmitter station on the Depot grounds in 1978 that remained active until 2010.

Few other locales could claim the presence of four different military services. This obscure, remote region was saturated with military establishments.

The Depot

Seneca Army Depot Bunkers, a.k.a., Ground Zero
(Public Domain)

By road, Seneca Army Depot is 31 miles from Canandaigua. Traveling between the two requires looping around the north shore of Seneca Lake, making a right-angle turn south, then heading down the east side of the lake to the main gate. However, as the Soviet Bear bomber flies, the distance between Canandaigua and the Depot is the hypotenuse. Applying Pythagoras' theorem, $a^2 + b^2 = c^2$, the distance is only 22 miles. Close enough to guarantee Canandaigua's total destruction.

It is reasonable to say that the Soviet Union would have targeted the Depot with at least one multi-megaton hydrogen bomb in order to be certain to wipe out the largest repository of

America's nuclear arsenal in a first strike. Given the concrete bunkers housing the warheads, with walls three feet thick, the bomb would have likely been one of the largest in the Soviet cache. The largest bomb the Soviet's ever tested was the humongous, 50-megaton "Tsar Bomba," which was detonated over the remote Arctic Sea island of *Novaya Zemlya* on October 30, 1961 (see Chapters 8 and 16).

The bomb was dropped by a Bear bomber and exploded at an altitude of around 15,000 feet. By the time it detonated, the plane was more than 100 miles away, but still felt the blast wave that almost destroyed it. The fireball was visible more than 620 miles away.

The Soviet "Tsar Bomba" detonation seen from a distance of 100 miles (Wikipedia)

All of the buildings in the village of *Severny*, 34 miles away, were destroyed. Wooden houses were leveled several hundred miles from the blast. Soviet scientists calculated that any human beings within 62 miles of the explosion would have suffered third-degree burns which, if they affected at least 24 percent of the body, would have been fatal.

Shockwaves from the explosion traveled around the world three times and broke windows in Finland and Norway.

If a bomb of this size were dropped on Seneca Army Depot, Canandaigua and most of its 8,000 inhabitants would have been wiped out by the bomb's initial effects. Those who survived the blast probably would have succumbed within a few days or weeks to fallout. Although unlikely, bomb shelters might have saved some of them, but only to die an agonizing death rather than having been instantaneously vaporized by the blast or follow-up 30,000 degree F. fireball.

Had I known growing up that Seneca Army Depot was a high-value Cold War target, I might not have been so dismissive of the ground observers doing their plane spotting or the Taj Mahal fallout shelter aficionados. I apologize, folks.

Postscript

Seneca Army Depot had an up-and-down history in its 50 years of serving as a U.S. Army ordnance repository. From its beginnings as a storage site for radioactive materials used in the Manhattan Project to its designation for closure by the Base Realignment and Closure Commission (BRAC) in 1995 (it officially ended its top secret existence as an Army facility in 2000), it went from bucolic obscurity to national news story and back.

In the early 1980s, local activists discovered what had really been going on at Seneca Army Depot for four decades, and they were not happy about it. On July 4, 1983, the first of a series of very vocal demonstrations by anti-war and anti-nuclear protesters took place just outside the Depot. These gradually escalated into civil disobedience led by a newly formed group calling itself the "Seneca Women's Encampment for a Future of Peace and Justice." The Encampment set up a headquarters operation in an old farmhouse on Route 96 in the village of Romulus, New York on the Eastern side of the Depot.

During an October 1983 protest, Dr. Benjamin Spock and a host of other less famous people climbed the fence surrounding the Depot and were arrested. The non-violent ones were quickly released after being given "ban and bar letters" telling them they would be charged with trespass if they were caught inside the Depot a second time. Feminist artist Helene Aylon and writer Grace Paley were also among the demonstrators.

The demonstrations continued for several years and from time-to-time made the evening TV news shows. The protesters demanded that the facility be closed. In 1995, they got their wish.

When the Depot closed down in 2000, a spirited debate arose about what to do with this huge piece of property and its many igloos. As with many BRAC-designated bases, the Depot was turned over to a local economic development authority for disposition.

The debate raged for years and, to an extent, still remains unresolved today. At various times, the property was leased by the Sports Car Club of America for racing competitions and by a Cornell University (Cornell is just over a halfhour distant from the Depot) Urban Challenge Team for testing autonomous (self-driving) vehicles. A few igloos have been leased to a storage and shipping business. Much of the base housing has been sold to private developers. The extensive railroad tracks and rail yards are being used for railroad car storage. The airfield is now a New York State Police training center. A plan to build an ethanol plant died due to the rising cost of corn. There is a possibility that the Army's 10th Mountain Division based at Fort Drum, New York about 90 minutes north of the Depot might use a portion of it for combat training. The Seneca County Redevelopment Authority would like to rent the igloos to entrepreneurs as start-up business space. However, if you have ever been inside one (I have), it would require a massive amount of "build-out" for that to be viable.

The White Deer

Following the closure of the facility and its partial transfer to the county economic development agency, The U.S. Army Corps of Engineers maintained the remaining undeveloped 7,000 acres and the 24 miles of fencing surrounding it. In 2016, this property was sold to a local Mennonite businessman for $900,000 and established as Deer Haven Park, LLC pursuant to an agreement between the new owner and the Seneca White Deer Foundation. The Foundation today leases part of the land and operates it as a conservation park for the largest herd of non-albino white deer in the world. The herd is estimated at somewhere between 200-600 deer. In late 2017, the Foundation opened a welcome center and museum and began conducting bus tours of the park. Having taken the tour, I can say that the white deer are elusive, but when you encounter them, they are a dazzling, ghostly sight.

The white deer began appearing after the Depot fence was erected in 1941. A handful of white-tailed deer that carried a recessive gene for all-white coats was isolated within the depot. The white deer live alongside 600 brown white-tailed deer.

The Spectacular Seneca White Deer
(Public Domain)

Remorse

A half-a-decade after I graduated from high school, still deriding Canandaigua's Cold War defense exertions, I found myself serving in a U.S. Army nuclear weapons unit in Germany. One day when on duty at our secret weapons storage site in Northern Bavaria's Franconian Forest, I saw a notation on the clipboard hanging on a nail in one of the bunkers where my platoon's tactical nuclear weapons were stored. It was a "chain of custody" log of one of the bombs in the bunker. The last entry indicated that the particular bomb in question came to us directly from Picatinny Arsenal in the Delaware Water Gap on the border between Pennsylvania and New Jersey, where the final bomb assembly was accomplished. The notation before that read: "Seneca Army Depot."

Apologies again to Canandaigua's plane spotters and shelter builders.

Chapter 5
The Wrong Direction

What's the best feature of a Trabant? — There's a heater at the back to keep your hands warm when you're pushing it.
—East German joke about the country's workhorse vehicle

The Worker's Paradise

Defections to the West from the captive nations of the Soviet Bloc were a constant Cold War phenomenon and propaganda weapon exploited very effectively by the United States. Why, if the Soviet Union and its Warsaw Pact neighbor nations were such workers' paradises did so many millions of their citizens move heaven and earth, often risking their lives, to defect to the West? The answer was simple: life behind the Iron Curtain sucked. They were Hobbesian horror shows. The life of men and women within the Soviet leviathan was guaranteed to be "solitary, poor, nasty, brutish, and short."

Soviet-era jokes say a lot about the rigors of the subsistence struggle that most of its unfortunate citizens had to endure:

We pretend to work and they pretend to pay us.

Q: *How do you deal with mice in the Kremlin?*
A: *Put up a sign saying 'collective farm.' Then half the mice will starve, and the rest will run away.*

Q: *Is it hard to be in the gulag?*
A: *Only for the first 10 years.*

Q: *What's the difference between a capitalist fairy tale and a Marxist fairy tale?*
A: *A capitalist fairy tale begins, 'Once upon a time there was . . .' A Marxist fairy tale begins, 'Some day, there will be . . .'*

Q: *Is it true that there is freedom of speech in the Soviet Union, just like in the USA?*
A: *In principle, yes. In the USA, you can stand in front of the White House in Washington, DC and yell, 'Down with Reagan!' and you will not be punished. Equally, you can also stand in Red Square in Moscow and yell 'Down with Reagan!' and you will not be punished.*

Q: *What is the difference between the Constitutions of the US and USSR?*
A: *Both of them guarantee freedom of speech, but the Constitution of the USA also guarantees freedom after the speech.*

These jokes paint an accurate picture of life behind the Iron Curtain. The barrage of Washington propaganda about how difficult it was to live under Communism embedded itself deeply into virtually every American's DNA.

But not everyone.

The Other Germany

During its 41-year existence, the German Democratic Republic (GDR) developed a reputation as the most repressive and dismal of the captive nations. Photographs taken during the Soviet era of the grand boulevard, *Unter den Linden*, which bisects the heart of Berlin from East to West, are strangely bereft of people. It looks as if a neutron bomb exploded there, wiping out humans but preserving the grand edifices like the Brandenburg Gate and the storied Hotel Adlon.

The end of World War II saw the beginning of one of the largest migrations of human beings in history. Ethnic Germans fleeing or expelled from what was to become the Eastern Bloc numbered around 15 million. This was a mass movement of people to which the Allies had agreed as the war wound down. More than two million of these people perished during their march westward, primarily those racing ahead of the Red Army as it advanced toward Germany, fearing Soviet reprisals against Germans, a fear that was real but also inflamed by Nazi propaganda. A large number of these Germans finally settled in what was to become the German Democratic Republic (GDR).

The Brandenburg Gate, Berlin
(Public Domain)

The establishment of a number of Communist buffer states occupied by and in thrall to the Soviet Union following World War II did not sit well with their populations, most of whom yearned for freedom. For ethnic Germans, this was especially acute. Four million of them found themselves outside what would become East and West Germany and prevented from further movement west by the Red Army. Many of these folks were subsequently forcibly deported to Siberia, Stalin fearing a fifth column.

Between 1945 and 1950, however, millions of people left the Eastern Bloc for the West at a time when borders could still be crossed relatively easily. Applications for political asylum in West Germany skyrocketed, and asylum was readily granted. By 1953, asylum applications had reached new highs coincident with Stalin's increasing paranoia.

During the 1948 UN debate leading to the Universal Declaration of Human Rights, the Soviet Union vigorously fought against the inclusion of the following language: "Everyone has the right to leave any country including his own." Only two nations supported the USSR (Poland and Saudi Arabia), so the language made it into the final Declaration.

By 1961, when the Berlin Wall went up, more than 3.5 million East Germans had fled to West Germany. It appears that a grand total of 11 West Germans defected to East Germany during the same period, along with four UK subjects (other than a handful of spies such as the "Cambridge Five"). Voting with one's feet meant that while the East experienced a flood of escaping humanity, the West felt not even a trickle.

Wagons East

During the 1950s, when the GDR was unquestionably the title holder for most repressive Eastern Bloc regime, a grand total of five Americans came to the conclusion that the East German workers' paradise was "it." One was Victor Grossman (née Steven Wechsler), a 24-year old U.S. Army draftee who grew up in a Socialist family and was a Harvard graduate. He was assigned to a unit at Warner Barracks in Bamberg, West Germany, but transferred to a U.S. base in Austria once the Army got wind of his left-wing leanings. From there, he deserted, swam the Danube and went to the Soviet Union. The Soviets then sent him to the GDR to become a journalist. He has lived there—and in what is now unified Germany—ever since.

My loose connection to Mr. Grossman is that I was also stationed in Warner Barracks in Bamberg almost two decades after him. I never had much interest in defecting, but I would have loved to travel to nearby Dresden and Leipzig. My security clearance did not allow that.

So, technically, Mr. Grossman did not defect to East Germany, but ended up there at the direction of his Soviet handlers. That leaves only four other candidates for the honor of being the only Americans during the 1950s to prefer the GDR to the USA. All were from Canandaigua, New York.

Dr. and Mrs. K were German Jewish refugees from the Nazis who were granted asylum in America and ended up settling in Canandaigua, where Dr. K, a psychotherapist, found employment with the big Veterans Administration mental hospital that was our town's largest employer. He and his wife and two children (both daughters if memory serves me) lived in one of the so-called "temporary" World War II Quonset huts that housed a number of VA physicians.

Canandaigua Veterans Administration Medical Center
(Public Domain)

The Ks became friends (acquaintances is probably the more accurate term) of my parents, who had pulled together an interesting circle of European refugees from all over Western New York State and met frequently to discuss current affairs and gossip about their peers. The group often gathered at our house where I listened from around the corner in the hallway to their bi-lingual (English and German) exchanges, which were often quite fascinating even to a young child.

Both Ks, however, were different from the rest of the gathering. It was clear that they were not happy U.S. campers. When the rest of the group expressed their relief—if not always their gratitude—at living in America and contrasted their safe existences with what they had endured in Europe, the Ks consistently argued the opposing point of view. They were critical of virtually everything American, its consumption obsession, its hucksterism, its anti-intellectualism, you name it.

The last time they came to our house, they were especially condemnatory of America and Americans. I remember the conversation descending into an angry debate where they were decidedly outnumbered. That was the last time my parents ever saw them . . . in person.

Two weeks later, there was another gathering of the refugee group at someone else's house. The Ks did not appear. One of the group members, another VA psychiatrist, reported that Dr. K had not shown up for work that week and no one knew where he was. The VA security contingent had gone to his Quonset hut and, when over the course of several days no one answered the door, broke in and found the place largely empty. The Ks had flown the coop.

Several weeks passed. Then, one evening during the nightly television news broadcast, we watched a clip from East Berlin. It featured Walter Ulbricht, the First Secretary, i.e. the leader of East Germany, announcing the defection of the family K, both parents and children positioned on either side of him. I thought my father was going to have a coronary.

Monsters' Ball: Mao-Tse-tung, Josef Stalin, Walter Ulbricht
(The Wilson Center)

I have no idea what happened to the Ks following their opting for the workers' paradise. I hope they found whatever it was they were seeking.

Chapter 6
Spasiba (Спасибо), Sputnik

Oh little Sputnik, flying high
With made-in-Moscow beep,
You tell the world it's a Commie sky
and Uncle Sam's asleep
 —Governor G. Mennen Williams (D-Mich.)

The Final Frontier Gets Breached

On Friday, October 4, 1957, I returned from home with my parents from a long vacation necessitated by my father's totally debilitating hay fever attacks. If he did not escape Western New York State—a.k.a. Ragweed Central—in mid-August when the ragweed bloomed and remain away until early October, he found himself bed-ridden and sometimes hospitalized.

Wait a minute, you might ask. What about school?

Until I was in what was then labeled junior high school (7th and 8th grades), I never saw the month of September in school, always absent until October. The older I got, the more embarrassed I became by being singled out to such an extreme extent. As the child of recently arrived Jewish refugees who spoke with heavy German accents, I stood out enough already. I certainly did not need an additional reason to be deemed "different."

When we arrived home, we sat down to dinner accompanied by the nightly news on television and learned that the Soviet Union had beaten us to space by launching a 28-lb beeping metal orb with tentacles called "Sputnik" (translation: "traveling companion"), a benign moniker for what to most

Americans—especially our national security establishment—was a decidedly non-benign but rather threatening piece of machinery. At least that's the way our government portrayed this "calamity" of mythic proportions to the public.

The government breathlessly informed us that history had changed. When they shared the dimensions of this shiny new orbiting object, I became a tad skeptical about the whole deal. Sputnik was about the size of a beach ball, just under 23 inches in diameter and weighing only 184 pounds.

It took 98 minutes to orbit the Earth. My first inclination was to go outside after dark and look for it.

Sputnik: The Dawn of the Space Age
(Public Domain)

The skies above Canandaigua were not exactly overflowing with airplanes on a flight path to nearby Rochester or anywhere else, and the lights of town did not exactly illuminate the night sky and blot out the stars, so I figured that my chances of seeing the little guy were pretty good. They weren't. I saw nothing moving across the night sky, so I went back inside and called my friend, Ben, with whom I had shared multiple musings about space travel over the years.

He had been following the frothy, hysterical radio broadcasts since he got home from school and filled me in on the national tumult Sputnik was generating. We spent several hours on the phone mulling over the implications. By the time we hung up, I had changed my opinion so much that I sat down and wrote a letter to President Eisenhower telling him that he better get on the stick now that we were so far behind in the all-important space race. If someone had held a gun to my head, I would have been unable to provide a compelling reason why exactly we were behind the eight ball.

Two years earlier, the U.S. had announced its intention to launch an Earth-orbiting satellite in the very near term. Several months later, the Navy's Vanguard rocket was selected to carry the payload. The Vanguard, however, proved to be a flawed design. The news media went overboard showing us images of failed launch pad attempts to get the thing to even fly. Despite that, the Soviet launch basically achieved nothing more than giving our Cold War adversary temporary bragging rights. All that happened to us was that we were caught off-guard.

The U.S. Reaction

Sputnik abruptly altered the American psyche while simultaneously shattering the post-war illusion that we were anointed by God to be the number one nation in every arena of human endeavor. It ushered in several entirely new ways of looking at things in the political, military, technological, scientific and educational spheres.

Then, before America was able to exhale, the Soviets struck again. On November 3, Sputnik II was launched, carrying a much heavier payload, including a dog named *Laika* who, sadly, died upon re-entry.

The public, fueled by media speculation borne of ignorance and lousy reporting, feared that if the Soviets could launch a heavy satellite, they must also be able to hit the U.S. with ballistic missiles carrying nuclear weapons.

Laika, the First Dog in Space
(Hungarian Stamp—Author's Collection)

Despite that conclusion requiring a leap of faith worthy of the closing scenes of *Indiana Jones and the Last Crusade*, the political world made much of the public anxiety. Twenty seven months later, Senator John F. Kennedy of Massachusetts announced that he was running for President. One of his central themes was that the Eisenhower administration, in which his opponent, Vice President Richard M. Nixon, was a key player, had carelessly allowed the Soviet Union to forge ahead of the U.S. in ballistic missile development. The Soviet Union actually launched the first ICBM in August 1957 and used the same R-7 rocket to put Sputnik into space two months later. But then the Soviet ICBM program ran into problems while U.S. missile technology leapfrogged ahead. During the 1960 presidential campaign, Kennedy kept harping on the "missile gap" whereas Nixon, constrained by classified information, was unable to respond with the facts, namely that if there was a missile gap, it was overwhelmingly in the U.S.'s favor.

On January 20, 1961, the day John F. Kennedy was sworn into office as the nation's 35th President, the relative missile strengths of the two superpowers were as follows:

- Soviet Union: 3 ICBMs capable of striking the U.S.
- U.S.: 123 ICBMs capable of hitting the Soviet Union. Only a week later, the first Minuteman missile was successfully tested. One thousand Minutemen would be deployed over the next six years.

JFK got an enormous amount of political hay out of his campaign oratorical fiction. Less than a month following the inauguration, Defense Secretary Robert McNamara said, at a Pentagon news conference: "I [have] concluded that if there was a missile gap, it was in our favor."

Going back to 1957, America was totally freaked out by Sputnik. Something had to be done.

First, the U.S. Defense Department responded by approving funding for another U.S. satellite project. The Navy was still permitted to slog ahead with the much-maligned Vanguard, but the new fair-haired boy was Werner von Braun, the reconstructed Nazi scientist who, along with a hundred of his Nazi scientist colleagues, the U.S. secreted into the country following World War II in order to (1) develop vehicles that could drop atomic bombs on our pending Soviet enemy, and (2) keep these rocket scientists out of Josef Stalin's hands. Von Braun had been the head of the German V-2 rocket development program that had wreaked so much destruction on English cities during the war from his *Peenemunde* redoubt where 7,000 slave laborers were worked to the bone (and many to death) putting his rockets together. Rehabilitated, he quickly became the darling of the deluded U.S. media.

On January 31, 1958, less than four months after Sputnik I, the U.S. successfully launched Explorer I, a modest-size satellite that actually contributed a significant scientific breakthrough, the discovery of the Van Allen magnetic radiation belts that envelop the Earth. The Explorer program continued to successfully launch lightweight, scientifically useful satellites.

No matter that we had largely caught up to and in many respects actually exceeded the Soviet achievement. They were first into space and that was all that counted.

The second major impact of the Sputnik launch was the creation by Congress of the National Aeronautics and Space Administration (NASA).

The NASA Logo
(Public Domain)

The Personal Effect

The National Defense Education Act

Finally, and most important for me because it had a direct and immediate impact on my life, was the enactment of the *National Defense Education Act (NDEA)*, which President

Eisenhower signed into law on September 2, 1958, just in time for me and the rest of the advance team of the Baby Boom generation (those of us born in its first year, 1946) to begin seventh grade. The law was a more sober and intelligent response to Sputnik than all the hoop-de-doo that had transpired in the immediate, panicky aftermath of the Soviet's surprise launch.

The Act was quite well-designed for a legislative pronouncement (having worked with Congress on legislation and spent a career dissecting bills, I can say with absolute confidence that most of them are as muddled and indecipherable as the Rosetta Stone). Its main purposes were to (1) restore public confidence in America's resolve and capabilities, and (2) fund more—and more robust—science and math education beginning in the junior high school years.

My junior high school lost no time in implementing a new program and finding ways to spend the sudden infusion of funds that quickly came its way. The powers-that-be quickly selected around 30 incoming seventh graders to receive an extra injection of science and math education. We were directed to rise early and get to school by 7:00 AM for two sequential science classes taught by the best junior high science teacher, Mr. Blake, and one of the best high school science teachers, Mr. Russell. The program continued into my eighth grade year and I felt as if I learned a lot in addition to my routine science classes during the regular school day.

The math component was offered during the regular school day. I felt well-prepared for high school math and found that feeling to be warranted once I arrived in secondary school.

A Minor (League) Adjustment

Beisbol Been Belly Belly Good to Me
  —Garrett Morris (playing "Chico Esquela"
    on *Saturday Night Live*)

At first, waking up early for extra classes was difficult because I was sneaking my transistor radio under the covers every night in order to listen to Rochester *Red Wings* baseball broadcasts, some of which did not end until after midnight. Lack of sleep did not bother me, though. Had I forgone the baseball broadcasts, I would have missed the last-ever professional baseball game in Havana, Cuba. It involved the Triple-A, International League Havana *Sugar Kings* playing the Red Wings in *El Gran Estadio del Cerro*. The game ended early when Red Wings manager Cot Deal pulled his team when one of his players, Frank Verdi, was shot and wounded by a raucous, gun-toting Cuban fan while leading off third base. The Sugar Kings went on to win the league championship, but had to play all of their remaining games away from Havana.

Official Havana Sugar Kings Logo
(Twitter.com)

Verdi wound up with only a flesh wound, but an esteemed and hallowed place in baseball trivia history. *Note: Long-time baseball fan Fidel Castro, a halfway decent pitcher during his college days, played in an exhibition game at "El Gran" the day before. He pitched two innings and got two strikeouts.*

The league moved the Sugar Kings to New Jersey for the 1960 season, once Castro declared himself a Communist

Fidel at the Exhibition Game
(Wikipedia)

and nationalized everything in Cuba that was not tied down. They resumed their existence as the Jersey City *Jerseys* (creativity not being an International League strong suit). The Jerseys lasted all of two seasons in Jersey City, then moved to Jacksonville, Florida, having discovered that Jersey City was more dangerous than Havana.

Lingua Not My *Franca*

I found the advanced classes stimulating. But more significant, I felt as if I was doing my patriotic part to defeat the Soviet menace. Some day, I fantasized, my extra science classes might enable me to design a bomb or a missile that could be lobbed into the men's room in the Kremlin and take care of the "problem" once and for all.

By eighth grade, the school was receiving more NDEA money from the U.S. government than it had anticipated. It decided to spend it on another accelerated program, this one in languages. A handful of us were selected to begin studying French in eighth grade rather than having to wait until high school to take a foreign language. The result was that I had five years of French under my belt by the time I graduated from high school.

I never questioned why French was selected instead of Russian. I had been under the impression that the French were our Cold War allies. I did not anticipate any chance that we would soon be bombing the Eiffel Tower, but I deferred to the superior information available to the school's administrators.

Despite the excellence of my teacher (I had the same teacher for all five years), nothing could overcome my tin ear for foreign languages. I went on to take two years of advanced French in college, this time from genuine Frenchmen. I did well my freshman year, but my sophomore year I found myself in a meat grinder of a graduate course for which I was hopelessly unprepared. The students included several from France. The course capstone was a 1-hour presentation on a literary subject of our choosing. I was so intimidated that I opted in September to give my presentation in May during the last week of classes. Big mistake. I lost a lot of sleep that year worrying about it and trying to scope out how I was going to survive this ordeal. I finally came up with a theme that enabled me to cheat: instead of standing up in front of the class and speaking without notes for a whole hour, I chose a topic that allowed me to read poems and prose passages that supported my argument that there were parallels between the governance of French King Henri IV and the classical literature of the era. If I could have avoided this trial by fire by bringing a doctor's note to the professor requesting that I be excused because of bone spurs, I would have. Despite all of this, I survived, albeit with a less-than-stellar grade.

Education Crashes

The accelerated science classes continued into high school, where I was able to take Biology, Chemistry and Physics a year early. The ultimate goal was to be able to take an Organic Chemistry class my senior year. However, the student attrition rate was such that, by the time senior year began, there were only three of us left from the original 30 students selected for the accelerated science program six years before. We each had spent the summer working on a special project that we would continue honing once senior year Organic class began. Mine was a study of marine bioluminescence, the unique biochemical phenomenon whereby an organism produces and emits light. I was very excited by what I had learned over the summer and was eager to move forward with actual experiments once back in school. It was not to be.

The local school board cancelled the Organic class after only two days, stating that it could not justify spending money on a teacher, equipment and materials for only three students. I felt bitter and betrayed. It cast a dark cloud over my senior year. I could not wait to blow town and get to college.

The abrupt termination of my science education was just the beginning. My accelerated math preparation allowed me and a number of other "surviving" students to take Calculus during our senior year. It was the first time that Calculus was offered by the high school. However, after the first semester, during which there was some attrition, history repeated itself and second-semester Calculus was cancelled.

My last semester in high school I had only two classes—English and French. The rest of my school day consisted of study halls.

Despite my less than glamorous experience with the waning stages of the NDEA, the Act nationally had a very positive impact on American education. I only discovered that once I arrived at college, where many of my peers came armed with something called Advanced Placement courses under their belts. I had never heard of the AP concept. That enabled them to be placed into higher level courses our freshman year.

I, in contrast, was assigned to a class snarkily known on campus as "Immigrant English." The professor was a closet homosexual (no one dared come out in those days) who took a lengthy break at the beginning of the second semester to go on a tryst with his boyfriend. That mattered little to me. What concerned me more were his selections for our reading and discussion assignments. For the Shakespeare component of the class, he assigned the plays that never get performed very much (for good reason): *The Winter's Tale*; *Cymbeline*; *Timon of Athens*; and *Titus Andronicus*. If the Bard had had to rely on just those third-rate dramas for his livelihood, he would have had to supplement his income by shoveling excrement in a Stratford suburb.

Legacy

America benefited greatly from the NDEA. We produced a legion of highly competent scientists, engineers and mathematicians. We quickly erased any lead the Soviet Union had in the space race. They may have beaten us to the punch again by catapulting the first man into space (Yuri Gagarin), but we beat them to the Moon by the end of the 1960s and they have never really caught up since.

More important, the NDEA launched us on the road to becoming the planet's technological and innovation leaders, a position we still hold today despite the anti-science and anti-education attitude of several recent presidents and their administrations. Unfortunately, our lead will soon disappear if those troglodytic attitudes continue to govern where and how we spend the limited funds reluctantly made available for scientific research and development.

Presidents Eisenhower and Kennedy deserve a great deal of credit for stepping up to the plate and realizing the importance of investing in education. The return on that investment propelled American prosperity and strength to previously unrealized heights. We won the race to the top with our Soviet adversaries largely because of that.

Chapter 7
American Apogee

We went to the New York World's Fair, saw what the past had been like, according to the Ford Motor Car Company and Walt Disney, saw what the future would be like, according to General Motors. And I asked myself about the present: how wide it was, how deep it was, how much was mine to keep.
—Kurt Vonnegut, *Slaughterhouse-Five*

If you graph American power looking for its peak, the year 1964 would probably be the mountaintop. That year we were at relative peace (the Gulf of Tonkin Resolution would not be approved by the cowed and clueless 88th U.S. Congress until August). The missile gap with the Soviet Union reached yawning chasm proportions—we were light years ahead of our adversary and it would require them to redirect much of their economy to military spending in order to play catch-up. We had not yet experienced the full impact of the justifiable discontents that fueled the civil rights movement and the women's movement. Cities were not yet burning. Daily anti-Vietnam protests were in the future. Drugs and the sexual revolution were still down the road. We were at the peak of our global power, albeit far from being able to call ourselves a just society.

America dominated the world not only militarily and in terms of our ability to project force anywhere. The U.S. economy was roaring. Gross Domestic Product growth that year was an incredible 5.8 percent, an achievement we are not likely to experience ever again. Our GDP for the year was seven times that of second-place Great Britain and logarithmically beyond what the Soviet Union could boast (even bearing in mind that Soviet economic statistics were largely bogus and invariably exaggerated).

If you wanted to grasp the differences between the two competing societies and ideologies, you had only to compare a U.S. grocery store groaning under the weight of fully stocked shelves and almost limitless options with a Soviet market, a misnomer . . . there was no such animal. If you went food shopping in Moscow, you had to go to the meat store, cheese shop, bread store, fish store, milk store, etc., stand in line for hours and, if you were lucky, actually come home with something to show for your ordeal.

In sum, the U.S. was the world's oyster, the envy of the planet.

Nowhere was this more evident than at the 1964 New York World's Fair, the last time the U.S. went all out to boast about "The American Way of Life." I couldn't wait to visit this marvel. I must admit that

The 12-Story High Unisphere at the New York World's Fair
(Wikipedia – photo by Anthony Conti)

my interest was focused almost exclusively on the U.S. pavilions. I was dismissive of what the other 79 exhibiting countries brought to display in New York. Even before I saw them, I was convinced that they could not hold a candle to what America was able to do.

In addition to the 140 pavilions, most of them gauzy ads for U.S. companies, there were marvels to jaw-drop over such as computer terminals with keyboards and CRT displays and even telephone modems. I was dazzled by American technology and innovation.

When I left the fairgrounds, I felt a lot better about the Cold War. There was no way the Soviets could defeat us.

Chapter 8
Channeling Vienna

Nobody intends to put up a wall!
—East German Premier Walter Ulbricht,
two months before the Berlin Wall was put up.

Nikita Khrushchev Misreads JFK's "Deer-in-the-Headlights" Affect in Vienna
(Public Domain)

The moment that the Cold War took its most dangerous turn down the path toward global annihilation occurred during a series of meetings on June 3-4, 1961 in Vienna, Austria between the first two men in the history of the planet with the ability to cause the extinction of the entire human race and every other species. If they miscalculated, the Cold War could instantly turn hotter than the sun and burn all of us to death.

My family hails from Vienna. They first arrived there in the 1890s and were only able to stay around for less than 50 years, when those who were savvy and lucky enough to be able to leave escaped the onrushing Holocaust and got out, most coming to America.

I first visited Vienna when I was 20. The only places I was interested in seeing were my parents' street growing up (they were born and raised in neighboring apartment buildings) and the Great Gallery at *Schönbrunn* Palace where President John F. Kennedy and Soviet Chairman Nikita Khrushchev, accompanied only by their interpreters, met during their Vienna Summit and took the measure of one another.

I was obsessed with the summit meeting place because it was there that, in my opinion, the most dangerous events of the first several years of the tumultuous and dangerous decade of the 1960s germinated. More on that later in this chapter.

Schönbrunn Palace
(By Thomas Wolf, www.foto-tw.de
CC BY-SA 3.0 de
Wikimedia Commons)

The Run-Up

Nixon and Nikita in the Kitchen

The events leading up to the Vienna summit began two years earlier during the Eisenhower administration. After almost a decade-and-a-half of escalating Cold War tension, the possibility of a warming of relations between the Soviet Union and the United States suddenly emerged. Soviet Communist Party Chairman Nikita S. Khrushchev appeared to be reaching out to the West now that he had more or less consolidated his power domestically. What had spiraled into fear of nuclear annihilation since both adversaries had developed The Bomb now seemed poised for a pause.

Khrushchev invited Vice President Richard M. Nixon to Russia, a first step toward reciprocal visits between the two leaders, Khrushchev and Eisenhower. While in Moscow at an exhibit of Americana at the July 24, 1959 opening of the American National Exhibition at *Sokolniki* Park, Nixon and his host engaged in an impromptu debate about the relative achievements of their two competing systems, Communism and Capitalism. The American exhibitors had constructed an entire house, claiming that it was one any American could afford. It contained all of the labor-saving and recreational devices intended to demonstrate state-of-the-art American consumerism. The debate was filmed and subsequently broadcast in both countries, but not equally. Tens of millions of U.S. viewers watched it and felt good about what they saw, which was that their country was far ahead of its rival when it came to quality of life. In contrast, in Russia the debate film was shown only late at night and only in Moscow. Very few Russians saw it and they were not able to discern much about what went on because the Soviets did not provide a translation of Nixon's remarks.

Khrushchev and Nixon Debate the Merits of Their Respective Systems
(Wikipedia - Public Domain)

Khrushchev's U.S. Visit

Two months later, Khrushchev flew to the United States, becoming the first Soviet leader to ever do so. He stayed for two weeks during which he met with President Eisenhower, publicly praised him, re-emphasized that the Soviets sought "peaceful co-existence" with the U.S., and agreed that Ike would visit the Soviet Union the next year.

In their private sessions, Khrushchev alternated between arrogance and bombast on the one hand, and sweetness and light on the other. His tough guy persona may have been a façade to disguise the fact that the Soviets only possessed four ICBMs capable of reaching the continental United States versus 123 for the U.S. (See the discussion of the "Missile Gap," above.)

Khrushchev also traveled outside of Washington, visiting, among other venues, an Iowa farm. When he left, both the administration and the media slapped the label "The Spirit of Camp David" on the meeting, deeming it a success and the first foray by both sides into someday trusting one another. Khrushchev left a favorable impression on Americans. For the first time since the beginning of the Cold War, there was a glimmer of hope and an opportunity to relax . . . a little.

Ike, Khrushchev, Mamie and Nina at the White House State Dinner
(Wikipedia - Public Domain)

You Too?

The relaxation of tensions did not last long. Less than nine months after Khrushchev's successful U.S. visit, all of the good feeling and optimism that resulted came crashing down along with a CIA-sponsored U-2 spy plane shot down over the Soviet Union. Exacerbating the situation, Ike's advisors convinced him initially to lie about the U-2's incursion deep into Soviet airspace (the plane was downed over *Sverdlovsk* [now *Yakaterinburg*] more than 2,300 miles inside the Soviet

Union), claiming that the U.S. government had no knowledge of the flight, a weak and ludicrous response that was quickly debunked.

Within days, Eisenhower was forced to admit that the plane was on a reconnaissance mission, taking off from Pakistan with the objective of landing in Norway. The pilot, Francis Gary Powers, survived the downing of his aircraft. He did not inject himself with the instantly lethal, shellfish-derived *saxitoxin*-tipped needle he carried with him in a modified silver dollar. A show trial was held, Powers was convicted and sentenced to ten years. He was in a Soviet prison for only one year when he was exchanged for Soviet "master" spy Rudolf Ivanovich Abel in a dramatic, nighttime transfer in Berlin. *Note: Abel had been feeding information back to Moscow for years when he was caught. There is considerable evidence that his "spying" consisted of full days spent at the New York Public Library reading openly available U.S. media sources like the New York Times and Time magazine and relaying what he learned to Moscow Centre.*

Eisenhower had grudgingly approved the spy missions two years before and requested permission from Pakistan to establish a secret base at Peshawar from which the planes could take off. He was initially opposed to the spy missions, worried that if a plane were shot down it might be viewed as an act of aggression. What finally convinced him to allow the flights was the substitution of British for American pilots. The first two missions were flown by Brits and were successful, pinpointing Soviet missile sites. Ike then allowed additional missions. However, in the months leading up to his scheduled May, 1960 Paris summit with Khrushchev, he grudgingly authorized the CIA to fly only two more missions.

The first one, on April 9th, was flown by an American pilot without incident. It provided a gold mine of information, as the plane was able to fly over and photograph four top secret Soviet military facilities. By this time, however, U-2 flights were being routinely detected and tracked by Soviet Air Defense Forces and prompted attempted interception by Soviet fighters. These invariably failed because the fighters could not fly high enough to threaten the U-2s.

The fruits of the flight were so valuable that the second flight was quickly scheduled for late April. Bad weather forced a postponement, so Powers' did not get airborne until May 1, only 15 days prior to the Paris summit.

This time, the Soviets, anticipating another mission, were ready. All units of the Soviet Air Defense Forces went on high alert. Once the plane was detected, an all-out attempt to bring it down went into action. Its high altitude again caused fighter interceptor efforts to fail. However, a surface-to-air missile (SAM) scored a direct hit and Powers ejected. He was captured when he landed in Russia.

The U-2 Spy Plane Cruising at 70,000 Feet (Not High Enough)
(History.com - Public Domain)

The cover-up, first implemented by NASA and then picked up by Eisenhower, blew up in America's face when Khrushchev produced Powers and the plane's wreckage. Eisenhower was deeply embarrassed. Khrushchev at this point, however, still wanted to preserve the scheduled summit and so directly blamed not the President, but his CIA chief, Allen Dulles.

Word began circling that Eisenhower was not in control of his own administration, a terrible condemnation that deeply hurt the general who masterminded the World War II victory in Europe. The President even contemplated resigning. He decided to go public with his own direct role in the affair and gave a speech to that effect on May 11, at the end of which he announced that he was still going to Paris.

But his admission of complicity in the U-2 debacle and subsequent cover-up made a successful summit impossible. It only lasted one day, during which Khrushchev blasted the U.S. at every occasion. He rescinded his invitation to Eisenhower to visit Moscow.

The Ultimate Spy Plane, the Incredible SR-71 "Blackbird," Replaced the U-2
(Wikipedia)

Pigging Out

In its waning days, the Eisenhower administration was beset by one Cold War crisis after another. The U-2 embarrassment and subsequent escalation of East-West tensions was the beginning of a cascade of dismal events that did not wind down until the 1970s efforts at "détente." The Cold War, which appeared to be warming a bit in 1959, was back on.

The next setback was Fidel Castro's coming out of the Communist closet. When his Cuban revolution triumphed on January 1, 1959, he was hailed by both a clueless Washington and dazzled media who labeled him a pro-American folk hero. The U.S. intelligence failure regarding Castro and his revolution's true Marxist-Leninist nature ranks as one of the worst blunders of the Cold War era.

In April, Castro visited the U.S. in a charm offensive that firmed up the mistaken belief that he was America's best friend. At the same time, he began to institute policies back home that showed beyond any doubt that he was much farther to the left than the U.S. government believed: nationalizing healthcare; redistributing wealth and income; radical land reform; etc. He began to appoint avowed and overt Marxists to senior government positions.

A befuddled U.S. began to be concerned that Fidel was not going to turn out to be America's "BFF." This was confirmed beyond any doubt toward the end of 1959 when Castro began openly aligning himself with Moscow.

By 1960, with the Cold War raging at a fever pitch, Castro began openly expressing his hostility to the U.S. He reached an agreement with the USSR to provide sugar and other items to his new benefactor in return for oil, agricultural and industrial goods and a $100 million low-interest loan. When U.S. refineries on the island refused to process Soviet oil, he nationalized them. The U.S. retaliated by cutting off sugar imports, whereupon Castro nationalized almost all remaining U.S. assets.

Castro and Che Guevara Enter Havana, January 1, 1959
(Wikipedia)

This was the last straw for the Eisenhower administration. Fearing the growing Soviet presence and influence just 90 miles offshore, Eisenhower in March 1960 directed the CIA to overthrow Castro's government. He even authorized the CIA to work with the Mafia, who also lost all of their billion-dollar Havana investments in casinos and brothels. This was followed up in October by a total economic embargo of Cuba.

In September 1960, Castro visited New York City for the opening session of the UN General Assembly, where he met with Nikita Khrushchev. The two of them sucked up all of the media attention with their on-camera denunciations of "U.S. imperialism."

A few weeks after the tumultuous Castro visit, the first-ever presidential debate took place between Vice President Nixon and Senator John F. Kennedy. Nixon believed that he was by far the superior debater, having bested Nikita Khrushchev in the kitchen exhibit in Moscow. However, Kennedy prevailed thanks to his looks, his demeanor, his demonstration that he was Nixon's equal, and his incessant criticism of the "missile gap" (see above).

Contrasting Images at the First Presidential Debate, September 26, 1960
(tutorialspoint.com)

When the government transitioned from Eisenhower to Kennedy on January 20, 1961, JFK inherited the Bay of Pigs operation, the CIA's plan to overthrow the Castro government, and decided to go ahead with it. On April 15, CIA-owned B-26s bombed Cuban military airfields. The next night, the CIA's 1,400-strong Cuban exile army—Brigade 2506—left its secret training base in Guatemala and landed at Cuba's *Bahía de cochinos*—Bay of Pigs—on the island's south coast. The rag-tag army had no air support, which had been pulled by Kennedy. It took only three full days for the Cuban army to overwhelm the brigade and force its surrender.

The Bay of Pigs, Cuba—Nothing Like Ceding the High Ground to the Defenders
(History.com)

Castro's victory stunned the world and embarrassed Kennedy, making him look weak, inexperienced and indecisive, not the best trifecta with which to travel to Vienna for a summit meeting with the Communist world's chief.

Summit Prep

Kennedy's perceived ineptitude was precisely the reason why Nikita Khrushchev was eager to extend an invitation to meet him in Vienna in early June. JFK, for his part, was even more eager to accept Khrushchev's invitation, viewing it as an opportunity to rehabilitate his shattered reputation and demonstrate that he was a formidable player on the world stage.

Kennedy dove into the briefing papers like a man possessed. They included psychological profiles of Khrushchev and additional mountains of material his staff and the bureaucracy had prepared for him. He was probably more prepared for the Vienna meeting with his antagonist than any other president facing any other issue at any other time.

At the same time, however, he was in excruciating pain resulting from his chronic ailing back and his well-hidden-from-the-public Addison's Disease. Addison's is a rare insufficiency wherein the adrenal glands don't produce enough Cortisol, a steroid hormone that regulates metabolism and the immune response and plays an important role in helping the body respond to stress, and too little Aldosterone, the lack of which can have a devastating effect. Addison's in JFK's time was life-threatening. Treatment today involves supplementing the missing hormones, a therapy that did not exist in the early 1960s. Symptoms include: extreme fatigue, weight loss, decreased appetite, hyperpigmentation (JFK's ruddy complexion deluded the public into believing he was the picture of health; in fact, the opposite was the case . . . outside the bedroom); low blood pressure; low blood sugar (hypoglycemia); gastrointestinal distress; abdominal pain; muscle and joint pain; irritability; depression or other behavioral symptoms; and a compromised immune system that made it challenging to fight off infections. He had also suffered from venereal diseases for twenty-five years. To combat these maladies, he had been consuming megadoses of antibiotics and received constant cortisone injections for most of his life. In sum, Kennedy was a mess.

He compensated for his severe health problems by enlisting the assistance of a physician originally recommended to him during the 1960 presidential campaign, according to some sources, by his brothers-in-law, Peter Lawford, an actor and member of Frank Sinatra's "Rat Pack," and Stanislaus Radziwill, the husband of Jackie Kennedy's sister. Dr. Max Jacobson had become something of a Hollywood and Broadway icon and counted among his patients stars and celebrities such as Marilyn Monroe, Elvis Presley, Alan Jay Lerner, Andy Warhol, Anthony Quinn, Bob Fosse, Cary Grant, Cecil B. DeMille, Eddie Fisher, Elizabeth Taylor, the Everly Brothers, Frank Sinatra, Ingrid Bergman, Jerry Lewis, Judy Garland, Leonard Bernstein, Marlene Dietrich, Mickey Mantle, Otto Preminger, Peter Lorre, Richard Burton, Sharon Tate, Tennessee Williams, Tony Curtis and Yul Brynner, among others.

Jacobson, a.k.a. "Miracle Max" and "Dr. Feelgood," had devised a cocktail of illegal substances to which he added amphetamines ("speed"), with which he injected his clients. Investigative reporter Seymour Hersh, in this book, *The Dark Side of Camelot*, describes Jacobson thusly: "the doctor of choice in the early 1960s for many in fast New York society." That, as you can see from the partial client list above, is a major understatement.

Secret Service visitor logs show that Jacobson made more than 30 visits to the White House and also ministered to the President and First Lady in Palm Beach and Hyannisport. Eventually, he became the subject of federal investigators for alleged misuse of amphetamines; his medical license was revoked in the mid-1970s. Dr. Max also left JFK his "cocktails" and a bunch of needles and taught him how to inject himself. It is unknown how often the President self-medicated, but given his daily battles with pain and immobility, it is reasonable to assume that this occurred frequently. Sen. George Smathers, one of Kennedy's closest friends, said that the President needed the shots at six-hour intervals.

Any medication loses its punch the more it is administered. For it to remain effective, doses must be increased, and Jacobson was readily disposed to go to "DefCon 1" when it came to his most important patient.

Jacobson himself wrote that he first injected JFK just before one of his televised debates with Richard Nixon in 1960. He accompanied Kennedy to the 1961 Vienna summit and gave him multiple shots during the two-day affair prior to his meetings with his Soviet counterpart.

According to the ex-wife of one of Jacobson's patients, her husband injected himself with the Jacobson compound and got "flushed in the face. His eyes would get a glazed look—the whites would look full of mucus and be fixed—and his mouth would get dry." She went on to say that a certain zombie-like numbness and unresponsiveness set in.

The Meetings

Kennedy and Khrushchev met three times during the two-day Vienna summit, twice privately for substantive discussions, the last such meeting taking place on June 4, 1961 in the spectacularly appointed Grand Gallery at Schönbrunn. It was in this room that four of the most important Cold War milestones of the 1960s, occurrences that changed the course of history, got their start (more on that below).

By the time of the summit, Kennedy had been shooting up Dr. Feelgood's mystery medication for more than a year. Pharmacologists say that overuse of amphetamines over time can promote a partially opposite reaction to what the drug is designed to do, which is give the patient a "high" and a feeling of omnipotence. Given the hundreds of injections administered and self-administered, it is likely that JFK, while temporarily pain-free from whatever pain-killers were included in the mix, was experiencing a "downer" that affected his mental faculties.

Khrushchev's post-mortem evaluation of the summit was that he had successfully intimidated his young, inexperienced adversary. Encouraged by Kennedy's non-responsiveness to his threats, bluster and bombast, the Soviet leader left Vienna, his principal takeaway being a conviction that he had JFK's number. It would not be long before he began to act on his assumption that Kennedy was a wimp.

Consequences

1. The Berlin Wall

Only 70 days after the summit, Nikita Khrushchev ordered the construction of the Berlin Wall. The wall was erected to stem the hemorrhage of East Germans escaping their country's repressive regime and fleeing to the West. In the 16 years since the establishment of the Soviet Communist East German puppet state, almost 3.5 million East Germans crossed over divided Berlin into a new life in the West. This was a tremendous embarrassment to the Soviets. Khrushchev, emboldened by his meeting with Kennedy, took the opportunity to stop the mass escape. Although the wall construction caused an escalation of tensions, there was little the West could do about it. To Khrushchev, American passivity confronted with this slap in the face confirmed the opinion of Kennedy he had formed in Vienna.

The wall came to symbolize the Cold War. For Khrushchev, its success encouraged him to take the next step in his competition for global supremacy.

2. 50 Megatons Here We Come!

On October 30, 1961, only weeks after the construction of the Berlin Wall, Khrushchev decided to rub Kennedy's nose in the dirt pile he had laid down in Vienna by conducting the largest nuclear weapons test in history. The "Tsar Bomba" blast over the Arctic Sea island of Severny just off *Novaya Zemlya* produced the equivalent energy of 50 megatons of TNT, more than 3,000 times more powerful than the Hiroshima bomb. Khrushchev's intent was obvious in the name he chose to give this monster weapon: "Kuzka's Mother," from an old Russian saying that you are about to teach someone an unforgettably harsh lesson.

See Chapter 16 for more about Tsar Bomba.

3. The Cuban Missile Crisis

On October 14, 1962, a CIA U-2 spy plane on a pass 70,000 feet over Cuba photographed the partial assembly of a Soviet SS-4 medium-range ballistic missile. The CIA photo interpreters were shocked by what they saw—an offensive, nuclear-capable missile only 90 miles from the United States. President Kennedy was briefed on the discovery two days later and immediately assembled a group of advisors that became known as the "ExCom." For the next two weeks, the world came as close to nuclear war and the extinction of mankind as it ever has. The Cold War had reached its apogee.

This was supposed to be Nikita Khrushchev's finest hour, his ultimate aggressive move founded on the perception of Kennedy he took away from Vienna as a weak adversary who would

Khrushchev and Kennedy Fiddle with the Fate of Mankind
(researchgate.net)

wilt if threatened. He badly miscalculated. The tables now turned. Khrushchev discovered that the perceived wimp had some junkyard dog in him.

Kennedy sensed that it was now or never. If he was going to expiate the impression he had left of himself with Khrushchev in Vienna and then underscored by his inaction following the building of the Berlin Wall, it had to be with respect to an offensive nuclear threat within spitting distance of the U.S. He imposed a ship quarantine on Soviet vessels heading to Cuba with missile parts and possibly nuclear warheads. In so doing, he also exercised restraint, vetoing his reckless ExCom advisors' consensus that we needed to take more aggressive action against the Soviet Union.

Following backdoor negotiations handled primarily by Attorney General Robert Kennedy and Soviet Ambassador to the U.S. Anatoly Dobrynin, an agreement was reached to the effect that the Soviets would dismantle their Cuba-based missiles in return for a U.S. quid pro quo to do the same with our missiles in Turkey, on the Soviet southern border. The U.S. reciprocal arrangement was done clandestinely, making it appear that Khrushchev had blinked first in the face of Kennedy's steadfastness.

4. The Vietnam Escalation

JFK was not done. His reversal of form did not end with his public triumph in the Missile Crisis. His confidence was only partially rebuilt. He knew, if the public did not, that removing the missiles from Cuba was nothing more than reciprocation for our stand down in Turkey. To Kennedy, that meant that Khrushchev might yet not respect him as a leader on a par with himself. He felt that he still needed to demonstrate his mettle and American resolve. Vietnam was going to be the locus of that demonstration. After all, in his 1961 inaugural address, he said America would "pay any price, bear any burden, meet any hardship, support any friend, oppose any foe, to assure the survival and success of liberty."

Kennedy is hardly the only president to blame for the tragedy of U.S. involvement in a war that should never have happened. Like a slowly metastasizing cancer, Presidents from Truman through Nixon shared much the same philosophy.

If we want to date the beginning of our slippage down the slope into the black hole of a horrific war that cost the lives of more than 58,000 Americans and an estimated 3-plus million Vietnamese, 1950 is probably our best bet. President Truman, in a startling reversal of Franklin Roosevelt's opposition to the continuation of colonial empires at the end of World War II, decided to help France retain its hold over Indochina, mistakenly believing that he was preventing Chinese Communist expansion into Southeast Asia. He based this on the false assumption that the Vietnamese nationalist leader, Ho Chi Minh, was a Chinese pawn. This display of acting on misinformation was yet another monumental U.S. intelligence failure borne of historical ignorance: Vietnam and China have been mortal enemies for 2,000 years. To the extent they were reluctantly pushed into each other's arms, it was because of French and American intervention in Vietnam. In fact, even at the 1954 Geneva Conference convened to settle the Vietnam

Divided Vietnam
(alphahistory.com)

"problem," China pushed the Vietnamese Communists to agree to a partition of their country. One way to describe our blunder was that we were intent on containing a China that at the time required no containment.

By the time of the Geneva Conference, the French had suffered a shocking defeat at *Dien Bien Phu* and had had enough of Vietnam. U.S. Secretary of State John Foster Dulles and his brother, CIA director Allen Dulles, the chief proponents of President Eisenhower's global containment policy, stepped into the vacuum caused by the French abandonment of its colony and refused to permit agreed-upon elections to be held, fearing that Ho Chi Minh would win. Instead, the U.S. supported partition and began to view South Vietnam as a client state and potential bulwark against the naively assumed "domino theory" that all of Southeast Asia would fall to the Communists if they prevailed in Vietnam.

The Geneva "solution" was really just a postponement of a final solution to the Vietnam problem. Having replaced France as the principal colonial power in (South) Vietnam, President Eisenhower felt that he needed to do something to support our new dependent state and a regime that was already being threatened by Communist *Viet Minh* guerrillas. He turned to a man who was already something of a legend in the region—Colonel Edward Lansdale, a charismatic alumnus of the wartime Office of Strategic Services (the predecessor to the CIA) whose reputation was made by helping the Philippine leader and later president, Ramon Magsaysay, crush the *Hukbahalup* rebellion.

Lansdale's approach was "psychological warfare," the winning of "hearts and minds," a stunningly naïve approach labeled "counterinsurgency" that compounded the cluelessness of the Truman administration's misperception of the complex realities of Vietnam. Lansdale's superficial and wholly ineffective strategy was unfortunately endorsed by several otherwise respected journalists and authors.

Lansdale's original coterie consisted of only 12 soldiers and intelligence agents. However, they were the germ that by the mid-to-late 1960s expanded into a massive, 500,000 man military force.

The group violated the Geneva accords with impunity, making forays into North Vietnam to sabotage oil shipments and helping to rig elections in the South, among other transgressions.

Gradually, the American mission grew in size until, at the changeover of U.S. administrations in early 1961, it consisted of several hundred "advisors," a handful of whom lost their lives in skirmishes with the Viet Minh. When Eisenhower handed the baton over to Kennedy, the latter considered Vietnam a relatively low priority. That, however, quickly changed thanks to Col. Lansdale's return to Washington armed with an alarming report about the deteriorating situation in Vietnam. Kennedy was unnerved by what he read.

While Eisenhower, a military strategist perhaps unmatched in the twentieth century, was not really a fan of Lansdale, JFK in contrast was smitten by him and bought into his charisma and counterinsurgency-hearts-and-minds strategy without much of any due diligence. Sadly, this was also one time that being an avid reader misled a president down the wrong path.

Kennedy was familiar with accounts of the successful British anti-guerilla efforts in Malaya the decade before, which appeared to have also heavily influenced Lansdale. The "Malayan Emergency" was a jungle conflict that has often been compared to and contrasted with the Vietnam War. The differences that led to British success and American failure were, however, stark:

- The Malayan rebels came from the country's ethnic Chinese population and looked different from the ethnic Malays who supported the colonial government. In Vietnam, both sides were of the same ethnicity.

- Malaya's geography was very different from Vietnam's. Instead of borders with sympathetic countries like China, Laos and Cambodia (supplies for the North and Viet Cong came through China; Laos and Cambodia provided safe havens for the insurgents as well as relatively safe pathways into South Vietnam), Malaya's only border was with Thailand, which supported the British.
- At its peak, the Malay insurgency numbered only 8,000 fighters, vs. 1.1 million North Vietnamese and Viet Cong troops.
- The Brits set up a Jungle Warfare School and put their troops though extensive training. The Americans largely stuck with their conventional training programs with little emphasis on the unique conditions troops would confront in Vietnam.

Had Kennedy or his "best and brightest" advisors bothered to absorb these lessons, history might be very different. He did not live to see the results of this disastrous intervention and his successor felt bound by his pledge to pursue Kennedy's domestic and foreign policy goals come what may.

Destroying a Country in Order to Save it
(Wikipedia - Public Domain)

Postscript

Kennedy continued to receive injections of Dr. Feelgood's "cocktail" throughout his presidency. The confidence he gained via his Cuban Missile Crisis "triumph" might have been augmented by the feeling of invincibility that often accompanies massive ingestions of amphetamines and whatever else Dr. Jacobson was pouring into the president's pain-wracked body. JFK went into Vietnam feeling that victory over a bunch of peasants who wore straw hats and flip-flops was inevitable.

There is a cohort of revisionist historians who claim that, had he lived, Kennedy would have pulled our growing number of advisors out of Vietnam and thus avoided the calamity that ensued. I don't buy that at all. Every one of his instincts, his history (see, e.g., his bellicose inaugural address) and his fantasies point to just the opposite: an escalation of our involvement in a place where we never should have been.

At the beginning of the Kennedy administration, the U.S. had only a few hundred military advisors in Vietnam. By November 22, 1963, the day JFK died, we had 16,000.

Sic transit Gloria mundi.

When I walked alone into the Grand Gallery at Schönbrunn only five years after it served as the scene of one of the most momentous summits in history and the take-off point for some of the most significant events of the second half of the twentieth century, I was so excited that I began hyperventilating. This is par for the course for me whenever I stride into or through a place of great historical significance. But this was special.

At that time, the Schönbrunn tour managers retained the two chairs in the same places in the gallery where John F. Kennedy and Nikita S. Khrushchev sat while, *mano-a-mano*, they played great power games with the future of mankind. I visualized them in the center of the huge room with the fate of the planet hanging in the balance. I felt their auras. It was both heady and bone-chilling.

Upon exiting the gallery at the other end, my respiration returned to normal and my brain agitation gradually subsided. I began to contemplate the implications of what had happened in that room that afternoon in June 1961. Since then, I have returned to thinking about it often, but it took me until well into the twenty-first century to realize just exactly what those discussions signified. To this day, I think with amazement and not a little bit of outrage about the reckless disregard for humanity that marked Kennedy's and Khrushchev's behavior and the impunity with which they toyed with the planet and its billions.

An Historical Aside

The Vienna Summit was a momentous meeting, on a par with the Versailles Peace Conference at the end of World War I and an early nineteenth century gathering that carved up Europe after the chaos of the Napoleonic interruption, the 1815 Congress of Vienna.

For that Vienna meeting, Austria and its Habsburg emperor pulled out all the stops and put on one of the greatest shows in history. The Congress lasted many months and included the brightest luminaries, political and otherwise, of the era: emperors, tsars, kings, princes, dukes, foreign ministers, glitterati from all walks of life, entertainers from Salieri to Beethoven, and an assortment of wives, girlfriends, mistresses, camp followers and the nineteenth century equivalent of *paparazzi* and gossip columnists who kept their readers breathless with their descriptions of both the gala parties and the interminable negotiations.

The participants, including the Duke of Wellington, had to take a breather when Napoleon escaped from his casual exile on the island of Elba and re-energized his troops for what became known as the "100 days" that culminated in the decisive Battle of Waterloo. Afterwards, the Congress of Vienna completed its work of restoring monarchies and realigning the map of Europe. It must be considered a success because Europe avoided a major war for the next 99 years.

The Vienna Summit of 1961, in contrast, proved to be a disaster of massive proportions. It was the first such meeting where the participants convened mindful, but with reckless disregard, of the fact that any misstep might mean curtains for humanity.

This chapter focused on weighty events of global and even existential significance, *macro* material that stressed even the author in writing about them. The next chapter affords a bit of a breather in the form of a *micro* description of how the Cold War impacted on college life in the mid-to-late 1960s.

Chapter 9
G.I. Joe College

I came from Yale, where you get an extracurricular degree in self-importance because you went there.
—Larry Kramer

The Freshmen Arrive on the Old Campus
(Yale University)

Clouded by Vietnam

The "bright college years" would have been a lot brighter absent the culmination of what the Vienna summit wrought, namely the Vietnam War. It—and the possibility of becoming cannon fodder following graduation in what we almost all considered a huge, tragic mistake—loomed like a Sword of Damocles over our heads for most of the four years we spent on campus. It was always there and it began to hit home fairly soon after we arrived for our Freshman year in the fall of 1964, less than a month after Congress approved the Gulf of Tonkin resolution and gave President Lyndon B. Johnson carte blanche to proceed with escalating the Vietnam War into the greatest U.S. foreign policy blunder of the twentieth century.

Aside from two brave Senatorial dissenters—Ernest Gruening of Alaska and Wayne Morse of Oregon—no one really understood the ominous implications of the Tonkin Gulf Resolution. We too were among the duped. When Johnson ran as the "peace candidate" in 1964 and won by a landslide over the perceived warmonger, Sen. Barry Goldwater, a feeling of relief swept the campus. Our rear ends were now safe for the time being.

Note. The only elective I was permitted to take during my first college semester (those were the days of the core curriculum) was a "Chinese History and Politics" course taught by an eminent "China hand," Professor David Nelson Rowe. When he took a leave of absence to advise the Barry Goldwater campaign on foreign policy during the fall of 1964, we complained about losing a renowned teacher and having to be saddled with his stand-in, a young Ph.D. candidate named Jonathan Spence, who wound up doing a stellar job substituting for a genuine luminary. In the ensuing years, Spence went on to become the greatest American Chinese scholar of the twentieth century and the author of a now-classic work, "The Search for Modern China," among many other ground-breaking books. FYI, he was the spitting image of another Scotsman, Sean Connery. Generations of Yale women signed up for his class just to ogle him.

If this sounds like whining, it is. The whole time I spent in college, I was acutely aware that many less fortunate than me were being drafted and shipped to Southeast Asia to fight and perish in a stupid war. That does not excuse the "better them than me" attitude that underlay everything we proclaimed and protested about the war.

But the threat was real, as an incident during those college days underscored. Two classmates decided to crash a reception at the college president's house sporting raincoats. When they took off their raincoats, they were revealed to have nothing on underneath except a pair of socks each. For that, they were expelled from school. One of them was welcomed back, unchastened by his experience as it turned out, after only a year (he was expelled a second time for a subsequent transgression; however, Mother Yale was forgiving once again and readmitted him a second time). The other one was immediately conscripted upon leaving school and, within a few months, found himself in Vietnam, where he was killed soon after arriving in country.

Running with the Enemy

It is hard to believe that a book about the Cold War could twice talk about running track as a core topic. Nevertheless, it can and does.

My college track coach, Bob Giegengack, had just returned from being the head coach of the United States men's track and field team at the 1964 Olympics in Tokyo several weeks before my matriculation.

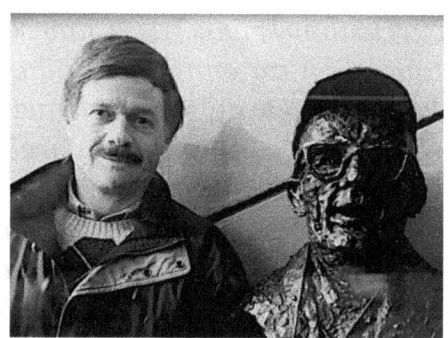

The Author by a bust of Yale (and U.S. 1964 Olympic Team) Track Coach Bob Giegengack
(Author Collection)

The Olympics were a very big deal for my class in any event because far-and-away the most famous member of the incoming Freshman class was a young man named Donald Schollander, who had just hauled in four swimming gold medals at the Tokyo games. We were all in awe of him, having only weeks before watched him dominate the swimming world on television. Knowing that "Gieg" had come back after coaching the greatest assemblage of track athletes in Olympic history, with a record haul of medals to prove it (U.S. athletes won 14 of the 24 gold medals), was icing on Yale's cake.

When I met Gieg at my first track practice that fall, I was so in awe that I was unable to speak. He quickly calmed me down with an anecdote from the Olympic Games, but more so because of his rich, endearing Brooklyn accent. By the end of that first day of practice, I would have followed him into battle.

While in Tokyo, Gieg and his Soviet counterpart, head coach Gavril Korobkhov, became good friends, a rare Cold War phenomenon. This was especially the case because Gieg coached a bunch of amateurs—all-time Olympic greats like Bob Hayes, the world's fastest human, Billy Mills, the Native American upset winner of the 10,000 meters, long jumper Ralph Boston and discus thrower Al Oerter—while Korobkhov managed a team of professionals whose livelihood was totally consumed by training.

The friendship continued once both teams returned to their respective motherlands and culminated in a very unusual arrangement: my Sophomore year, the Soviet national track and field team spent the winter in New Haven, training with us every day. Legends like high jumper Valeri Brumel, long jumper Igor Ter-Ovanesyan and the Jewish Press sisters, Tamara and Irina (we called them "the Press brothers" for reasons that will be obvious if you Google them and have a gander at a few photos) were now grunting and sweating in our indoor facility every day. It was both exhilarating and defeating to know that, every single day you are going to get the shit kicked out of you by some of the world's greatest athletes.

Tamara and Irina Press, Holders of 26 world records
(genderverificationinsports.com)

Ter-Ovanesyan, a 27-foot long jumper and world record holder, was the only English speaker on the Soviet team and something of an intellectual, being very well-read and eager to discuss books and ideas with anyone who would listen. He gave me a few tips on my long jump technique and I actually improved marginally as a result. I was eager to break bread with him outside of practice, but that was impossible because the Soviet team was kept on an extremely tight leash by its KGB "handlers," burly fellows who accompanied the team everywhere and stood off to the side at practice, making sure that none of its charges slipped out a back door and defected. Igor T-O was under special scrutiny by the thuggish operatives keeping watch over the team because of his worldliness and language prowess.

The Soviets stayed at the New Haven Holiday Inn and never emerged unless they were traveling by bus to or from practice. It was also apparent that, despite the hotel being well-equipped with all the modern conveniences like showers, this was something alien to Russian hygiene. After a couple of days of training with the Soviets, our indoor facility reeked.

Other than what Ter-Ovanesyan taught me, the lesson most deeply imprinted on me from sharing the track with our supposed enemies was that fear is a great motivation toward superior performance. It was obvious that the standards by which these Soviet athletes were judged were quite different than what applied to us rank amateur college boys. Lose and it's off to Siberia.

Of course, for the Soviet Union, athletics was just another Cold War weapon, a means of demonstrating the superiority of what they branded Communism (Karl Marx would have been appalled) and the Soviet Way of Life. The great track and field stars with whom we trained that winter were mere pawns in the great game between East and West. Along with my deep admiration for their incredible abilities, I felt deeply sorry for them.

Beauty and the Beholders

By the beginning of the second semester of Freshman year, it was apparent that U.S. involvement in Vietnam was well on its way to quagmire-dom and that the Johnson administration was in the process of turning a really bad mistake into a far worse one by several orders of magnitude. Of course, there was a powerful dose of self-preservational interest motivating us.

Several months later we were paid a visit by the First Lady, Lady Bird Johnson, who came on campus to promote her "beautification" campaign. Campus opposition to the war was widespread and becoming rather vocal. It proved an inopportune visit for all concerned, most of all the First Lady.

The First Lady Doing Her Oblivious Beautification Thing
(National Park Service – Public Domain)

Lady Bird was scheduled to give a speech outside on what came to be called Beinecke Plaza, a paved open space named after the dazzling new Rare Book Library that had just opened its doors shortly before. A very large crowd of students showed up to protest the war. A heavy representation of signs noting opposition to the war were in attendance, many with blown-up photos of Vietnamese suffering atrocities at the hands of our troops with captions reading "Beautification???" or some such. Lady Bird was barely able to get a word out, drowned out by chants such as: *"Hey, hey, LBJ, how many kids did you kill today?"* and the ubiquitous *"One, two, three, four, we don't want your fucking war!"* Lady Bird looked visibly shaken, as if she was suffering from a combination severe migraine and acute constipation. She had to cut short her beautification speech, drowned out by the derision of several thousand angry students.

This was the first protest demonstration I ever attended. It would not be the last.

The Fire in the Lake Heats Up

Fire in the Lake was the title of the Pulitzer Prize-winning book about the Vietnam War written in the early 1970s by Frances Fitzgerald. It documents in excruciating step-by-step stupidity America's gradual immersion into the Vietnam morass. It is also an apt description of the raised consciousness on campus of the Vietnam debacle and what it might mean for us in a few short years.

As our Sophomore year hurtled to an end, LBJ announced that continued draft deferments for college students would henceforth depend on performance on a new exam, the *Selective Service College Qualification Test*, unfondly known colloquially to male college students of the era as the "War Boards." As if a bunch of students at a highly demanding and competitive university needed any additional pressure as final exams loomed.

As the needs of the military for bodies to fuel the Vietnam bone crusher expanded dramatically in late 1965 (more than 33,000 men were drafted in October 1965), the 2-S student deferment began to look tenuous. LBJ and the Selective Service System decided that, if a student wanted to retain the 2-S designation, he would have to meet a certain class rank threshold or pass this new national examination with a high-enough score (70 for undergrads; 80 for graduate students) on the 150-point War Boards to continue to be draft-exempt while in school. Neither Yale, Harvard nor a number of other schools ranked their students so we all had to take the test and pass it.

Suddenly, almost two million draft-deferred college students had another preoccupation to add to whine, wine, women and song. The test was given on several dates toward the end of our second semester and in the early summer. It bore a strong resemblance to the Scholastic Aptitude Test (SAT).

It meant that Yale students would be competing against one another as well as against students from across the country, presumably a big advantage in our favor given that we thought we were God's gift.

The War Boards turned out to be mainly a big annoyance rather than a pressure cooker. I know of no Yalie who did not pass the test. Nevertheless, it was yet another impetus for us to be anti-war and royally pissed off at our government.

Turning Point

The specter of Vietnam did not recede over the next two academic years. The campus, like many throughout the land, became increasingly roiled by anti-war outrage powered, it must be admitted, by very subjective concerns about our own skins. Many late-night bull sessions debated whether we were truly opposed to the war or motivated by the fact that our asses might be on the line. I concluded that it was a combination of both. No one wants to be subjected to getting killed or maimed. At the same time, by the beginning of Junior Year (fall 1966), it was pretty much unanimous that America had wandered into a meat-grinder for no apparent rational reason and to no apparent end. It was incomprehensible to us that a disaster continued only because a bunch of politicians did not want to admit how badly they had screwed up.

The cynicism about politics and its practitioners and skepticism about government that Vietnam spawned in my Baby Boom generation became permanently embedded in our DNA. I and most of my colleagues henceforth assumed that anything that came out of Washington was probably a lie and not in the best interests of the citizenry.

Gene McCarthy and Bobby Kennedy, 1968
(Wikipedia—Public Domain)

Skepticism eventually trickled up to include a growing number of members of Congress. When Sen. J. William Fulbright (D-AR), chairman of the Senate Foreign Relations Committee, launched a 5-year series of hearings on the Vietnam War in 1966, he immediately became not only our hero, but also what we hoped would be our lifeline. It was not to be. Despite the committee's revelations about the origins and conduct of the Vietnam misadventure, bolstered by increasingly critical daily media coverage of the unfolding catastrophe, as well as increasing public anxiety about and opposition to the war, it went on for another nine years. Tens of thousands of additional Americans died for nothing along with two million more Vietnamese during these years.

By the beginning of our Senior year (fall 1967), it was apparent that the war would still be an issue for us when we graduated, when many of us would lose our 2-S deferred status. Consequently, it became time to buckle down and find ways of avoiding the whole lame exercise. We spent more quality time searching for alternatives to the draft—VISTA, Peace Corps, teaching, medical school, the Coast Guard, Canada, Sweden, prison, etc.—than we did enjoying our last year of being able to act like irresponsible idiots. I applied for the Coast Guard and VISTA and was accepted by both, but only after (by one day for VISTA) I received my draft notice. Once tagged for conscription, it was too late.

Our last semester was a time of mental turmoil, national torment and personal preoccupation. Shortly after it began came (1) *Tet*, when the reality of what Vietnam was doing to America hit home with a vengeance, (2) the Gene McCarthy presidential campaign when the man who to this day remains my political hero boldly went where no other political leader dared go and challenged an incumbent president, basing his entire effort on Johnson's disastrous Vietnam adventure, (3) LBJ's retreat from the presidency when confronted with

McCarthy's primary success, (4) the assassination of Martin Luther King, (5) Bobby Kennedy's belated entry into the race for the Democratic nomination, (6) his untimely death immediately after prevailing in the California primary, and five days later, (7) graduation on my birthday, a singularly sad event for many of us who that day received notice to report for our draft physicals.

Note. After being "Clean for Gene" in the run-up to the New Hampshire primary, I spent spring break in Wisconsin handling accommodations for the thousands of McCarthy volunteers who flooded the state. When I met the candidate, shook his hand and exchanged a few words with him, I thought I was in the presence of one of the great men of history. Despite his eccentric post-Vietnam career, I still do.

Dean Rusk, Lyndon Johnson and Robert McNamara possibly contemplating eternity in Hell during a meeting in the Cabinet Room of the White House on Feb. 9, 1968
(Wikipedia – Public Domain)

Evaluation

College was a great experience for a country boy from a public high school who probably would not have been admitted without the relaxation of the "Jewish Quota" that since the 1920s had restricted the number of my co-religionists able to attend Yale. However, it would have been orders of magnitude better without the nagging feeling that we had better make a helluva lot of hay because in short order following graduation we might all be dead.

Chapter 10
Just the Basics

I am going to take a shit in a box and send it to your parents for sending me theirs!
       —Unnamed Drill Sergeant to a New Recruit

You're so dumb, if you fell into a barrel of tits, you'd come out sucking your thumb.
       —Drill Sergeant J. addressing the Author

Stats

(Library of Congress – Public Domain)

In 1968, more than 300,000 young men were drafted into the U.S. Army and Marine Corps. The military's need for cannon fodder was desperate. The Selective Service System had, by then, run out of the poor and non-college educated who had so unfairly borne the burden of the folly foisted on us and on Southeast Asia by four (soon to be five) U.S. presidents. Now it was the turn of those of us fortunate enough to have had four years of student deferments.

The need for bodies was acute because 550,000 troops were on the ground in Vietnam serving one-year deployments. More blood was squandered in 1968 than in any other year of the war: 16,592 Americans killed; 27,915 South Vietnamese soldiers killed; an estimated 200,000 Viet Cong and North Vietnamese combatants dead; and more than $77 billion ($557 billion in 2019 dollars) frittered away by a President and Congress terrified of doing the responsible thing and raising taxes to fight the war.

The vast majority of the potential draftees (including new college graduates Bill Clinton, George W. Bush, Donald Trump and the author) received their draft notices beginning in June immediately after college graduations. What made 1968 even more unusual was that more than half of my college class wound up in the military within six months of graduation.

Despite being armed with six letters from physicians attesting to my very real asthma, allergies and bad back (alas, no bone spurs), I passed my draft physical exam, the Army having determined that my right index finger was in fine shape to depress a trigger. When I provided my urine sample, I asked a nurse for a pen to write my name on the bottle. "No worries," she replied. "Just put it on the shelf with all the others."

When I showed up at the Armed Forces Examining and Entrance Station in New Haven, Connecticut, a non-commissioned officer (NCO) ordered us to count off 1 through 7. He then ordered the number 7s to step forward and announced: "Congratulations, gentlemen. You are about to be sworn in as United States Marines. Parris Island here you come!" I was a number 6.

I was ordered to Fort Dix, New Jersey for Basic Combat Training.

A Brief History of Military Training

Vietnam Era Army basic combat training was designed to take an otherwise reluctant and highly individualistic and assertive young man out of his civilian comfort zone and, in very short order, turn him into an automaton willing to follow any orders, no matter how irrational. It worked.

Echo (The Author's) Company Preparing for the 150-Yard Man Carry at Fort Dix, January 1969
(U.S. Army)

The approach to military training that came to be known as "boot camp" traces its origins to the late nineteenth century in a prison in Upstate New York. In 1888, the warden at the Elmira Reformatory (not too far from where the author grew up) decided that he needed a more effective way to keep his inmates—mostly juveniles—in line and occupied, free from boredom and inactivity. He instituted a training methodology that became the model, many years later, for Army basic combat training.

In World War I, men entered the Army at recruit depots all over the U.S. and then reported directly to their service units where they were sometimes trained and then sent overseas. Following the initial overseas deployments, new enlistees were kept at the recruit depots where they were supposed to be trained to be loss replacements. Little actual training took place. The Army did not have enough men to fill regular deployment units, so instead it tore apart existing units and reassigned men to units ready to go overseas. Soldiers were thus shuffled around so much that training became an afterthought. The result was that highly inexperienced "green" recruits were sent into battle without much, if any, training.

During the interwar years, initial Army training consisted of nothing more than swearing an individual into the military and handing him fatigues and a weapon, followed by a modicum of lip service about how to march in formation. That same system was still in place when World War II began.

As the U.S. anticipated its impending involvement in World War II, the Army decided that it needed designated places where soldiers could be trained before being assigned to regular units. Beginning in 1940, soldiers were trained at replacement training centers. Within a short time, the training process was standardized for each Military Occupational Specialty (MOS). In addition, field training exercises with live ammunition were added.

However, by early 1942 the Army ran out of the necessary manpower to fill deploying units. It reverted to the World War I haphazard system where, upon joining the Army, soldiers were immediately assigned to a unit and were sent overseas without any training. This continued for the duration of the war.

After the war, the Army was finally able to devote attention to developing a formal, structured training program. Following a number of fits and starts, it devised the training program that endured for almost the entire first thirty years of the Cold War.

By the Korean War, the system of sending soldiers through Basic Combat Training followed by a roughly equal amount of time receiving Advanced Individual Training in an MOS was introduced. In 1963, with the Vietnam War looming, the Army introduced drill sergeants and specialized experts to manage training cycles. Drill sergeants were selected for their leadership abilities and accomplishments in the field. They became the day-to-day supervisors of basic training. Specialized instructors taught specific skills such as hand grenades, infiltration, rifle marksmanship, night firing, close combat, individual tactics and subjects such as first aid.

This training program was the one that I experienced. A few years later with the advent of the All-Volunteer Army, initial training was modified to equip soldiers with lifelong skills transferable to the civilian economy as an inducement to enlist.

Baby Its Cold Outside . . . and Inside

Former Main Entrance to Fort Dix
(U.S. Army – Public Domain)

Don't let the photo above delude you into thinking that Fort Dix was Happy Valley. A dismal place under any circumstances, Dix was even worse during the record bad winter of 1968-69 when I was there.

The memories that most imprinted on me from Fort Dix have to do with the cold (apropos since this is a book about the Cold War). I and my colleagues fought and lost our own micro-cold war against bitterly freezing conditions. There were days when the wind chill temperature was -30° F.

Marching several miles to the rifle range while wearing long underwear (Army-issue long johns, FYI, are the best in the world—I still have mine 50 years later), fatigues and a field jacket and carrying a rifle and backpack meant that by the time we arrived at our destination, we were sweating profusely (does anyone ever sweat un-profusely?) with nowhere for the perspiration to escape our bundled-up selves. Once you stop moving in the bitter cold, your captive perspiration begins to freeze against your skin. That is not a pleasant feeling.

At night in the barracks, we slept in our skivvies, were allowed only one thin wool blanket and were ordered to keep our windows open. Some of us took to donning several layers of clothing, but this proved impractical given that drill sergeant bed checks exposed our subterfuge and compelled us to remove the extra clothing. The consequence was "URI," short for Upper Respiratory Infection. Virtually everyone in my company and the whole post came down with URI and felt miserable as a result. The option of going on "sick call" was unattractive, frowned upon by the drill sergeants who threatened that if we missed any training days we ran the risk of being "recycled" through another entire basic training cycle, and subjected anyone who showed up at the post infirmary with more harassment from the physicians and nurses than even our company cadre gave out. Thus, very few trainees went to sick call. Instead, we all just suffered until we recovered toward the end of the training cycle.

The historical weather records for January and February 1969, which accounted for most of my time at Fort Dix, confirm that it was one of the coldest winters on record. Adding to the misery was a record setting month of February, during which Fort Dix suffered 18 consecutive days of snowfall, an all-time record for the area. This made slogging through knee-deep snow to get anywhere a capstone ordeal on top of the snow and bitter cold. How any of this prepared troops to fight in a jungle where the average temperatures was often triple digits is a mystery.

A Praise-Worthy Aside

> *"The common soldier does not change too drastically from one era to another or from nation to nation or war to war."*
> –Jaroslav Hacek, *The Good Soldier Schweik*

Before reciting some of the M.A.S.H.-worthy absurdities of basic training, it needs to be said that the U.S. Army does a remarkably effective job of taking undisciplined, often aimless and frequently clueless civilians off the streets and, in just over two months, turning them into reasonably well-disciplined and well-coordinated fighting men that meet or exceed the threshold of military competence demanded of a modern army. They do this through time-honored techniques of stripping away the individuality that defines us as human beings and replacing it with group-think. Three factors play a major role in this rapid transformation:

1. *The first-day haircut.* If you entered the Army when I did in 1968, you came in with a group of hirsute young men sporting either very long hair, Afros, mohawks and other assorted locks and looks reflective of the temper of the times. Then came the trauma: the forced visit to the post barber shop, a venue where the barbers needed to know nothing about haircuts and styles. In fact, the best possible preparation for the job is sheep-shearing. All that was necessary was the ability to wield clippers that produced an outcome where the subject's head wound up looking like an egg yearning to become a peach. By the end of the exercise, everyone looked like everyone else. A mirror was irrelevant. If you wanted to know what you looked like, you had only to look at the guy standing next to you.
2. *New clothes.* The next stop on the road from unrepentant civilian to faceless grunt was the supply room where we were issued our Army clothing, which consisted of (1) everyday training uniforms: fatigue shirts and pants, field jackets, pile caps with ear flaps like those worn by the yelling Chinese People's Liberation Army hordes that poured over the Yalu River and surprised General MacArthur's troops as depicted in what few Korean War movies exist; and socks—all in a color labeled "olive drab" (emphasis on "drab"); white, V-neck T-shirts that made us all look like

dweebish nerds; "swinger" undershorts that would have caused otherwise willing young ladies to run away screaming; and two pairs of combat boots (the best footwear in the history of the universe!). In addition, we were issued olive drab dress uniforms for special occasions, mindful that boot camp offered few opportunities to don such garb.
3. *Routine and Sameness.* The Army wastes no time getting its newbies into a rigorous routine. Waking and bedding down at the same time every day. Morning formation. Eating at the same time. Moreover, everyone's personal effects are precise clones of everyone else's: soap; toothpaste; shoe polish (lots of shoe polish); etc. And everyone's personal area must look the same.

All of this happens so rapidly that you are rendered a more-or-less mindless automaton before you realize what has happened. Individuals whose whole lives up to this point were spent raising hell and waxing contrarian generally fall into grouchy obedience without much protest. Individualism, a characteristic Americans take to the bank as being uniquely their preserve and what renders them exceptional, is washed away with stunning suddenness. It is a remarkable psychological brainwashing that amazed me at the time and still does today.

Volunteering

We arrived at the Fort Dix Reception Station at dusk. After processing in and filling out a sheaf of redundant paperwork, we were assigned to a holding company, the jumping off point for reassignment the next day or two to a basic training company. Idle time being anathema to the Army, we were divided into groups of about twenty men and followed a drill sergeant off to one corner of the barracks.

The sergeant asked: "Is anyone here a runner?" Foolishly, I raised my hand and announced that I ran track in high school and college. "Good," said the sergeant. "You can run errands for me all night long." I not only felt like a moron; it was obvious that the more sophisticated of my new colleagues typecast me as one.

Over the next two years, I never volunteered for anything again.

Sno-Men

The next day, our first full day at Fort Dix having turned into evening, we were informed that we were slated for overnight KP. Grumbling over the lack of sleep that portended, we were nevertheless curious about KP, about which we had all grown up hearing horror stories. Nothing, however, could have prepared me for what I was about to experience.

My new friend Mike and I found ourselves at the end of the line when we entered the mess hall. It turned out our cohort had been mistakenly ordered to KP because another company of novice troops arrived there before us. Nevertheless, the mess sergeant found something for everyone to do until he arrived at the end of the line where Mike and I waited.

"Let's see," said the NCO. "I think I'll make you two snowmen."

We stared at him blankly, not comprehending what he had in mind.

"I'm going to write 'Snowman' on the back of your field jackets so you'll know what your assignment is."

He took a piece of chalk and wrote the following on the back of each of our field jackets: "SNO MAN." Spelling not being his strong suit, he handed each of us a shovel.

"But drill sergeant," Mike said. "There's no snow on the ground."

"Bullshit!" said the sergeant. "You two must be fucking blind. Now get out of my mess hall and shovel the sidewalks all around it. I'll be checking on you."

Absent any viable alternative, Mike and I stepped outside and began shoveling the air off the clear, dry sidewalks. We exchanged some choice opinions about the army as we toiled.

About an hour later—it felt like an eternity—the sergeant appeared outside and yelled at us for not shoveling fast enough. "Fucking trainees!" he grumbled as he walked back inside. He came outside a few more times during the night and once even praised the fine job we were doing.

Mike and Me
(US Department of Defense – Public Domain)

Dawn finally arrived, finding us as exhausted as if we had shoveled actual snow all night. The only distraction was Mike's humming of arias from his civilian career as an opera singer.

I wanted to find a pay phone and beg my mother to come and pick me up. Looking ahead to two full years of this insanity was disturbing. But there was no exit.

Drill

I'm not sure why armies spend so much time drilling: marching in step; double-timing (not to be confused with two-timing); "forward march!;" "to the rear, march!;" "left face!;" "right face!;" "about face!;" and so forth. I suspect it has to do with transforming the individual into a groupie, but it also might have to do with an excuse to rhyme and sing time-tested marching ditties such as:

> *I know a girl who lives on a hill*
> *She won't do it but her sister will*
> *. . . two, three, four.*

Drill was actually a challenge for some trainees. One of our company members, a fellow the guys nicknamed "Cyclops" because his eyes were so close together that at a distance he could pass for having only one, never got the hang of it. Many a "forward, march" led him to execute an "about face" and crash into the soldier directly to his rear.

My favorite command was "road guard, post!" which was shouted as we approached an intersection, at which command the second soldiers in a "column-of-twos" formation would jump out and run up to the intersection to ward off any vehicle otherwise inclined to run over us.

Cadre

Drill sergeants are theoretically selected from the *crème-de-la-crème* of the Army non-commissioned officer corps. The drill sergeants assigned to Echo Company were, shall we say, of uneven talents and temperaments.

Not all were bad guys, poor leaders, borderline crooks or totally unhinged lunatics. But enough were to make me wonder how they arrived at positions they had no business being near.

Sgt. R was a Puerto Rican lifer who grumbled that he should receive overseas pay for serving in the continental U.S. He was a Vietnam veteran who claimed that, following one battle, he was the only survivor of his company. He had been busted in rank numerous times and as a result was still only a buck sergeant after 18 years in the Army. He had no patience for anyone who was slow to follow orders or who fit his definition of a "poo-sie." To demonstrate his toughness, he beat his dog with a whip in front of our formation. The list of trainees who would have loved to kill him was long.

"Are There Anyone Down Range?"

Before you criticize me for poor grammar, know that the title of this section was the standard query shouted by the rifle range NCO before ordering us to begin firing at targets. Of course, if there was someone dumb enough to be hanging out down range, s/he would soon have been rendered a non-issue.

The Rifle Range
(U.S. Army – Public Domain)

Until my initial meet-and-greet with the rifle range, I had never touched a firearm in my life and was in fact intimidated by the very thought. However, after only several minutes toting a rifle, I felt very much at home. I almost developed a soft spot for the Second Amendment.

Our first day at the range, there actually was "someone"—a cute little bunny—romping around down range, but not for long. When the order to "lock, load and fire" was given, the company opened up on the poor creature, instantly vaporizing what might have made a fine if dainty entrée. I only pretended to shoot at it.

At the beginning of boot camp, we were issued the M-14 rifle, an unwieldy apparatus that had a kick and was, for me, a huge challenge. Before firing, it had to be adjusted for what the Army designated "windage" and "elevation," using a couple of dials on the weapon that remained an unfathomable mystery to me. I had trouble hitting anything with the damn rifle and, when it came to the final test on the weapon, received the lowest possible passing score and a qualification badge to put on my uniform and announce to the world that I was a mediocre shooter. If I remember correctly, the hierarchy of marksmanship badges went from Expert to Sharpshooter to Marksman to "*Oy Vay.*" I received a "*Nebbish*" badge.

However, my reputation as a rifle range *schlemiel* suddenly took a dramatic turn for the better. During boot camp, our M-14s were replaced by the M-16A1, the rifle issued to the infantry fighting in Vietnam. No more agonizing over windage and elevation. I mutated into a crack shot with the M-16 and, on the final marksmanship test, hit 35 out of 35 targets that were designed to be silhouettes of Viet Cong fighters at pop-up distances of 50 to 400 meters. I received an Expert badge and abruptly retired my "Nebbish" badge.

We learned to fire our weapons assuming four positions (61 fewer than the *Kama Sutra* and nowhere near as interesting): standing, sitting, squatting and prone. One member of the company had a written waiver from the squatting position from which, if he had had to assume it, he would never have been able to stand up. The drill sergeants and the company's resident dumb-asses gave him an immense amount of grief about it. For more about this tragic figure, see Appendix A, "Chillin' with the Coldest Warriors."

Classroom Instruction

We spent a good deal of time in a classroom, where we watched instructional films, broke down and reassembled M-14s and M-16s, and listened to lectures by our officers and drill sergeants. It was a welcome break from the frozen tundra outdoors. Before being allowed to sit down after we marched into the classroom, we had to shout out our company slogan/mantra: "Echo, Echo Eagles...Proud Rifles All the Way!...Rah!"

Following which one of the drill sergeants would yell: 'TAKE SEATS!"

The only film I remember was one about safe driving, replete with horrible traffic accidents and head-on crashes that dismembered crash dummies whose heads then rolled down the highway until they were crushed by oncoming vehicles. The lectures covered a

Learn While You Earn (A Pittance)
(U.S. Army – Public Domain)

variety of subjects that someone at Army headquarters thought necessary to creating soldiers. This included a dose of Vietnam War propaganda that made it clear that if we did not stop the Commie hordes pouring into South Vietnam from the North, the next battle would be against the Russians in Kansas City. So fighting this proxy war was a no-brainer.

The most fascinating class—American History—was conducted by one of the drill sergeants, a nice but simple fellow who stood up on the stage and shouted out the following:

"Fourteen Ninety-Two!"
"Seventeen Seventy-Six!"
"Eighteen Twelve!"
"Eighteen Sixty-One"
"December Seventh Nineteen Forty-One!"
"Nineteen Fifty!"

That was it. No elaboration about what happened on those dates followed. I felt like a fly on the wall in a Salvador Dali painting watching a limp watch try to crawl over the lid of an open box.

Eye Teeth

The Army does virtually everything in a group, a very totalitarian and fairly efficient approach to life's problems. This was certainly consistent when it came to healthcare. Sick call was an assembly line process with each soldier receiving a cursory examination that was then repeated with every other soldier. When most of Echo Company came down with URI, the few that dared go on sick call reported back that they were diagnosed while in line in a cold hallway and provided with a handful of aspirin, a process that took virtually no time at all and was hardly conducive to healing.

I observed this phenomenon manifesting itself most nefariously when we were directed to (1) see the post optometrist, and (2) visit the dentist. We were called out alphabetically and sent off to the infirmary to have our vision tested. At least half of the company returned with a set of Army-issue spectacles that were so ugly that it was difficult even for men to look directly at them without turning away.

I never realized the value of being eight letters down the alphabet until the day that was designated for Echo Company to have our teeth checked. By the time the roster drilled down to the letter "H," I was able to incorporate feedback from the returning "A's, B's and C's." A disturbing number of them emerged from the dental clinic absent most, and in some cases all, of their teeth. Apparently, the Army believed that it was more efficient if a cavity was discovered to pull teeth rather than fill them.

Hence, when my name was called, I left the formation and walked down the street toward the dental clinic. When I turned the corner from the barracks, I ran behind a parked truck and crawled under it. Thirty minutes later, I reported back to the company, teeth intact.

Godliness

The First Amendment does not apply in the U.S. Army. At least according to our First Sergeant, who rejected a list of grievances unwisely crafted and brought to his attention by a member of our company. His concise response as he tore up the list was: "Fuck the Constitution." The petitioner wound up doing several punishment tours on KP.

Needless to say, there was no appeal.

So it was not totally shocking when we discovered that the First Amendment's Free Exercise (of Religion) Clause also had no place in the military. Our first Sunday in boot camp, the First Sergeant made the following announcement at our morning formation:

"Attention. Church services are at 10:00 AM. You *will* attend."

To which one of the Jewish members of the company piped up:

"Excuse me, First Sergeant, but some of us are Jewish."

"So?" asked the First Sergeant."

"That means we don't go to church. We go to a synagogue instead."

"OK," responded the First Sarge. "At 10:00 AM all you Jewish will go to your church or whatever it is."

"But First Sergeant, we go to temple on Friday night, not Sunday."

"I thought you go to syn-a-what."

"Temple is another name for synagogue."

"Oh. Well then, you can stay here and get started doing laundry while everyone else is in church."

He had a quizzical look on his face as he dismissed us.

The next morning during formation, the First Sergeant made an announcement:

"Attention, all you Jews! You will attend Friday night services at 1900 hours at the chapel." He had obviously done his homework.

When Friday evening arrived, Echo Company's four Jews headed off to the chapel where we were greeted by an Airborne Ranger rabbi from Rochester, New York who looked like he could have fended off the Romans at Masada all by himself. There were about 25 additional Members of the Tribe present from other basic training companies. The Rabbi performed a perfunctory service, ending it by saying he had a surprise for us: he pulled back a folding wall and it was as if the gates of Jerusalem in its Second Temple hey-day had opened. There, laid out on a long table, was a feast for the eyes, stomach and most of all for the soul: bagels, lox, gefilte fish, brisket, kosher pickles, smoked whitefish. Heaven! Best of all, the servers were *zaftig* young ladies from the Camden County, New Jersey Jewish community. After more than a week eating the swill that passed for food in the mess hall, this was Nirvana. We gorged ourselves on the food, not the women, although efforts toward that goal were undertaken to no avail. It was look-but-don't-touch. They announced that they would be back the next Friday.

Returning to the barracks, we mentioned our good fortune to our *goyim* colleagues. The next Friday, Echo Company's Jewish community had increased by several members, an expansion that continued for the next succession of Fridays.

The Spirit of the (Irrelevant) Bayonet

In the history of modern warfare, only a tiny percentage of soldiers died from either hand-to-hand combat or being skewered or filleted by a bayonet. In every war, the largest number of deaths is attributed to artillery (almost 60 percent in World War II). Next come rifles, followed by grenades and far down on the lethality list, which it barely makes, the bayonet.

Mindful of that, one needs to ask why we spent such an inordinate amount of time practicing killing with bayonets, thrusting them at dummies, clobbering each other with what were known as "pugil sticks" that simulated attacking an enemy with a bayonet and responding whenever a drill sergeant shouted out: "What's the spirit of the bayonet?" "To kill, drill sergeant, to kill!"

During one of our pugil stick training days, Sergeant J, a fellow who had a particular obsession with singling me out for harassment, decided to hold a contest to determine the top pugil stick fighter in the company. We were randomly put into brackets similar to what "March Madness" uses to determine the NCAA basketball champion. I made my way through my bracket with relative ease and somehow wound up the overall winner, whereupon Sergeant J challenged me to fight him. When I beat him, too, he challenged me to a sprint race, having heard from some

Trainees Duking It Out with Pugil Sticks
(U.S. Army – Public Domain)

unknown source that I had been a track athlete in my civilian incarnation. I beat him at that too, whereupon he spent the remainder of basic training doing his damnedest to do me in.

G.I Schmo

Sergeant J's personal vendetta directed at me put me on high alert with respect to going the straight and narrow, which I also believed was a good idea because I wanted to learn as much as possible that might save my behind in Vietnam. The result was that I ended boot camp winning the award for being designated the top trainee, initially in my platoon, then successively up the line to Echo Company, 1st Battalion, 2nd Brigade, and eventually all of Fort Dix. I had been awarded expert badges for firing the M-16 rifle and for grenade throwing. I maxed the PT (Physical Training) test, which consisted of five events topped off by running a sub-6-minute mile in fatigues and combat boots and for which I received a much-coveted, 24-hour pass to Philadelphia.

However, toward the end of boot camp I had become so cynical that these so-called honors did not really resonate with me. I could not see that I would gain any real advantages from these accolades. I was jumped up in rank two grades to Private First Class, which did little for me other than let me advance in rank later on a little faster than the norm.

I was now the darling of every drill sergeant except J. Seargent R, however, was so impressed that, after the battalion award was conferred and I was up for the Brigade honor, he took it upon himself to spit-shine my shoes so that I would "dazzle" (his word) the interlocutors. I was exempted from all further training and company obligations for the last week of boot camp so that I could concentrate on preparing for the final two levels of the "Soldier of the Cycle" competition.

I was also invited to the Fort Dix commanding general's quarters for tea with him and his wife, a decidedly awkward occasion made more so by (1) his asking if I planned on making the military a career, and (2) his invitation sent to my parents to fly them down for the graduation ceremony during which he would put them up in his quarters and I would parade around with a golden rifle and do some fancy left, right and about faces while also receiving an accolade designating me as the "Proud Rifle." A duller individual than the general I have never met.

Mercifully, my parents declined the invitation, expressing shock and amazement and not a little concern that I was such a crackerjack soldier, not exactly something predicted by my DNA. Both they and I were a bit embarrassed by my "achievements." Despite that, when I returned home after being discharged from the Army almost two years later, I discovered that my mother had given away all of my sports trophies, medals and ribbons and retained only the large trophy I received for being the "Soldier of the Cycle" at Fort Dix. I did not dare ask her what that was all about.

Proficiency (Pro) Park

"Pro-Park" constituted our final exam. Testing covered all major areas of military competence: guard duty; military justice; drill; first aid; infiltration; chemical, biological and radiological (CBR) warfare; military courtesy; and more.

While almost everyone graduated from basic training, some did not. One of those was sweet, gentle and utterly clueless Cyclops, who had been drafted out of his city sanitation worker job and found himself in a mystifying environment that he simply could not grasp. As I mentioned above, when we drilled and were ordered to do a simple maneuver like a "left face," he invariably turned right. A "column left march" command invariably had him slamming into a colleague and getting whacked for his mistake.

He struggled mightily to absorb the barrage of information thrown at us, difficult enough for some trainees to master if they were not being harassed, called names and shouted at constantly. To no avail.

The night before Pro Park, I stayed up with him and we reviewed everything he would have to know to pass the tests. The next day dawned sunny, bright and warm for a rare change. Marching with the company to Pro Park was actually quite pleasant. When we arrived, we were divided up into small groups, each one rotating through the various testing stations simultaneously for efficiency's sake. My group, which included Cyclops, was assigned to go through the Guard Duty exam first. Cyclops survived. He *did not* hand over his rifle to the drill sergeant who demanded it (a huge "no-no" when on guard duty for obvious reasons). We had rehearsed that several times the night before. I had high hopes that he would make it through the entire Pro Park since that appeared to be the concept that gave him the most difficulty.

Cyclops did well until we arrived at our final testing station, which consisted of an exercise where a drill sergeant would shout out a situation and you had to respond appropriately. For example, if he yelled "leg wound—blood spurting," the correct response was to grab a piece of cloth long enough to tie a tourniquet on the victim's (in this case a humanoid dummy) upper leg in order to reduce blood flow from the femoral artery while also shouting for a medic. If the sergeant shouted "gas attack," the proper response was to immediately unhook your gas mask from your belt and don it. If he screamed "nuclear attack," you jumped into a foxhole and covered yourself with your poncho (duck-and-cover still lived!).

When Cyclops stepped forward, the drill sergeant yelled "sucking chest wound!" Cy grabbed his poncho, jumped into the foxhole and covered himself with it. It was not a good look.

Cy was not with us when we were marched back to the barracks. The next day, graduation day, he was one of three soldiers absent from Echo Company. I was unaware of his absence during the ceremonies because, as the "Proud Rifle," I had to perform. It was only after the festivities that I learned that he had been taken to a holding company following Pro Park in preparation to be recycled through basic training a second time.

Instead of celebrating with the company, I went to see him at the holding company. We both cried.

Aftermath

I never had any more contact with either Cyclops or S, the other soldier that my colleagues and I tried to help through boot camp. I don't know what happened to Cyclops, but assume he survived recycling intact and graduated. I do know what happened to S. Sadly, this unfortunate who had no business being drafted, died of a heart attack during recycling. I assume that the brutal harassment he suffered during his first basic training go-round continued in part two, where every trainee was automatically deemed a "fuck-up" and treated accordingly. More about sad S in Appendix A.

A Brief Word about A.I.T.

The Army called the next training phase "Advanced Individual Training" (AIT). We knew it as "Advanced Infantile Training."

I received orders for Combat Engineer School at Fort Leonard Wood, Missouri. I naively assumed that this meant that I would be studying engineering in a classroom, i.e., that I was about to get as close to a civilized learning environment as was possible in the Army. I even asked my mother to send me my high school slide rule.

Boy was I wrong! It quickly became apparent upon arrival in mid-country that a combat engineer was an unglorified coolie best equipped to haul heavy bridge-building components around combat zones.

Foxtrot Company was comprised of three major demographics: a contingent of rural Southern white guys; an approximately equal-size contingent of urban Northern blacks; and a slightly smaller collection of college graduates. It was a mix destined to cause serious problems. Racial tension was high and during the eight weeks of AIT escalated so much that whites and blacks designated men who would take turns staying awake all night to make sure no one was assaulted. The worst incident occurred when a group of black soldiers decided to hold what they called a "black power meeting" in the latrine.

A Latrine Aside. The latrine in our World War II-era wooden barracks was like nothing I could ever have imagined. Commodes were organized in a half-circular pattern and were open to view. There were no partitions or stalls. Try being regular under those conditions! Worse, the latrine also served a dual function as the laundry room. Yuck!

One lazy Sunday afternoon, I was on the second floor of the barracks schmoozing with some friends when we heard a primal scream coming from the latrine. We ran down the stairs and into the latrine, where a group of black soldiers were beating the daylights out of one of our buddies. I tried to pull him out of the melee only to find myself confronted by one of his assailants carrying a knife. We circled around each other for what seemed like an eternity but probably were only a few seconds when he lunged at me with the knife. When the drill sergeants broke up the fight, I saw that my hand was bleeding. Adrenaline flowing like lava from a volcanic eruption, I had been unaware that I had been slashed by my knife-wielding assailant. I was transported to the infirmary and stitched up. When I got back to the barracks, I found out that our friend had had both of his arms broken in the brawl.

Our company commander took no action against the perpetrators, fearing being labeled a racist. He proved that Officer Candidate School does not always produce leaders. My contempt for him was intense and I and some of my colleagues purposely defied his orders from then forward. He dared say nothing for fear we would "out" his cowardice up the chain of command to his superiors.

I suspect that the knife attack lingered for quite a while as a form of Post-Traumatic Stress Disorder (PTSD). For years following my Army discharge, I did not do well in the presence of knives, even when watching a dramatization of a knife attack.

Meanwhile, What Was Ivan Doing?

Welcome to the world of strategic analysis, where we program weapons that don't work to meet threats that don't exist.
—Ivan Selin, Head of the Strategic Forces Division, Office of the Assistant Secretary of Defense (Systems Analysis), 1966.

It's time to consider our adversary, "Boris," the Soviet soldier whom, we were often informed, was a fighting machine *par excellence*, his prowess being such that we had to train all that much harder just to stay up with this prodigy.

The reality, as I discovered much later, was not quite up to the image with which we were presented. In his superb book, *The Threat: Inside the Soviet Military Machine*, analyzing the readiness of the Soviet foe, Andrew Cockburn says that the Soviet grunt was one sorry-ass, weak, disorganized, woefully undertrained dude with poor weaponry, poor health, inept leadership, and little interest in defending the motherland. Cockburn relates his interviews with several hundred former members of the Soviet military who emigrated to the United States and settled primarily in the Brighton Beach section of Brooklyn, which had become and still is a microcosm of a Russian community. Its alias is "Little Odessa."

To a man, these veterans regaled Cockburn with tales of total ineptitude from the top down; of desultory training, reluctant trainees, lame-brained policies such as a vodka ban that prompted the troops to sneak out of their barracks after dark and siphon rocket fuel as a booze substitute, a practice that rotted out stomachs and hospitalized a large chunk of the Soviet forces, putting them out of commission for weeks and months.

After poring over Cockburn's book, you cannot help but think that the "Soviet threat" was the paper-est of tigers, on a par perhaps with Peter Sellers' "Grand Fenwick" army that declared war on the U.S. in *The Mouse That Roared*.

The quotation cited at the beginning of this section could just as easily apply to the contrast between the U.S. Army and its Soviet counterpart.

I received orders for Vietnam, which were magically rescinded about ten days later. I only told my parents about my Vietnam orders after I returned from active duty two years later. They would have made a fuss and my mother would have been all over me for not going to Canada or jail.

One final point about Army training: one develops very close and often intense friendships, however fleeting. Mutual hardship and its corollary, joint suffering, induces men who have endured it together to feel a comradeship that is much closer than anything in civilian life.

I finished AIT as one of the company's honor grads.

Now You Tell Me!

While writing this chapter, I attended a dinner where Lewis, a friend and contemporary of mine revealed that when he was drafted in 1969 and reported to the Armed Forces Entrance and Examining Station in Milwaukee, he did something so brilliant (my assessment) and unique that I was blown away. When it came time for the NCO to swear him into the Army, he announced (following consultation with his attorney): "On the advice of counsel, I refuse induction."

The NCO asked him for the name of the law firm representing him. Upon his response, the NCO said that it was the top firm in the state with respect to battling Selective Service local draft boards, so the Army was not going to fight it. Lewis went home a free man.

The only other person I was aware of who did this was heavyweight boxing champion Muhammed Ali. Ali, however, was convicted of draft evasion, sentenced to five years in prison, fined $10,000 and banned from boxing for three years. He stayed out of prison while his case was being appealed and never served any time. In 1971, the U.S. Supreme Court overturned his conviction after the government deprived him of three years in his prime.

During the Vietnam era, approximately 570,000 young men were classified as draft offenders. Around 210,000 were formally accused of draft violations. Only 8,750 were convicted and only 3,250, or fewer than one-half of 1 percent, went to jail.

Lewis, in contrast, did not face trial or any other adverse consequences as a result of his announcement. His attorneys advised him that the Selective Service process, which was delegated as far down the line as it could possibly go—to local community Draft Boards—was so fatally flawed due to the local yokels' ignorance of the law and almost preternatural ability to fuck anything and everything up that he could safely refuse induction and get away with it. It was just too much of a pain in the ass for the Army to fight it.

Lewis was quite obviously much smarter than me.

Chapter 11
Baby Boomer Bomber

Mankind invented the atomic bomb, but no mouse would ever construct a mousetrap.
—Albert Einstein

Atomic Demolition Munitions

It was kismet or karma or something that a young man who spent his childhood and adolescence fraught with worry about The Bomb would wind up becoming a "nuke." But that's what happened after I completed Basic Training and AIT.

Following a six-week training program in Atomic Demolition Munitions (a fancy way of saying "nuclear land mines"), my Military Occupational Specialty was changed from "11 Bravo," the designation of every Army infantryman, to "12 Echo 20," Atomic Demolition Munitions (ADM) Specialist. There were only six ADM platoons (an Army platoon consisted of around 30-35 soldiers) deployed in the world: three in West Germany, one in Italy and two in South Korea. I was eventually assigned to the one in West Germany closest to the Iron Curtain in the small, beautiful, medieval city of Bamberg in the *Oberfranken* (Upper Franconia) region of Northern Bavaria.

The SADM, America's "Backpack" Atomic Weapon
(U.S. Army – Public Domain)

Bamberg was the largest German city (population: 60,000) to escape Allied bombing during World War II. The city was lucky. It sat equidistant from two cities—Schweinfurt to the west and Nuremberg to the south—that suffered perhaps the most devastating bomb attacks of the war. Both were reduced to rubble. Schweinfurt had the misfortune to harbor Germany's principal ball bearing factories. The destruction of Nuremberg was largely symbolic: it was the "Holy of Holies," the Jerusalem of the Nazi movement, where the *Parteitage* ("party days") rallies were held annually. Those newsreels you often see of Hitler addressing hordes of soldiers and SS men holding high swastika banners while blondes fawn with orgasmic ecstasy are of Nuremberg.

Our platoon had two missions: the first, a defensive one, whereby we would detonate our big weapon, the Medium Atomic Demolition Munition ("MADM") in the Fulda Gap, one of two passes through which Warsaw Pact (i.e., Soviet) tanks would have to come in order to invade West Germany; the other an offensive mission whereby we would airdrop into an Eastern bloc capital city and detonate our smaller, backpack weapon (the "SADM") like the one in the photograph at the beginning of this chapter. The offensive mission smacked to us of being quite likely a suicide one.

MADM Component Parts Requiring Assembly in Order to Arm
(U.S. Army Atomic Demolition Munitions School, Ft. Belvoir, VA – Public Domain)

When I found out that I had been tabbed to attend the CONUS (continental United States in army parlance) ADM School, I was very excited. The first thing that occurred to me was my strong sense that there weren't any nuclear weapons in Vietnam. It was therefore unlikely that I would be assigned there. Many years later, I began to hear that I might have been mistaken. Former Secretary of the Air Force Thomas Reed, in his book, *At the Abyss: An Insider's View of the Cold War*, wrote: "Some say that a string of Atomic Demolition Munitions were set for deployment along the Chinese-Vietnamese border." He goes on to express regret that, if deployed, they were never detonated, arguing that this would have sent "an unmistakable message to the leaders of the Soviet empire: 'We are serious.'" Nothing like trying to provoke World War III. Once a domino theorist, always a domino theorist, I suppose.

I am by no means adept at things mechanical. In fact, I am an inept boob when it comes to using my hands to put stuff together or use tools. Nevertheless, I found that I was a star when it came to assembling and arming nuclear weapons, in some cases a several-hours long, fairly complex and intricate undertaking. I have no idea how I came to be good at something so alien to my background and tribal deficiencies dating back at least to Abraham's troubles wielding the knife he intended to use to cut his son's throat. His father being Jewish, Isaac did not know how lucky he was. No way could Abraham have accomplished this cruel, God-directed infanticide.

Unlikely as it seemed, I was good enough at this surreal stuff that I was one of the honor graduates of the school.

Moose and Squirrel

When ADM training ended, I spent a couple of weeks in what was called a "holding company" at Fort Belvoir awaiting assignment orders. During my time being "held," the only duty I did not evade was two days in Manassas, Virginia helping to build a swimming pool for disabled children. Otherwise, I hid out every day in the Fort Belvoir library. Discipline was sufficiently lax that no one bothered to notice or punish me.

I received orders for West Germany and reported to McGuire Air Force Base adjacent to Fort Dix for out-processing in preparation for a flight to Frankfurt. We had to go through the shot line twice because the Army either misplaced or lost our first shot records. Consequently, we boarded the plane to Europe with sore and swollen arms, a small price to pay for going in the other direction from Vietnam.

After several days in Frankfurt and then Stuttgart, I found myself in the easternmost ADM unit in the country, within spitting distance of the East German and Czechoslovakian borders.

One of the first things to which I was exposed was a training film on recognizing Soviet spies and how to avoid being blackmailed by them. We had fairly high security clearances and the feeling was that the enemy would be very interested in our knowledge of the bombs, their storage locations and our unit missions and tactics.

The film was surreal and hysterical. The actress playing the female Soviet spy was a vamp who bore an uncanny resemblance to "Natasha Fatale," the animated spy who, with her husband, "Boris Badanov," were the foils of Rocky the Flying Squirrel and Bullwinkle T. Moose in the classic TV cult cartoon series, *The Adventures of Rocky and Bullwinkle*. Natasha was tall, dark, slinky, bosomy, and poured into a purple dress that left little to the imagination. In the film, she sashayed up to a GI nursing a drink at a bar, hailing him with a heavily accented: "Gud iffnink, soldier." She may as well have been wearing a sign around her neck that said: "I'M A KGB SPY."

Boris, Natasha & Fearless Leader
Wikipedia.org
The Adventures of Rocky and Bullwinkle
© Jay Ward Productions

In the film, she invites the unsuspecting soldier back to her hotel room and seduces him. Meanwhile, the male KGB agent with whom she works leaps out of the closet and snaps a few pictures of the couple *in flagrante*. Next, the two Soviet operatives blackmail the soldier, threatening to send the photos to his wife back home if he does not spill his guts about his unit's deepest secrets.

All of this, of course, had me and the other new arrivals rolling in the aisles gasping for breath and bordering on incontinence. The only thing missing from this sidesplitting film was a monocled "Fearless Leader."

In my entire time in Germany close to the Iron Curtain, I never encountered anyone who remotely resembled a Soviet agent, much less someone as alluring as Natasha. Hope never triumphed over experience.

The only other training film that came remotely close to the Boris-and-Natasha comedy show was the instructional one on how to put on a condom, starring a well-endowed banana.

Alpine Interlude

Less than a month after arriving in Bamberg, I found myself back in another ADM training school. I informed Personnel that this had to be a mistake since I had recently completed ADM training back in the U.S. "We don't make those kinds of mistakes," replied the personnel specialist looking over my orders. "Says here you've never been trained on these weapons systems. So, off you go."

When you're an Army peon, you don't argue the point. Resistance is futile. Instead, you shut your mouth and do what they tell you, no matter how irrational. Keeping my mouth shut was one of the best decisions I ever made.

Aside: Silence in the face of absurdity greatly advantaged me later on when Personnel made its second major mistake in my favor. Soldiers earn 30 days of leave for each year of military service. By the time I became a "short-timer" (someone blessed with only a few months to go in the Army), I had used up all of my 60 days of leave. I was stunned when Personnel warned me with about four months to go that their records indicated that I had never taken a day of leave. Great. The result was that I spent two months traveling around Europe beginning when I had nine weeks left in the Army. But that was not the end of Personnel's SNAFUs. When I exited the Army on my last day, I went to the pay window back at Fort Dix and received two months of pay in addition to my "severance" that covered my last half-month. The two months of undeserved compensation were because Personnel's records revealed that I had never taken any leave during my two-year tour of duty.

Oberammergau—"O-gau" to the troops—the high Alpine village that was the site of the European ADM school as well as an assortment of other NATO training schools, was drop-dead beautiful, with snow-covered mountains all around, great weather (I was there for six weeks in June and July), spectacular blue skies, and the atmosphere of a village lost in time. It is also the locus of the world-famous Passion Play, which takes place at 10-year intervals at the change of every decade, a ritual that had been going on almost continuously (there were only two cancellations and one postponement) since 1634 (the locals quickly adjusted so that the play would be performed in the last year of each decade—the year ending in zero). That explained why every male in the village during this run-up year (1969) was growing a beard . . . almost everyone with a pulse participated in the performance.

Oberammergau
(Wikimedia - photographer Andreas Praefcke
license CC BY-SA 3.0)

When I heard about the Passion Play and found some literature about it, I saw right away that I needed to keep a low profile in O-gau. The play's 16 acts are littered with negative images and pronouncements about Jews. Some but by no means all of this has been cut back over time. Despite that, I became friendly with some of the locals who frequented the same *Gasthäuser* and *Weinstuben* where I spent many evenings. Classes were pretty light fare, rendered even lighter and more relaxed by the fact that this was an exact repeat of my training "back in the world," as soldiers serving overseas used to wistfully refer to the U.S. Having seen it all before, I did not bother studying in the evenings. Instead, I spent virtually every evening out on the town with pals from other NATO countries who were in O-gau learning all sorts of non-ADM stuff. They also forewent evening study, but for different reasons. They—especially the Beneluxers—were the laziest bunch of really fun reprobates I ever encountered.

Note. Until O-gau, I never knew what repeating an educational experience meant. On graduation day at the European ADM School, I was presented with two awards: one for being at the top of the class; the second for achieving the highest grade in the history of ADM training. I said nothing about being a recidivist.

Three weeks into school, we received a three-day pass. I went down the mountain to *Garmisch-Partenkirchen*, site of the 1936 Nazi Winter Olympics. Garmisch sits at the foot of the *Zugspitze*, Germany's highest peak at around 10,000 feet. I signed up for a technical climbing course, at the end of which our class scaled the mountain with our instructor.

Alas, all good things must come to an end. The bus ride back to base in Bamberg was almost as gloomy as the one to Fort Dix to begin boot camp.

"Turnkey"

Under German Noses

Our "war reserve" weapons—the real deal with the plutonium cores—were stored at what was called a Special Ammunition Storage Site ("special" being a euphemism for nuclear) deep in what remained of the Franconian forest about 25 minutes by jeep or "deuce-and-a-half" (Armyspeak for a two-and-a-half-ton truck) out of town. Getting there required negotiating what amounted to a narrow logging road for the last part of the journey. From time-to-time we would encounter the local *Jagdaufseher*—game warden—a throwback, apoplectic little fellow decked out in *lederhosen* and a green Tyrolean hat with a feather in it. He could never understand what U.S. Army vehicles were doing in his woods, and of course we could not tell him. Instead, we threatened him, occasionally brandishing our sidearms in order to induce him to move off.

The Site consisted of an outer fence buttressed by triple-concertina barbed wire and a front gate with a big old Sergeant and Greenleaf padlock (more on this ubiquitous military locking device below). The outer courtyard (I can't think of another descriptive term for it) included a headquarters shack, guard barracks and a tiny Access Control shack resembling a phone booth. Slightly elevated wooden steps connected the HQ shack to the front gate and back to the Access Control shack. Just beyond this shack was a gate and fencing that contained the "inner sanctum" within which a series of bunkers consisting of concrete and earthworks harbored the site's *raison d'être*, MADMs, SADMs and nuclear warheads designed to be fired by Honest John missiles.

Guards were assigned to the site for 6-month tours, during which they alternated being on duty for two hours with being off for four hours. Their only relief when they could be away from the site was one day each weekend when they could go back to their home units at Warner Kaserne in Bamberg and take a real shower, do their laundry, and go downtown. Getting drunk was not that much of an attraction because the guards were high most of the time on the top-of-the-line hashish and opium that the many Turks working in Germany brought into the country. Visiting a bordello, in contrast, was an immensely popular extracurricular activity, as evidenced by the number of times there was a "crab" epidemic running riot in the site's guard barracks. Every such episode mandated a liberal dousing of the area with "crab powder," a mysterious substance that was apparently anathema to the little, pubic hair burrowing critters. This was also the reason why neither we access controllers nor the HQ shack personnel ever slept in the guard barracks, preferring to take our chances on uncomfortable desks or chairs in the shacks.

Both my unit—the ADM platoon—and the Honest John artillery company shared access control (a.k.a. Turnkey) duties at the site. That meant that I had to be there for a 24-hour stint approximately every third week. My sole jobs were to let people and vehicles in at the main gate, inspect the roving and bunker guards and their weapons and open the inner gate for the existing and replacement guards when they changed over every couple of hours, and once each 24-hour period employ a galvanometer to check the pre-wired circuit that circumnavigated the site. The wiring connected a series of conventional explosives designed to blow the site to kingdom come in the event either the Warsaw Pact attacked it or, much worse, the West Germans discovered that a slew of atomic weapons was secreted in their midst and decided to march on the site. I had replaced a good bit of the wiring myself during my time in Germany, since I enjoyed scampering up the tall Scotch Pine trees at the site using a climbing belt and crampons. I was one of the few soldiers unafraid of heights, a phobia that I now share after a lifetime of (literally) looking down with some contempt on my fearful colleagues.

The rest of the time at the site was my own, during which I hunkered down in the Access Control shack and read while listening to the *Leipzig* (East Germany) *Gewandhaus Orchestra* play excellent classical music selections. On occasion, when I ran out of books and the East Germans were taking a performance break, I wandered into the HQ shack to schmooze with the handful of guys assigned there or to stretch out on a desk for some shuteye.

Also, from time-to-time, a handful of ADM troops were sent out to the site to go into the bunkers and inspect our weapons.

The high point of every evening at the site was the arrival of the pizza truck, the only vehicle that did not have to show a special set of orders to get inside the main gate. Bamberg, with a heavy Italian *gastarbeiter* (guest worker) population, was known for really delicious, thin-crust pizza. The pizza delivered to the site every night was among the best I've ever eaten. If anyone had any nefarious intentions requiring penetration of the site, the pizza truck would have been the way to do it.

Russia Calling

I only faced one crisis at the site. While relaxing in the phone booth that passed for the Access Control shack, I was summoned to the HQ shack to take a phone call. To my amazement, the call originated in Leningrad, USSR and was from a lady friend who was going to be traveling through Munich the following weekend and wondered if we could meet there. When I asked how she got the phone number (everything concerning the site was highly classified), she told me she had called the office in the barracks to which my platoon was assigned and they had put her in touch with my platoon administrator who freely gave out the number of the site.

After I hung up, all hell broke loose. Within 45 minutes, a squad (not mine) of soldiers arrived at the main gate, led by a full bird colonel who was frothing at the mouth. My first "mistake"—my second actually if you count having taken the phone call—was to deny him and his people entry because they did not have the proper credentials. Once the colonel calmed down after threatening me with a general court martial, he began grilling me from the other side of the gate about the nature of the call from the Soviet Union, who did I know there, was I a Soviet agent, blah, blah, blah? I felt like telling him it was Natasha Fatale, but managed somehow to restrain myself. He demanded that I be relieved of my duties and accompany him back to the base. I refused since he was not directly in my chain of command. When I pointed this out to him, he became completely unhinged and began waving his sidearm around, thankfully not in my direction. Finally, he backed off in frustration and informed me that I had not heard the last of this. I never heard from him again. Later, I discovered that the general/brigade commander in far-off Ludwigsburg had a talk with the flighty full bird and told him I had acted appropriately in denying him entry into the site, and to let the incident go.

Routine . . . and Not So Routine

Our daily routine back at our workspace beneath the barracks consisted of lectures, the occasional film depicting the Trinity or Bikini Atoll bomb test or something similar, and practicing arming our weapons. The larger weapon, the MADM, took hours to arm properly, so those days went by pretty quickly. If my Team Two had ever been called upon to deploy the MADM, we would have been able to arm it very competently, the problem then being that in training we were never able to simulate a successful detonation. That was true even when we used all the redundant arming procedures—wire, radio waves, and manual timers. None of them ever worked.

The SADM, a 50-lb backpack weapon, was another story. It could only be armed by a manual timer and we did not have any means of assuring that it would actually explode. Fortunately, we never had to find out.

Two-Man Control

A brief digression is in order here. The concept of "two-man control" has been a central precept of U.S. nuclear doctrine since the advent of the Atomic Age. This was designed to be the ultimate fail-safe mechanism, the idea that two minds—and two pairs of hands—must be aligned and act in concert before a nuclear device can be deployed and detonated. If only one person could execute that decision, the danger of perpetrating a global Armageddon was too great.

The movies depict this very well. Two Air Force officers man the missile launch controls in a silo in the remote reaches of North Dakota. The controls are far enough apart that even basketball center Dikembe Mutombo (who was 7'8" with an 8-foot "wingspan") could not simultaneously turn the keys to send an ICBM on its way to Moscow. It required both officers (1) agreeing that their orders directed a launch, and (2) turning the keys in unison in order to launch a nuclear missile.

At least with respect to ADMs, it did not work that way. While our MADM required an entire ADM team to arm and then detonate the weapon, two-man control was out the window when it was a SADM that needed to go bang. One of the SADM's capabilities was that a single soldier could parachute out of an airplane with it in his backpack. When he hit the ground, the weapon was intended to be emplaced and armed by him alone. It would have been completely impractical to do anything else. Two-man control became one-man control, the only such "violation" of doctrine extant.

That was inevitable and perfectly in accordance with SADM deployment doctrine. But it also affected my ADM unit in two other very important ways:

1. *Opening the safes and retrieving our deployment orders.* One of our training exercises consisted of receiving a "Teletypewriter Exchange Service" (TWX) action message, or telex, from brigade headquarters that instructed us to open a safe in our training area and remove an envelope. The envelope contained instructions for weapons deployment in the event of war. Two-man control came into play because the safe could not be opened unless two locks were disengaged. Two ADM soldiers, each having memorized one of the lock's combinations, were on duty at all times in the event such a training message was received and required action.

This procedure worked well during daylight hours. However, when night fell, things changed. None of us particularly enjoyed being awake during the night shift, so the typical *modus operandum* was to share the lock combinations so that only one of us had to be awake at any given time. So much for two-man control. However, since these were mere training exercises, denoted by a "Code Blue" heading the TWX, this was not deemed a big deal.

Except for one time when the TWX was headed by a Code Red, which meant that this was the real deal, no longer just a training exercise. I happened to be on night duty with another soldier, albeit asleep in a chair, when the TWX machine began buzzing. My colleague never gave a second thought to the fact that the message was ordering us to open the safe and extract the envelope marked "Red Dot Five," which would instruct our ADM unit to go to the special weapons site, open the bunker doors, remove our weapons, load them on trucks, proceed to designated coordinates, arm the weapons and set the timers for detonation. In short, go nuclear.

I woke up when I heard his combat boots clattering across the concrete floor toward the safe. "What's going on?" I asked.

"Brigade just sent us a Red Dot Five."

"Whoa," I said. "Hold on. That can't be correct. Let's send a message back up to Brigade and ask them to confirm that they didn't just make a mistake."

"And get in trouble?" He replied. "No fucking way. I'm opening the safe."

"This is bullshit," I argued. "Think about the international situation. All's been quiet. You don't just go from calm to global thermonuclear war in a heartbeat."

"You got a point," he admitted.

I went over to the TWX machine and tapped out a message to Brigade. In less than two minutes, we received a response that, to paraphrase, said: "Oops. Sorry."

2. *Opening the bunker doors at the site.* I never learned who figured this out, but it must have been a genius. Two-man control also found its way into one of the more important activities involving our nukes: extracting them from the bunkers. Once again, the fundamental fail-safe construct designed to prevent a calamity failed to work as intended.

One of the platoon veterans claimed that If you took a Sargent & Greenleaf lock of the variety that were ubiquitous around ADM platoons, and set it to zero, then pounded on top of it with a hammer, it would spring open. I tested this assertion once when I was performing access control at the site and, *voilà*, he was absolutely correct!

Warner Barracks: The ADM Platoon lived and worked in the middle beige building (upper left)
(U.S. Army – Public Domain)

Map Reading 1.0

Another routine task that occupied an occasional work day was reading maps in order to stay up on where we were supposed to go and how to get there in the event of various Defense Readiness Conditions (DEFCONs). DEFCONs were and still are a central component of nuclear doctrine. They define different stages of U.S. armed forces emergency readiness.

The President establishes the DEFCON level and transmits any change in it through the Secretary of Defense and then via the Chairman of the Joint Chiefs of Staff and the Combat Commanders. Each DEFCON level defines a set of specific security, activation and response instructions for our troops.

There is no single DEFCON level that applies to the entire U.S. military establishment. Different services, commands or bases can be activated at different DEFCONs. Even during the Cuban Missile Crisis, when the world came as close as it ever has to nuclear annihilation, the only-ever DEFCON 2 declaration did not apply to the entire world.

DEFCON 5 (Code-named FADE OUT) is the norm, the lowest state of readiness. DEFCON 4 (Code-named DOUBLE TAKE) mandates an increase in our intelligence watchfulness and security measures. DEFCON 3 (Code-named ROUND HOUSE) increases force readiness above the peacetime norm and requires the U.S. Air Force to be ready to hit the skies in 15 minutes. DEFCON 2 (Code-named FAST PACE) is when things begin to get really interesting. It is one step closer to nuclear war and requires designated U.S. armed forces, in particular nuclear forces, to be ready to deploy and engage in under six hours.

And then there is DEFCON 1 (Code-named COCKED PISTOL), which signifies that nuclear war is imminent and calls for maximum readiness.

Our map study was intended to prepare us for any of the dicier, stomach-churning DEFCONs. Instead, we took it as an opportunity to find ways to safety. Those of us who were designated to drop into Eastern Europe, arm our backpack SADMs and then run like Hell understood that this was a suicide mission and also a silly one, given the likely impossibility of doing this clandestinely. Moreover, some of us learned from our Honest John nuclear missile battery counterparts at the weapons site that one of their missions was to blow those same targets to kingdom come while we were there. Patriotism aside, we were not particularly enamored of getting vaporized by friendly fire.

Consequently, while our cadre of lifer sergeants and junior officers marveled at how diligently we studied our maps, we were planning escape routes to places like neutral Switzerland, mindful that as the repository of both sides' booty and other valuables, the oft-declared neutral and decidedly perfidious Gnomes of Zurich were not likely to experience a leveling of the Alps by either side's nukes.

My route, carefully planned out, had me going south by *autobahn* in my POV (privately-owned vehicle—the Army has an acronym for everything) to the shores of the *Bodensee* (Lake Constance) where I intended to steal a watercraft, even a rowboat, and cross the lake to Switzerland. My plan was to reach the lakeshore around *Friedrichshafen* on the German shore, drive northwest along the shore to a relatively sparsely settled rural area, and get myself across one of the narrowest parts of the lake to the Swiss side. Being young and naïve, I never bothered to ponder how I would explain myself to the Swiss *polizei* who were certain to confront me at some point.

Bamberg is top center; Bodensee (Lake Constance) is Bottom Left
(Wikimedia Commons - By NordNordWest from Landkreise 07-2007.svg by Fremantleboy, license CC BY-SA 3.0)

Inspections (They Were a Blast . . . or Not)

In addition to the periodic barracks inspections to which we were subject because we were loosely attached to the 82d Engineer Battalion for administrative and support purposes, the ADM platoon had to endure four one-week-long inspections of our nuclear prowess (or lack thereof) each year. These were rather demanding ordeals that were the closest thing to a figurative proctological examination I have ever had to undergo. The inspectors scrutinized every facet of our mission and operations to determine if we were a fit bunch of nukes.

Passing the inspection earned us a really huge benefit: one week off from work. If we failed the inspection, our punishment was . . . one week off from work. If this sounds totally irrational, rest assured that it was. I never elicited an adequate explanation aside from one that our cadre subscribed to: we were a highly sensitive bunch of prima donnas who would be rattled by anything smacking of real punishment, whereas treating us with kid gloves might ensure that unit morale remained positive and that we would continue to do our jobs, grateful for having avoided sanctions.

There was, however, one rather draconian price to be paid by any ADM platoon that flunked an inspection: the immediate relief from command of our two officers (both lieutenants) and their rapid reassignment to . . . Vietnam, where there was a very serious shooting war going on. Because we flunked these inspections more frequently than we passed (passing required being perfect in everything thirty guys did for a full week), we had a high turnover of officers. Moreover, because our officers knew from the first day on the job that if we screwed up they were on their way to the rice paddies, they generally treated us exceptionally well. While fraternization between officers and enlisted men was frowned upon to the point of occasionally court-martialing an officer who partied with the grunts, our officers quietly fraternized to an extreme and were never punished for it. We partied together, played together, drank and ate together (just not at the mess hall), etc. We were a pretty tight bunch.

The temptation to send one of our officers away to Southeast Asia only surfaced once. A new First Lieutenant showed up as a replacement for our platoon leader whom we liked, but who had the misfortune to fail an inspection when one of our platoon mates decided one afternoon to curl up in a MADM casing, which was roughly the size of a 55-gallon drum, and catch a few zz's. An inspector found him and that was that. Nothing we could do thereafter could rehabilitate us. We flunked.

The new guy was a bit of a martinet and had trouble adjusting to our unusual unit full of pretty smart guys, many college-educated and beyond, who were preternaturally inclined to do things their own way, which was often decidedly not the Army way. The last straw during his brief tenure was sending two platoon members on a seven-mile round trip walk to a storage shed at the extreme other side of our base to count the number of floor mats we had stored there. When they reported back several hours later, he ordered them to go back to the shed and retrieve two mats. They quite properly (in my opinion) refused and an impasse ensued. He then ordered the rebellious duo on KP for a week, which struck the rest of the platoon as an over-the-top punishment for the lieutenant's own screw-up (since he could have asked them before their initial trip to the shed to bring back two mats).

The platoon bided its time before exacting revenge. During our next quarterly inspection, we went out to our special weapons storage site, where one day of each inspection was devoted to examining how well our weapons were faring in their bunkers plus how we defended against a simulated assault on the site by irate Germans who suddenly discovered that they resided near a nuclear arsenal. As mentioned above, our mission in the event a German mob marched on the site was to blow it up. We had pre-positioned a hard-wired circuit of conventional explosives throughout the facility, largely near the top of the magnificent Scotch Pines that were the last vestige of the once extensive Franconian forest. The wires met in the headquarters shack, tethered to two dummy terminals on a shelf with a galvanometer that we used to test the circuit. Below that lurked our blasting machine which, when hooked up to the wires, was intended to blow the site to bits. Whether such a detonation would cause a multitude of dirty bombs to spread plutonium all over the place and into the atmosphere was often speculated upon. Given the half-life of plutonium, the site might then become habitable again in about 125,000 years.

Our platoon leader was the only person authorized to depress the plunger on the blasting machine. When it came time for him to test the circuit and simulate the explosion, he was unable to locate the blasting machine, which had been removed from its location in the headquarters shack by a vengeful soldier. We flunked the inspection and the poor looie was off to the friendly confines of Saigon, Cam Rahn Bay, Hue and the Demilitarized Zone. As usual, we earned a week off for our incompetence.

A Pinch of SALT

In late fall 1969, one of my college roommates, an engineering grad, called me to announce that he was in Germany working for the Philco-Ford electronics company involving some highly classified aspect of the Strategic Arms Limitation Talks (SALT) that were going on between the U.S. and Soviet Union with the goal of putting some limits on nuclear weapons and delivery systems. He wanted to visit me in Bamberg, which of course was something I eagerly anticipated.

In the late 1960s, U.S. intelligence learned that the Soviets were hell-bent on a huge ICBM construction program designed to reach parity with us. At about the same time, we noted that they were constructing an Anti-Ballistic Missile (ABM) defense system around Moscow, which could change the balance of power by altering U.S.-Soviet nuclear war deterrence doctrine which was based on the utter lunacy of what was labeled Mutual Assured Destruction ("MAD"). An ABM system portended that one side could launch a first strike and then stop retaliation from the other by shooting down their incoming missiles.

The Defense Department went into freak-out mode. What emerged from DoD's panic was a call for SALT talks with the

Soviets designed to limit the development of both offensive and defensive strategic systems and thus stabilize relations. Formal SALT talks began in Helsinki in November 1969 and my roommate was sent over to Germany to begin work on some technical aspects of what eventuated in the SALT I Treaty of 1972, the first time during the Cold War that the two adversaries agreed to limit the number of nuclear missiles in their arsenals.

When he arrived in Bamberg, I was annoyed that he could not discuss what he was doing with me. Reciprocally, I could not discuss what I was doing in ADM with him. It was a Mexican standoff, but it did not prevent us from having a good time. I took him to the best hotel in town where we enjoyed a great meal followed by an absurdly expensive bottle of wine (more than $400 in today's dollars) that we charged to his expense account. It was the first and last time I tasted a top-of-the-vine wine because my uneducated palette could not discern any difference between *Chateau LaFitte Frumpelmayer* or whatever and the bottles of Ripple in the vending machines in some of the barracks on post.

After dinner, we went to a neighboring town where there was a raucous band concert and alcohol and drug-fueled party going on through most of the night. Because we did not have any drugs, the German girls were unimpressed, so we staggered back to my barracks in the middle of the night and collapsed.

SALT I was followed by SALT II, the ABM Treaty, START I and START II and the INF Treaty, all of which limited either warhead stockpiles or ballistic missiles. Watching the Trump administration abandon this long-standing and very salutary nuclear weapons policy is deeply troubling.

Trucks

We had much in common with our Soviet Cold War counterparts when it came to transportation. Both rival superpowers were less than super with respect to how they managed trucks.

Trucks were central to our activities. We needed them to haul our weapons back and forth from the storage site to the supply and maintenance base at the extreme other side of the country, as well as for military exercises. Each nuclear weapons team had its own deuce-and-a-half truck that could accommodate both the team and its weapons. Our trucks were kept in a motor pool directly across from our barracks. The motor pool was lightly guarded by whichever unlucky soldier was the recipient of punishment duty on any particular day.

Despite a 24/7 guard, the shenanigans that went on with respect to the trucks were constant. If a team needed a particular truck part—tire, engine, radio, etc.—the easiest way to obtain it was to sneak into the motor pool after dark and steal it from another team's truck. This went on constantly and caused no end of aggravation. Many were the times we would have to take our trucks out on a mission, only to discover that they lacked an essential part. No one ever thought of going through the time-consuming process of actually ordering a replacement part from whichever quartermaster depot served as the official repository of truck parts.

Several years later, I asked my father-in-law, who served in the Quartermaster Corps in World War II, if similar things went on and drove him nuts. He responded: "Yes" and "Hell, yes."

The American Trump Card

This is something I've thought about a lot beginning with my time stationed in Germany. I think what I am about to say might have been a contributing factor to our prevailing in World War II.

I had two experiences that pointed out the stark differences between how the lowest-level U.S. Army unit—in our case a squad (a.k.a. "team")—handled a problem vs. how comparable units from other NATO countries responded to the same problem.

1. At a conventional demolitions training school in the German Alps, one day we were divided up by country—U.S., Germany, Netherlands, Belgium, etc.—and given a simulated infiltration problem to solve. Our team not only finished first, but also received the "prize" for being the most innovative. The other nations' squads all flunked the test because they were not accustomed to improvising, which appears to come naturally to Americans.
2. During a NATO exercise, my team along with other NATO country squads was deployed along the Czech border. We encountered a problem of where to position ourselves when our original site was found to be unacceptable. We immediately made the decision to go to the high ground, set up a perimeter, and post sentries to watch for enemy movement. We learned during the post-exercise debriefing that all the other nations' comparable squads experienced a similar problem. However, instead of trying to solve the problem themselves, they insisted that they had to remain where they had originally been assigned and wait for a higher authority to come along and tell them what to do.

These anecdotes highlight something undefinable in the American psyche that differentiates us from others in almost every human endeavor. We are used to making decisions on the fly and at the lowest operational level. We are also innovative and entrepreneurial, which is why European nations send people over here to observe how we start businesses and make decisions.

Chapter 12
Czeching In

You can crush the flowers, but you can't stop the spring.
—Alexander Dubcek

The Great Alexander Dubcek Greeting His Adoring People at Old Town Square, Prague
(© Franz Goess, Austrian National Library)

Prague Spring

In August 1968, ten months before I arrived in Bamberg, my ADM platoon had actually received a "Red Dot Five" TWX message that was the real thing. After several months of increasing tension due to the declaration of "Prague Spring," "Socialism with a human face" in the words of the emerging Czechoslovak hero, Alexander Dubcek, Soviet Communist Party Chairman Leonid Brezhnev had had enough. On the night of August 20, 1968, the Warsaw Pact armies of the Soviet Union,

Poland, Hungary, East Germany, and Bulgaria invaded Czechoslovakia to put an end to Dubcek's bold democratic experiment. What happened next was the tensest moment in Cold War history since the Cuban Missile crisis six years before.

President Johnson ordered DefCon 3 (during the Cuban Missile Crisis, the U.S. went to DefCon 2, just one step from nuclear war), thus prompting TWX messages to go out from the Pentagon to U.S. forces worldwide. The TWX that traveled from Washington, DC to U.S. Army Europe headquarters in Heidelberg made its way down the chain of command at the speed of light to Seventh Army, VII Corps, Seventh Brigade and finally to the ADM Platoon in Bamberg.

When the two soldiers on night duty at our training facility opened the safes and the sealed envelopes, they found that they contained two sets of orders. First, the platoon was instructed to go to our storage site and retrieve its complement of MADMs from the bunkers. Then four of the six nuclear weapons teams were instructed to go to the Fulda Gap 70 miles to the north and prepare to arm the weapons.

The Fulda Gap is one of two narrow lowland corridors through which Warsaw Pact tanks would have to travel in order to attack the West German heartland and race to Frankfurt-am-Main, the German financial capital, and the Rhine River. It was one of the two most strategically important choke points in NATO's defense plans. After his defeat at the Battle of Leipzig in 1813, Napoleon retreated through the Fulda Gap and defeated an opposing army at the Battle of Hanau, near Frankfurt. From there, he escaped back to France.

The second set of orders instructed Teams One and Two (my future team) to travel to a set of coordinates on the West German-Czechoslovak border with their MADMs. When they arrived there, they watched as Soviet T-54 battle tanks several hundred yards away across the barbed wire swung around their turrets and pointed their big guns at my colleagues. The ones who overlapped with me the next year said that they were sweating bullets, believing that they were about to die.

The Soviet invasion of Czechoslovakia in 1968 was not the only time that the U.S. contemplated using my platoon's tactical nuclear weapons against its adversary. Back in 1959, when Khrushchev once again threatened a Berlin crisis, a secret NATO war plan known as *Live Oak*, the purpose of which was to maintain open Western access to Berlin, contemplated an alternative to the airlift that had worked so well in 1948: sending an armored division armed with tactical nukes down East German highways.

The Crushing of Prague Spring
(The Central Intelligence Agency - Soviet Invasion of Czechoslovakia - Public Domain)

The Soviet spy network found out about this plan and informed Khrushchev. The Chairman then cooled his Berlin bombast and a very dicey situation was avoided.

War Games

During my second year in Germany, Team Two was assigned to the staff of the Supreme Allied Commander, Europe (SACEUR) as his ADM unit to deploy as he wished during a NATO war games exercise. This dubious honor required us to spend at least one overnight somewhere in the field away from our home base in Bamberg. None of us were even remotely ready or eager to sleep outside our barracks, or even knew what that entailed. Lieutenant "Luke" was assigned to lead the six of us. He was easily the best and most easy-going officer we had experienced, and forever endeared himself to us when he suggested that several of us head downtown and pick up some meats to grill (he intended to bring his own portable grill) and some good, hard-crust German bread, cheeses and wines. Generally, troops out in the field ate C-rations, a miserable concoction of Spam-like gruel that any discerning hog would summarily reject in favor of swill.

We came back loaded down with gourmet goodies and packed up our gear, including a training set of MADMs and SADMs, and headed off to the coordinates sent us by the four-star general's aide. The coordinates, once we figured out how to interpret them, landed us in the middle of a farmer's fallow field smack up against the triple-concertina barbed wire denoting the border between West Germany and Communist Czechoslovakia. During the Cold War, the intimidating barriers, watch towers, no-mans' land, free-fire zones and *Volkspolizei* patrolling the border between West and East Germany became much more laid back as one traveled south to where Germany met Czechoslovakia.

Less than 15 minutes after our arrival at the designated place on the map, the irate German farmer appeared in his field armed with a shotgun and threatened to begin shooting unless we moved off his property. Notwithstanding that we were armed with M-16 rifles, .45 caliber sidearms and several *faux* nuclear weapons, we threw up our arms, and I yelled: "*schiessen Sie nicht!*" Don't shoot! (I was the only German speaker on the team.).

We threw everything we had taken out back into the rear of our truck and moved off up on a hill overlooking both the farm and the border. After we realized that we could not put up our squad tent because, "strak" soldiers that we were, we had forgotten to bring along the tent's center pole, we gave up on setting up a campsite, deciding to sleep either on the ground or in the back of the truck, and proceeded to grill our steaks, *bratwursts, weisswursts* and *mettwursts*, cut off some chunks of delicious cheeses, broke the bread into pieces, opened the bottles of Riesling we brought along (we saved the ice chest full of *Burgerbrau Bamberg* beer for later) and had a fine repast. When it got dark, we were surprised by a visit from two German girls—*junge mädchen*—from the nearby town of *Fürth-im-Wald*, who sat around our lighter-fluid-fueled campfire drinking beer and wine and flirting. After they said good night and gave us all teasing kisses, the longest serving member of the team regaled us with stories of August 1968 when Team Two had been deployed nearby with their war reserve nukes and found themselves facing off against Soviet armor during the Czech "Prague Spring" crisis.

We crawled into our sleeping bags after assigning one team member to sleep next to the radio, in case SACEUR (Supreme Allied Commander, Europe) communicated with us. At around 0400 (4:00 AM), we were awakened by a crackle of radio static. The SACEUR staff ordered us to pack up and move north to another set of coordinates where we were to prepare to simulate arming and detonating our MADM weapon. We were so comfortable in our sleeping bags that I suggested that we stay put, call into SACEUR headquarters in the morning and report: "mission accomplished." To our surprise, Lieutenant "Luke" said: "Good idea." We went right back to sleep.

Upon waking the next morning, we radioed SACEUR headquarters and reported: "Mission Accomplished!"

I was accustomed to a long run before breakfast and the terrain where we were looked very inviting. I ran down the hill and, paying no attention to the barb-wire border, ran through an opening in the wire and along a dirt path toward the rising sun. About a mile into my run, I encountered a grizzled, hunched-over gentleman with the mother of all chicken necks, driving a horse-drawn cart.

"*Was machen sie hier?*"—"What are you doing here?"—he asked in heavily accented German. I stopped and told him I was on my morning run.

"*Sind sie Amerikaner?*"—"Are you an American?" He did not need to be perceptive to see that my olive drab fatigue shirt read "U.S. Army" across one pocket.

I said yes.

"*Armée, ich glaube?*"—"Army, I believe?"

"*Ja. Sie haben recht.*"—"Yes. You're right."

It was then that he informed me that I was in Czechoslovakia. He went on to tell me that he went every morning through the gap in the wire that he himself had cut years before in order to sell his milk to the Germans at the farmer's market in *Fürth-im-Wald*, where he was able to get a much higher price—paid in *Deutschmarks*, no less—than he could get in Czechoslovakia. He offered me a ride back through the wire. I declined and sprinted back to our camp as fast as I could. If someone had had a stopwatch on me, it might have been "watch out, Roger Bannister." All the way, I imagined the headlines had I been caught by the Czech police.

When I got back from my inadvertent adventure on the wrong side of the Iron Curtain, it was time for breakfast.

While we ate grill-cooked eggs, home fries and more German sausage, soaking up the greasy residue with bread, and washed down with *orangensaft* and *apfelsaft*, Lieutenant "Luke" decided that, to be safe, we better head out for the coordinates ordered by SACEUR just in case anyone from his staff decided to check on us (unlikely since the friendly confines of Heidelberg, where SACEUR hung out, was more than 200 miles from where we were playing army).

We packed up and moved out. Given our inability to understand and interpret a simple concept like map coordinates, we weren't sure we had arrived at the designated location. We remained there for the rest of the day, finishing off our food, wine and beer. When the exercise ended late that evening, we packed up and trucked back to base.

A fine time was had by all.

Addendum

Being based so close to Czechoslovakia for two years, I was aching to visit Prague, a city about which I had heard all my life and one that fascinated me because I had so recently been enraptured by Alexander Dubcek's heroic attempt to break the shackles of Soviet Communism. My security clearance, however, prevented me from traveling inside the Iron Curtain (legally, at any rate). I was always wistful when I saw tourist buses leaving from the American Express office on post some Saturday mornings for day-trips to the Czech capital.

Charles Bridge, Prague- Insert, West Support (Where My SADM Would Have Been Placed)
(Author Collection and Sergey Ashmarin, CC BY-SA 3.0 - Wikimedia)

It took almost 50 years before I made it to Prague. In fall 2018, Prague had just a few days before celebrated the 100th anniversary of its independence from the Austro-Hungarian Empire and its initial plunge into democracy. I asked our tour guides about how the celebration of the 50th anniversary of Prague Spring had gone, which I assumed must have been a very big deal a few months before. I was surprised to hear their indifference to that epic event and that there had been very little celebration at all.

Soviet tanks can do that to you, not to mention that our tour guides had not even been born when the tumultuous events of 1968 had turned their country inside out.

Ruins of the Soviet War Memorial Column, Old Town Square, Prague, 2018
(Author's Collection)

Chapter 13
Back in "the World"

I'm so short I can sit on a piece of paper and dangle my legs over the edge.
 —The universal short-timer's creed

Soldiers stationed abroad often ached to be back home in what we called "the world," an expression of disdain for where they were forced to be and regret that they could not be back home. That was not me. I loved being able to travel around Europe on my off time and faced the prospect of returning to the U.S. with some ambivalence.

I was unable to get out of the Army in time to begin law school (a number of the schools that had accepted me when I originally applied in my last year of college kept those openings available because so many prospective law students had to satisfy their military obligation first). Instead, I decided to use my GI Bill education benefits to get a Master's degree prior to matriculating at law school the following fall. I needed a graduate program that began late enough to accommodate my Army separation date and also one that would allow me to complete a two-year graduate program in a year and a summer. I found one in the New School for Social Research in Manhattan.

The New School

An Inauspicious Beginning

The New School was a storied institution founded in 1919 by a pantheon of leading left-leaning luminaries: John Dewey, Charles Beard, Thorstein Veblen and a number of their progressive friends. Ever since, it has been positioned on the ideological spectrum somewhere between Karl Marx and Leon Trotsky. It was about as distant in its politics and that of its student body from the U.S. Army as it was possible to be. It was also probably more diverse than any comparable college or university at the time. While well-known as a haven for Jewish students, including many from Brooklyn's Orthodox and Hasidic communities (as alien to me as if they were extra-terrestrials), it also attracted young Arabs in town with UN diplomatic missions as well as other students from all over the world. An added bonus was that the male/female ratio was very favorable.

The New School for Social Research
(Beyond My Ken - Own work, CC BY-SA 4.0, Wikimedia)

A friend of mine, Janet Elsea, is the author of a very good book, *First Impression, Best Impression*, that I wished I had read before entering class that first day at the New School. The presence of so many women in class was a major culture shock for me, having spent the prior six years in all-male environments. I made myself famous the first day of class, only eight hours after being released from the Army when, exhausted from only an hour of restless sleep on the bus from Fort Dix to New York City and no longer accustomed to polite society, I was called on by the professor and asked to comment on a passage of required reading from Aristotle's *Politics*. My unedited response: "I haven't read the fucking book. I don't even know where to buy the goddamn thing. I just got out of the Army at midnight, for chrissakes!" When I realized what had come out of my mouth, I was horrified. After class, however, I discovered that my unfiltered outburst was popular among the distaff population of the class. Two young ladies invited me to parties at their apartments the next weekend. I don't know if it was my unfiltered language or the exotica that the New School might just have been the unlikeliest place on the planet in which to find an Army veteran.

Remembrance of Things Past

Early in my first semester, I was in the school's snack bar one day between classes when a well-dressed gentleman sporting a decorative handkerchief sticking out of his breast pocket—not the usual New School student or professorial garb—approached and asked if he could sit down at my table. After a few minutes of small talk, he stunned me by saying: "I understand you were stationed in Bavaria."

"Excuse me?" I said.

"With an Atomic Demolition Munitions team?"

"I don't know what you're talking about," I responded as I got up and left.

I never encountered him again, but the brief meeting unnerved me for a long time.

Bonding with Mentors

I had two great professors during my graduate program, unquestionably on a par with the top academics I encountered at Yale:

I immediately clicked with Saul Padover, from whom I took a course on the history and politics of the Franklin Roosevelt Era and how it set the table for the Cold War (Padover had been close to Eleanor Roosevelt and worked for FDR's Secretary of the Interior and friend, Harold Ickes). Saul was Jewish, from Vienna and was an Army veteran (OSS in World War II). He was a prolific writer. His books on his World War II experiences and on Karl Marx, Joseph II of Austria, Louis XVI of France, Alexander Hamilton, James Madison and especially Thomas Jefferson are great reads. Saul served as my advisor for one of my two Master's theses, *Presidential Disability and the 25th Amendment*. I admired him enormously.

The other academic luminary with whom I bonded was Jacob Landynski, with whom Saul co-authored the first book I ever read about constitutional law, *The Living U.S. Constitution*, which unlike any other book about our foundational document, also contains character sketches of the delegates to the constitutional convention written by their colleagues. I took several courses from Landynski, each one an eye-opener. He was a dramatic lecturer, unlike Padover, and combined the best features of the Socratic Method with Talmudic back-and-forth. Landynski served as the advisor for my second Master's thesis, *Search and Seizure in the Military: The Fourth Amendment in the Barracks*.

When I became a law professor, I tried to model my teaching techniques on what I had absorbed from these two educators.

Waging the Cold War in Lower Manhattan

By the time I arrived at the New School, its leftist orientation had become diluted. In one of my classes, I witnessed daily clashes between Hasidic students on one side arguing with Middle Eastern Arab students on the other. The Hasids defended democracy and American capitalism while the Arabs were equally vocal arguing the merits of socialism and, if truth be told, totalitarianism.

The professor was duly flummoxed. He tried to maintain order and enforce the ground rules of rational debate, but it was no use. It got so bad that, from time-to-time, the two sides came to blows. I along with other "moderates" attempted to restrain the combatants.

Fortunately, both sides' pugilistic skills were wanting. A pillow fight was more dangerous.

I concluded from these brawls that, if the opposing sides in the Arab-Israeli conflict had to depend on these inept warriors, we did not have to worry.

Ithaca and Irmgard

My first weekend in Bamberg, I was escorted downtown by two new friends from the ADM platoon. We first went to *Schlenkerla's*, the watering hole that, since 1405, has been the Mecca of Bamberg's famous *rauchbier* (smoke beer), a concoction that takes some getting used to. Accustomed as I was to American beer with its 6 1/2 percent alcohol content, I did not realize that a double-bock rauchbier came with an alcohol content of 25 percent. After two of them, I was only dimly aware of my surroundings. After Schlenkerla's, my new friends took me to the *Atlantik Bar* (the "A-Bar" to the American troop contingent), a dive that lived down to its name. It catered to "Ami" soldiers. The women who frequented the A-Bar were mostly girls who either played for pay or were on the make for drugs, mainly marijuana and hashish. What little I remember about the evening was moderated by my inebriated condition. I did, however, realize that this was not going to be the best place to find lasting female companionship.

When I returned from Oberammergau and the NATO Nuclear Weapons School, another friend suggested that we drive down to Erlangen, just north of Nuremberg, to the university where a girl he was going out with had invited him to a party. That sounded much more enticing to me than evenings at the A-Bar.

The partygoers proved to be of a single mind politically: way to the left. We two U.S. army guys were subjected to considerable criticism for the Vietnam War, capitalism, racism, support of Israel, etc. I became rather defensive despite my own centrist inklings. One of the fiercest interlocutors was a very serious, not bad looking young woman named Irmgard Möller. I never found out if she was in fact a student at the university, but she was by far the most outspoken person at the event. Once the grilling was over and we returned to base, I barely gave her or her hostility another thought.

A few years later, I was married and in law school in Ithaca, New York, about as distant as one could get from both Erlangen University and the extreme rage of Irmgard Möller. One day, the telephone at our apartment rang and my wife picked it up. The caller asked: "Can I speak to Irmgard Möller, please." When my wife related the call to me, the name meant little. I knew I had heard it before, but could not place it.

Irmgard Möller-German Wanted Poster
(Public Domain)

Over the next several years, we kept getting similar calls, always asking for Irmgard Möller. Coincidence? Who knows? I doubt that there are a lot of Irmgard Möllers loose in the world, and certainly not in backwater Ithaca. I wondered what message someone could be sending me? At some point during law school, I discovered that the Irmgard Möller I had encountered that evening at Erlangen University was third in command of the "Red Army Faction" (a.k.a., the Baader-Meinhoff Group), a terrorist organization that was wreaking havoc in Germany. In May 1972, she and a colleague entered police headquarters in Augsburg carrying suitcases that contained pipe bombs that they planted in empty offices. When the bombs went off, five policemen were injured and the building partially collapsed. A few days later, she and another colleague drove explosive-laden cars into Campbell Barracks in Heidelberg and parked the vehicles in front of U.S. Military Intelligence Headquarters. Three American soldiers were killed and five were wounded when the car bombs exploded. Two months later, she was betrayed to the authorities by a fellow terrorist who had flipped. She was arrested, tried and sentenced to a long prison term.

In 1977, Möller attempted suicide, stabbing herself four times in the chest. She survived, unlike her Red Army Faction colleagues, Andreas Baader and Ulrike Meinhoff, both of whom died in prison, allegedly by their own hands, but probably not. Irmgard Möller was released from prison in 1994.

Coding Most Foul

No matter where I went, the Cold War in various guises seemed to follow. Ithaca and law school were no exception.

When you complete your active military service and are discharged from the U.S. armed forces, you receive a document called the "DD-214," "Certificate of Release or Discharge from Active Duty," that among other information indicates the nature of your discharge: Honorable; General; Other Than Honorable Conditions; Bad Conduct; or Dishonorable. It also includes any medals and awards you won, your highest rank and pay grade, combat service, overseas service, Military Occupational Specialty, and a record of the training and schools you completed.

The DD Form 214 is used by various government agencies, primarily the Department of Veterans Affairs, to award veteran benefits, and may be requested by employers should a person indicate he or she has served in the military. It is also required by funeral directors in order to prove eligibility for interment in a veteran's cemetery, obtaining a grave marker and for providing military honors to a deceased veteran.

The DD-214 (Anonymous Example)
(Department of Defense)

This document is as critical to a veteran's making his or her way in the civilian world as a Social Security number or birth certificate. Employers, academic institutions, labor unions, etc. all want to see a veteran's discharge status. A Bad Conduct or Dishonorable Discharge is an enormous impediment to a successful existence. For many arbiters of one's future, anything other than an Honorable Discharge can mean automatic rejection.

At least that is the way it was until the military during the Vietnam Era resorted to a secret system of adding innocuous, small-print three-letter/digit codes to the DD-214. The codes supplemented the discharge narrative. Many were condemnatory in nature and were able to be added to the 214 without any vetting as to their veracity or review by a higher authority. If your commanding officer didn't like you for some reason—or for no reason at all—he (it was always a male back then) could arbitrarily add one of these disparaging codes to your 214. This was subjective in the extreme and a great revenge temptation.

I learned about this by accident when I was having drinks at a bar in New York with a former Army captain who revealed that he used these codes to "get back at" soldiers he did not like. That revelation stuck with me for the next three years. When it came time to select a topic for my 3L honors thesis in law school, I decided that I wanted to research these codes and argue that this was an abuse of power and denial of Due Process of Law on the part of the government. Fortunately, my thesis advisor was a wonderful professor, Harrop Freeman, who was on the progressive side of the ideological spectrum and a vocal opponent of the war in Vietnam. He encouraged me to go for it.

During the Vietnam Era, an army draftee had a 6-year military obligation consisting of two years on active duty, three years in what was labeled the Ready Reserve, and one year in the Inactive Reserve. The Reserve time meant that you were subject to being recalled to active duty under certain dire circumstances. The three years of Ready Reserve obligation required attendance at monthly meetings (one weekend per month) and a two-week summer assignment. When I separated from my two years of active duty, I never bothered joining a Reserve unit and no one ever checked to determine if I had. However, I still retained a military identification card and a DD-214. Armed with them, I walked into the Cornell University Reserve Unit building. There was no one around, so I walked into the vacant office of the colonel in command of the unit. Sorting through his file cabinets, I found the "Mother Lode:" a copy of the secret codes with an explanation of each one. I made a copy on his Xerox machine and walked out of the building with my copy in hand.

Studying the codes was a revelation. There were 3-letter and 3-digit codes for just about every bad thing a person could possibly have done:

- 21U – failure to demonstrate adequate potential for promotion
- 246 – Discharge for the good of the service
- 247 – Unsuitability, multiple reasons
- 256 – Homosexual
- 258 – Unfitness, ineptitude
- 260 – Unsuitability, ineptitude
- 261 – Psychiatric or psychoneurotic disorder
- 262 – Behavioral disorder
- 263 – Bedwetter
- 265 – Character Disorder
- 28B – Frequent involvement in incidents of a discreditable nature with civil or military authorities
- 293 – General court martial*
- 294 – Special court martial*
- 318 – Conscientious objector
- 367 – Aggressive reaction
- 383 – Criminalism
- 41A – Apathy, lack of interest
- 41E – Obesity
- 46A – Defective attitudes & inability to extend effort constructively
- 46B – Sexual deviate
- 460 – Emotional instability reaction
- 461 – Inadequate personality
- 463 – Paranoid
- 464 – Schizoid
- 480 – Personality disorder

*Even if acquitted

This is not the complete list, but you get the picture. If it doesn't make your blood boil, you probably merit a code on your driver's license.

The more I studied the secret codes, the angrier I became, thinking that one could have served with honor, received an honorable discharge, and still be coded. Worse, it turned out that, although the list was stamped classified "CONFIDENTIAL" at the top and bottom, it was often shared with civilian employers and university admissions officers, among other deciders of one's future. This convinced me that the list and its applications represented an unconstitutional denial of Due Process, which I argued in my thesis.

I also argued that this was unconstitutional for another reason: the Confrontation Clause of the Constitution's Sixth Amendment provides that "in all criminal prosecutions, the accused shall enjoy the right. . . to be confronted with the witnesses against him," and while the application of a code to a 214 was not a criminal prosecution, it had a similar adverse result. Generally, the clause is interpreted to mean that an accused has the right to a face-to-face confrontation with witnesses who are offering testimonial evidence against him or her at trial. My point was that this was in fact the imposition of a penalty comparable to a criminal sentence on someone who (1) did not even know that he was being charged, indicted and convicted of something, and (2) was being denied his right to confront his accuser. Perhaps a bit of a stretch, but so what? I wasn't arguing before the Supreme Court.

Professor Freeman was pleased with the resulting thesis and, several years later to my surprise, used it to support his testimony before a congressional Armed Services committee where he advocated getting rid of this injustice. The committee was amenable to his plea and, while it did not prohibit the practice via legislation, it publicly criticized the military services and secured their pledge to get rid of the codes. They did, and discharge documents remained "code-free" for some years. Unfortunately, they eventually stole back into use. I have not checked, but I suspect that they are again being unfairly applied to DD-214s to this day.

More Questions

Many years later, I was in my office when my receptionist buzzed me to announce that someone from the State Department wanted to speak to me. When I picked up my phone, a pleasant male voice engaged in about thirty seconds of small talk and then got to the point. I've re-created the conversation as best as I remember it below:

"Mr. Hermann, I'm with the department's Low-Intensity Conflict Division. I'd like to ask you a couple of questions."

Me: "Shoot."

"I understand that when you were in the Army, you were assigned to an Atomic Demolition Munitions platoon in West Germany, right?"

I hesitated because the question took me by surprise. Memories of the encounter at the New School as well as the Irmgard Möller phone calls flooded my brain. I worried that my interrogator might not, in fact, be from the State Department.

Me: "Why do you want to know?"

"I do *know*. I just wanted to make sure I'm speaking to the right Richard Hermann."

I said nothing.

"What we need to know is if you remember how many bombs your unit stored at the Special Weapons Site near your base."

Me: "Why do you need to know that?"

"We just want to know, that's all."

Me: "I have no idea what you're talking about."

"Look, it's a simple question. We've posed it to a number of your ADM colleagues from that time: Kenneth B; Sergio S; James C; Donald H. You want more names?"

Me: "That's enough."

It was apparent that whoever this guy was, he had done his homework.

"So, are you going to cooperate or not?"

Me: "OK. I don't remember the number. Sorry."

I really did not remember how many nuclear weapons we had at the site. And I did not want to guess.

"OK then, sorry to bother you, Mr. Hermann. Good bye."

When I hung up the phone, I sat at my desk thinking about the call. It quickly occurred to me that it was probably legitimate. I pulled out my copy of the *U.S. Government Manual* and learned that the Low-Intensity Conflict unit at State monitored stuff like skirmishes and battles that don't rise to the level of conventional war, which include terrorist incidents. The connection between its mission and the questions posed to me hit home: They were worried that someone, probably what they called a "non-state actor," had come into possession of one of our weapons. I knew that it would be difficult for any outside group to arm a SADM (the MADM was much too large and heavy to easily steal) and actually bring off a successful nuclear explosion (problematic even for those of us who trained daily on it). However, a conventional dirty-bomb detonation would scatter the plutonium core and hurt a lot of people. Was it possible that the U.S. government believed that a terrorist organization had gotten their hands on one?

The thought ruined my day, week, month, year, century and millennium.

Chapter 14
Puzzled at the Palace... and Beyond

More has been screwed up on the battlefield and misunderstood in the Pentagon because of a lack of understanding of the English language than any other single factor.
—General John W. Vessey, Jr.

The Best-Designed Building on the Planet
(Department of Defense)

The Path to the Pentagon

I lasted just under four years as a U.S. Government employee and another six as a senior legal consultant, i.e., a government contractor, working primarily on national security law matters. I was fortunate to be recruited for these consulting assignments while trying to build a private business because it assured an income flow until my company became profitable.

Seven of those ten years were with the Department of Defense (DoD) at the Pentagon, fondly known to its daily working population and its assigned ink-stained wretches and *paparazzi* as the "puzzle palace" (a moniker used equally to describe Fort Meade after the publication in 1982 of James Bamford's book by that name). This was, I discovered, an apt moniker. Although I later worked directly for two other federal agencies and consulted for and contracted with many more, the Pentagon was by far the most impenetrable and mysterious. I should add that it was also by far the best of a generally poorly administered lot. As to why this is will have to wait for another book.

My first job after law school was with the Department of Defense in Washington, DC (the Pentagon is actually located across the Potomac River in Arlington, Virginia). I returned for my second tour with the U.S. Army as an attorney with the Army Judge Advocate General's (JAG) Corps, enticed by the opportunity to get thrown into the criminal courtroom immediately, something that would not be possible in the vast majority of civilian practice settings. I had also discovered during the summer I spent abroad as a JAG Corps legal intern that this unusual immersion in trial practice translated very well into the civilian legal world after a few years.

As it turned out, I never stepped into a courtroom once I received my permanent assignment.

During my recruitment, my intrepid wife, who was then studying law in Buffalo, took it upon herself to march into the office where the JAG recruiter was interviewing graduating law students. She sought an assurance that I would be assigned to a location where she could continue her legal studies. She persuaded the recruiter that the JAG Corps would look favorably on her request provided that I performed reasonably well at the three-month long JAG School training program located at the University of Virginia Law School in Charlottesville.

One of the cities the recruiter suggested was New York, namely Fort Hamilton in Brooklyn. My wife rejected that, saying she was not about to travel through the city at night after evening classes or studying in a law library. The recruiter next mentioned Washington, DC. That satisfied her.

It was also propitious that, once he completed his law school recruiting tour, the JAG recruiter returned to the Pentagon to become the JAG Corps Director of Personnel, Plans and Training (PPTO). That made him the individual who had the final say concerning all Army JAG assignments.

I believed that I had kept my part of the bargain at the JAG School, finishing second in a class of 75 attorneys, being designated an Honor Graduate and receiving awards for being the top mock trial litigator and for finishing first in the class in two of the four core subjects. I smugly and confidently awaited my choice assignment, having completed my part of the bargain. Toward the end of the school, we filled out "dream sheets" indicating our top three assignment choices. Number one on my list was Washington, DC. It was thus a severe shock when I received orders to report to the legal office at the 18th Airborne Corps at Fort Bragg, North Carolina, adjacent to Fayetteville, which is not exactly Paris.

After recovering from the initial blow, I walked into the school administrator's office and complained about the assignment and related my wife's conversation with the recruiter. Several days later, I received a phone call from my future boss at the Pentagon saying that he was putting in a special request for me. My orders were quickly amended.

My wife was able to transfer to one of the DC law schools. Years later, when I encountered the recruiter with whom she had spoken in Buffalo, he mentioned how impressed he had been with her persuasive abilities.

An Officer and Maybe a Gentleman

Going from my former highest rank as a Specialist Fifth Class (a.k.a. "Spec 5")—the equivalent of a buck sergeant—to an

Army captain was traumatic. I morphed from "saluter" to "salutee," which took some getting used to. The first time I donned my officer's uniform, I was saluted by two enlisted men accompanied by a hearty "good morning, sir!" I was so flummoxed that I jumped behind a truck until they passed by.

Fortunately, once I arrived at the Pentagon, I was informed that wearing the uniform was optional. I opted for civilian clothes and thus never again had to experience the discomfort of being saluted.

I began my three-year JAG assignment as one of the attorneys in DoD's Federal Voting Assistance Division, the organization that protects the voting rights of members of the armed forces and their dependents and assures that they get their absentee ballots and that those votes get counted. The job was fairly undemanding—the legal issues were straightforward and repetitive—and came with a highly entertaining boss, a Navy commander who transitioned from taking off and landing on aircraft carriers to flying a desk.

He came from the hill country of Middle Tennessee, got married at 15, and could draw on a bottomless repository of colloquialisms that often had me doubled over with laughter. Someone who screwed up "stepped on his lizard." When we required a particularly persuasive argument to get what our division wanted, we needed a "leg spreader." And so forth. When he was reassigned back to the Navy about halfway through my tour, I was upset.

Legal Beagle

Within a short time after reporting to DoD, I began getting pulled away from my division for special temporary assignments that had nothing to do with my job. Requests for my legal services came primarily from our division's parent agency, the large and global Armed Forces Information Service (AFIS). AFIS encompassed every armed forces media outlet throughout the world, including several thousand base and ship newspapers, Armed Forces Radio, Armed Forces Television, the Armed Forces Network, numerous film and video production units and much more.

Some of my assignments proved highly stimulating:

- Writing the scripts for a 1976 television series called Bicentennial Minutes starring James Whitmore. These appeared on national television throughout the bicentennial year. The producer was Mel Blanc Productions in Hollywood. At the beginning of the script-writing process, I had to speak by phone with Mr. Blanc, whose major claim to fame was that he was the voice of Bugs Bunny, Daffy Duck, Porky Pig, Tweety and Sylvester, Yosemite Sam, Foghorn Leghorn, Pepe Le Pew, Speedy Gonzales, Wile E. Coyote, the Road Runner, the Tasmanian Devil, Woody Woodpecker and Elmer Fudd. After saying hello, he immediately transitioned into character, in this instance Foghorn Leghorn if memory serves. I was aching to say "dwatted wabbit," but was too intimidated. The series was awarded a coveted American Bar Association Gavel Award for its contributions to explaining the nation's constitutional and legal underpinnings to the public.
- Advising the *Stars and Stripes* bookstores on our bases in pre-revolutionary Iran about their rights and duties under the *Status of Forces Agreement* between the U.S. and Iran when the Shah suddenly prohibited them from selling *Playboy* and *Penthouse*. This involved a number of interactions with *Playboy*'s attorneys, but alas, no negotiations with centerfolds or trips to the Hef Mansion.

- Performing as the legal advisor for a major reduction-in-force (i.e., termination of employees) by the Office of the Secretary of Defense. One of those functions entailed one-on-one meetings with everyone on the SecDef's 700-person staff who might be subject to termination. The regulations governing such terminations are a bureaucrat's nightmare, so complex that (1) everyone affected had unique options under them, and (2) Talmudic scholars could have had a field day arguing about them. Often, the people I met with sought my advice about highly personal matters that had nothing to do with the RIF. A middle-age man destined for unemployment and likely unemployable given an assortment of personal issues brought in pictures he had taken from outside his bedroom window of his wife having sex with state troopers. A woman who eventually survived the RIF but had to take a grade reduction and lower pay asked me for advice about her son who had a thing for exposing himself to nuns. Attorneys can only do so much.
- Reviewing existing commercial contracts between the government and the 30 or so private sector establishments that were awarded the right to sell their wares in the Pentagon Concourse, a large open area just inside the main public entrance to the building. The Concourse perimeter was ringed by shops in which employees could buy virtually any good or service. These exclusive contracts were a gold mine for vendors, since 30,000 employees inside the building constituted a captive audience. In the days before the Washington area subway system began serving the Pentagon, these people had nowhere else to go during their lunch hour if they wanted to buy stuff.

The contracts all came up for renewal on a supposedly competitive bid basis every few years. I was asked to review a number of contracts about to terminate and suggest ways the government could improve its negotiating position with an eye to revenue maximization. Under each agreement, the government had the right to audit each business's financial records. I was hit with a lot of resistance when I requested those records: "proprietary information;" "unprecedented!" "All of our documents are in possession of our CPAs in San Francisco;" "So-and-so (your umpteenth-level superior [the SecDef? The President? God?]) says I don't have to provide them."

The first set of financials I was able to see were an eye-opener. They described the incredible bonanza the Concourse watch repair shop had enjoyed from its exclusive agreement. When I compared its revenue and profits with comparables (watch repair shops in communities of around 30,000 population), the differences were Brobdingnagian. Who ever heard of a small business like this reaping more than $1.5 million annually and returning a profit of over $1.3 million? I should mention that the rent the contracts called for were a tenant broker's equivalent of winning the lottery. I also discovered that the prices customers paid to have their watches repaired were almost 50 percent higher than "on the economy." Monopolies do in fact succumb to the temptation to price-gouge.

Once other Concourse businesses grudgingly handed over their financials, I found that the watch repair shop's behavior was replicated elsewhere. Pentagon consumers were being ripped off along with the government. The direction my recommendations took were thus predictable: real competitive bidding after a wide-ranging advertising campaign to alert bidders to the opportunity. No more sweetheart deals (I was flooded with rumors of kickbacks to government contracting officers that I could not substantiate). Rental rates comparable to outside commercial establishments. And, most upsetting of all to the existing shops, revenue-sharing with the government. My boss on this project loved my recommendations and a few of them actually survived higher-level review and were implemented. The revenue-sharing proposal went nowhere, notwithstanding that it would have expiated many sins.

Puzzling Vignettes

There are a million stories in the naked city; these are [a few] of them.
—Jules Dassin, *The Naked City*

Space limitations do not allow me to relate all of the interesting, quirky, weird or bizarre tales I chronicled during my decade-long association with the Pentagon. The ones I chose (below) describe the richness and flavor of the experience. After reading them, together we may marvel that we actually prevailed in the Cold War:

Reserved

From time-to-time, I ran into reservists who were doing their two-week summer tours on active duty at the Pentagon. The two most memorable were the following:

The Executioner's Song

RM's military career began in World War II. I met him in the mid-1970s when he was about to retire from the Reserves. He had been a hangman at the Nuremberg trials of Nazi war criminals. He sat with me one day and produced photographs he had taken of dangling Nazis and an original letter from German Foreign Minister Joachim von Ribbentrop to his daughter that he wrote the night before his execution. He had asked RM to mail it for him, but he never did. I was still then able to read German and found it a very moving missive from a monster to his offspring.

Dove e Il Gabinetto?

This most important of all Italian phrases means "which way to the bathroom?" It is a perfect summary of my two weeks' supervising a reservist who got lost in the Pentagon several times each day during his two-week tour. My boss (the Assistant Secretary of Defense for Reserve Affairs) at the time asked me to take this reserve JAG lawyer under my wing and give him a meaningless assignment to keep him occupied and far away from my boss. The reservist was the son of a major donor to Ronald Reagan's presidential campaign.

I assigned him to research the legal authority to establish a "Home Guard" to protect America in the event the Reserves and National Guard were mobilized and sent off to distant lands to fight. I got the idea from Hitler's desperate attempts to fill the Wehrmacht's depleted ranks in the last days of World War II. My charge took to the nothing assignment with great enthusiasm and parked himself in the Pentagon Law Library for the duration of his brief tour. I took the head law librarian (a friend of mine) into my confidence so that he would support the sham assignment. At the end of the exercise, the lawyer handed me a paper that was, given the Potemkin Village nature of the assignment, utterly irrelevant.

Years later, this gentleman was appointed Deputy Secretary of a federal cabinet department. When his boss resigned, he served for more than a year as the Acting Secretary. Be afraid; be VERY afraid.

Horseholder on the Hill

One of the jobs low-level flunkies do in Washington is to accompany their bosses when they travel to Capitol Hill to testify before a congressional committee. They sit behind them at the witness table and whisper in their ears when members of Congress ask questions the boss has trouble answering.

*A U.S. Senate Hearing
(Replete with Horseholders)*
(U.S. Coast Guard – Public Domain)

My second-level boss had to testify before the Senate Rules Committee (I forget the topic) and we staff grunts stayed up most of the night before cobbling together his written testimony. I asked one of our interns to collate the pages and put them into multiple loose-leaf notebooks—one for the boss; one for me so I could follow along while the boss testified; and the rest for members of the Senate committee.

The hearing began and my boss launched into his written testimony. A couple of pages in, he turned the page and continued speaking, but I noticed right away that there was a disconnect between the preceding page and the new one. He had segued from page three to page eight. I panicked and tapped him on the shoulder, but he waved me off. Fortunately, neither he nor the Senators noticed that anything was amiss. Unless there is some issue before a congressional committee that warrants a photo op, inattention is the order of the day.

I guess our intern had not yet encountered basic addition during his 17 years of education. The pages were numbered. That should have alerted him.

In and Out

My first DoD office was located in a high rise office building about two miles from the Pentagon (even though I had to be at the Pentagon virtually every day). The building was owned by two brothers who were "connected." They had been convicted of a variety of petty, mob-related offenses, but they must have had Clarence Darrow or Oliver Wendell Holmes for their defense attorneys. The arrangement they worked out with the sentencing judge was (at least until the late Jeffrey Epstein) unique and remarkably creative: Only one brother was required to do time at a time. The other was free to go about their business. In other words, they alternated time in jail. The reason behind this was because if they were to make restitution to the people they bilked out of their money, their business needed to continue.

Whenever one of the brothers was in the building, I studiously avoided getting in the elevator with him, having been exposed to far too many gangland movies where the elevator doors open and . . . bang!

Paging Mr. Bear

Down the hall from my office in the high-rise reposed a unique DoD outfit called the "National Committee for Employer Support of the Guard and Reserves." Later on, this unit, whose primary mission was to produce public service announcements for radio and TV promoting employer support of the National Guard and Reserves, became one of my internal legal clients. This was after I was assigned to the Assistant Secretary's office overseeing the National Guard and Reserves.

There was an Air Force captain who worked for the committee who was being persecuted by his female Air Force colonel boss, whom he referred to as "Col. Birdlegs" due to her stick-like appendages and Egret-like gait. He was determined to do her in before he voluntarily committed himself to an asylum.

His first foray into creative prankdom was to rotate Birdlegs' swivel chair one revolution each morning before she arrived at work. Birdlegs was tiny to begin with (a sub-five footer) and very Napoleonic/defensive about her vertical challenges. Over a few weeks, she became convinced that she was shrinking and sought a medical consultation.

Next, Captain "Quill" (his first name derived from a ballpoint pen) began calling her number and leaving messages such as "please call Mr. Bear at this number," which happened to be the main switchboard at the National Zoo. Birdlegs would dutifully return the call, only to be greeted by hysterical, fall-off-the seat laughter at the other end of the phone line. Quill got away with this ruse more than one might assume, but soon ran out of animal kingdom callers.

Calling Mr. Bear
(USDA National Agricultural Library – Public Domain)

Finally, he jimmied her windows so that the wind off the nearby Potomac would make loud howling noises as it attempted to squeeze through into her office.

Col. Birdlegs did not survive long in this decidedly hostile environment. She requested reassignment and the Air Force accommodated her.

I Am You . . . You Are Me

The colonel in charge of the aforementioned Support Committee was a very nice guy with whom I became friends. One day he brought me an exchange of correspondence between Secretary of Defense Donald Rumsfeld and honorary Chairman of the Board of the Support Committee James Roche, the chairman of General Motors. The first letter was from Roche to Rumsfeld thanking him for hosting a Support Committee dog-and-pony show. The response letter from Rummy to Roche thanked the latter for organizing the festivities.

My colonel friend wrote both letters at the direction of the two luminaries. He lamented that his military career had degenerated to where he ended up writing letters to himself.

Huks and Hucksters

The American Forces Information Service (AFIS) was headed by a gentleman who was "born-again" and wore his religiosity on his sleeve like a badge of honor. He made his bones as a broadcaster in the Philippines spewing out propaganda on behalf of Ramon Magsaysay, the future president of the country, who was embroiled in fending off a guerrilla band of leftist revolutionaries known as the Hukbalahap. The Huks staged a 12-year, unsuccessful war against the government. When the war ended, he came home to the U.S. His broadcasting background got him a job at the Pentagon, which by the time I arrived had made him something of a legend and a Pentagon power player.

As far as I could tell, he was the world's only "GS-18," a federal employee rank that put him at the very top of the pay and career employee scale. Today, the federal system only goes as high as GS-15, after which comes the Senior Executive Service. The scuttlebutt was that he rose to his stratospheric rank because he, like J. Edgar Hoover, "had something" on just about everyone, members of Congress included. Whatever the reason, he commanded an organization of thousands of employees as well as thousands of media outlets and products. His office was second only to the Secretary of Defense's in size.

Another rumor, one which was endorsed as true by people in the know, was that he was using the assets of the Armed Forces Radio and Television Service (AFRTS), one of the AFIS units, to produce Christian recordings that he allegedly then sold privately, pocketing the proceeds. While I had no direct evidence of this, people who worked at AFRTS headquarters swore to its veracity.

My first day working at AFIS, I was called over to his Pentagon office. He ordered me to a seat across a conference table, where we waited silently until the two-star general who headed the Army JAG Corps (a.k.a., "TJAG") walked in and took a seat next to him. I had no idea what was coming, only that I was now confronted by both my civilian and military bosses, the two of them several light-years above my pay grade.

"We have a serious crisis on our hands, Captain Hermann," He began. He pulled out a letter and began reading it to the TJAG and me. Its gist was that the writer's children had been kidnapped by *Hari Krishnas* and removed to another state. The woman had found his name in a directory called *Christians in the Corridors of Power* and reached out to him to help her get her kids back. He wanted me to outline the legal issues involved in this heinous kidnapping and advise him with respect to what could be done to retrieve the children. I thought I was going to collapse and did my best to conceal the violent shaking that I was sure would overtake me in the next seconds.

The Not-So-Good Book
(Photograph of Cover – Origin Unknown)

Panic tends to concentrate the mind, so I said: "I think one of the key questions is: 'who actually took the kids?'"

He hesitated as if he was reluctant to respond: "It says here that the father had joined the *Hari Krishnas*."

"Is she saying that her husband took them?" I asked.

"Er, it looks that way."

"If that's the case, then this is probably a matter for state jurisdiction since domestic relations matters such as custody battles are exclusively the province of the states."

"So you mean there's nothing we can do?"

"I don't think so, sir."

At which response, he turned to the TJAG and asked: "General, do you agree with your captain?"

I held my breath, envisioning all of the Hells that either boss could consign me to if I screwed up.

"Yes, the young man is absolutely correct. Nice job, captain."

The TJAG said his goodbyes and left.

The big boss dismissed me, obviously not very happy with what I had told him. I went back to my new office and into the men's room where I wiped the perspiration off my brow and body.

That first day was the worst by far of the thousand days I would spend in that job.

The Bizarro World of AFRTS

I became friendly with a number of the managers at AFRTS, the headquarters of which was in my building, due to the work I did on *Bicentennial Minutes* plus some other legal work I did for the organization. Two of the guys there were the life of any party. D and T both came from the commercial broadcasting world where they were TV anchors on local stations before gravitating into government radio and TV. They were the punch spikers at our Christmas parties (the big boss was a teetotaler, but always loved their punch, unaware that it was around 50 percent grain alcohol).

The two of them also moonlighted at the Columbia School of Broadcasting, one of those questionable businesses that advertised on matchbook covers. Their prize pupil had been Elizabeth Ray, a buxom bottle-blond who made a name for herself when she was hired for a position (no pun intended) on Congressman Wayne Hays (R-OH) staff ("literally on his staff," said the office wags) despite a total lack of typing skills. Her skills, it was revealed by intrepid *Washington Post* reporters, were restricted to other areas. As she herself put it: "I give great steno."

The capstone on my tenure as a Pentagon employee was achieved at one of my goodbye parties at a place called *Atilla's*, an Arlington establishment that advertised lunchtime belly dancers. When we sat down to eat, T suddenly turned pale. His ex-wife was the lunchtime entertainment, jiggling her exposed belly and other scantily-covered but impressive body parts. He had no idea she had changed professions.

George and the City

G served as the sports director of AFRTS. What that meant in practice was that he selected all of the sports programming that went out over the air to all of the troops around the world.

Monday			
5:00 Potpourri	6:30 Silver Wings	7:30 Beverly Hillbillies	
5:15 Kiddie Karnival	7:00 Evening News Report	8:00 Capsule News	
5:30 Edward Steichen — Photographer	7:30 My Favorite Martian	8:02 Rawhide	
6:00 Capsule News	8:00 Capsule News	9:00 News	
6:02 Andy Griffith Show	8:02 To be announced	9:05 Danny Kaye Show	
6:30 Vietnam Report	9:00 News	10:00 Late Report	
7:00 Evening News Report	9:05 Frank Sinatra: A Man And His Music	10:15 Late Movie: "Men With Wings"	
7:30 Dick Van Dyke Show	10:00 Late Report	12:00 News Final	
8:00 Capsule News	10:15 Late Movie: "Colonel Effingham's Raid"	**Thursday**	
8:02 Voyage To The Bottom Of The Sea	11:35 News Final	5:00 Potpourri	
9:00 News	**Wednesday**	5:15 Kiddie Karnival	
9:05 Milton Berle Show	5:00 Potpourri	5:30 Odyssey	
10:00 Late Report	5:15 Kiddie Karnival	6:00 Capsule News	
10:15 Johnny Carson Show	5:30 Science Report	6:02 Danny Thomas	
11:35 News Final	5:45 Social Security In Action	6:30 To be announced	
Tuesday	6:00 Capsule News	7:00 Evening News Report	
5:00 Potpourri	6:02 The Third Man	7:30 Bewitched	
5:15 Kiddie Karnival	6:30 Survival	8:00 Capsule News	
5:30 Biography	7:00 Evening News Report	8:02 To be announced	
6:00 Capsule News		9:00 News	
6:02 Roger Miller Show		9:05 Dean Martin Summer Show	
		10:00 Late Report	
		10:15 Late Movie: "Take A Letter, Darling"	
		11:47 News Final	

AFRTS Program Guide – April 17, 1967
(Department of Defense - *The Berlin Observer* – Public Domain)

While stationed in Germany, I often wondered why we received a constant dose of Yankee, Met, Knick, Nets, Jets, Giant and Ranger games to the exclusion of almost everything else. When I got to know G, I found out why. He was from the Bay Ridge section of Brooklyn, the heartbeat of the borough's

Italian community. While you can take the boy out of Brooklyn, you can never take Brooklyn out of the boy. G was a die-hard fan of the New York teams. Thus the bias in AFRTS broadcasts.

When I raised the issue with him, pointing out that the overwhelming majority of our close to two-and-a-half million servicemen and women were not from New York, his response was: "Nobody cares about the fuckin' Kansas City Royals."

Sidelines

Seconds after the first time I walked into the Reserve Affairs Assistant Secretary's offices in the Pentagon as a consultant, I was pulled aside by a colonel who guided me into his office, closed the door, and put up a large poster with photographs of shoes.

"Like any of them?" he asked.

"They look nice."

"They're very affordable."

"Let me think about it," I said as I beat a hasty retreat.

I was not completely surprised. Back in my JAG days at the Pentagon, I was stunned at how many of my colleagues had launched commercial businesses using government resources. In most cases, these were real estate enterprises. I didn't quite know what to make of this phenomenon and said nothing about it.

However, nothing that I experienced in that job prepared me for the creative energy invested in side businesses by the staff at Reserve Affairs. In addition to the standard real estate undertakings, there was another colonel there who took the grand prize when it came to ancillary businesses. He was engaged in two such operations:

- A pickle business. He kept a large vat in his office in which giant dills floated around; and

- A "multi-level marketing" scam, a sanitized way of describing an Amway-like pyramid scheme where the downline participants chase dreams of big dollars, but the only people who get rich are the ones at the top of the pyramid who launched the con in the first place. Only instead of selling soap, this guy was selling religion. He had purchased a bishop's designation in some supposed church and was hawking priesthoods to anyone gullible enough to buy into the fraud.

Given how open these people were about their side businesses, I was surprised that there was never a crackdown. It was inconceivable that the higher-ups were unaware of what was going on. Had these abusers of their employment and the public trust worked as hard on their jobs as they did on their businesses, the U.S. might have put the Soviet Union in its rear-view mirror much earlier.

Flipping Boris

The Pentagon Courtyard was a nicely-appointed, open-air space smack in the middle of the building and shaped like . . . a pentagon. It had grass, trees and park benches where employees often went on nice days to eat lunch outside.

It was also known to those of us who worked inside the building as "ground zero," almost certainly the aiming point for many potential megatons of Soviet atomic malevolence. It was well-known that a Soviet spy satellite passed directly over the Pentagon several times a day. A Defense Intelligence Agency "spook" I was friendly with claimed that he knew the exact fly-over times, so several of us would, from time-to-time, gather in the courtyard to point an operative finger up at the sky.

A Cold War Follies *Pot Pourri*

The High Ground

When you work in, or as an outside advisor to, the Office of the Secretary of Defense, it is as if you are flying above the constant fray that constitutes the inter-service rivalries between the Army, Navy and Air Force that daily roil the Pentagon. One of the first things I noticed as I made my way down the hill from the Sheraton Hotel where I stayed overnight to the Pentagon to report for duty my first day was a funny-looking building on a rise that loomed over the Pentagon like a hulking gargoyle. My impression was of a starving architect who went overboard designing the ultimate fork.

This was the Navy Annex, the *de facto* headquarters of the sea service that feels that it is superior to its Army and Air Force equals and thus should not have to demean itself by being housed in the same building. As I learned my way around the DoD bureaucracy and had occasion to visit the Navy Annex, I discovered that it was even more of an architectural train-wreck on the inside. To negotiate your way from an office in one fork prong to an office in a neighboring fork prong that might have been only a few yards distant, you had to walk all the way to the one bridge that connected the two prongs. It was the land equivalent of turning around an aircraft carrier.

The Navy Annex
(U.S. Navy)

The Annex was first constructed in 1941, the same year ground was broken for the brilliantly designed Pentagon (which took only 16 months to complete), as a warehouse. Over time, it became the place where the Navy did much of its business. For a long time, it also served as the headquarters of the Marine Corps, which much to the annoyance of *Semper Fi* alums, is a Navy subsidiary.

While the Chief of Naval Operations maintained a Pentagon office, a lot of other admirals preferred the Annex. When they had to come over to the Pentagon for meetings, they came accompanied by a large retinue of captains, commanders, lieutenant commanders, lieutenants and ensigns. Unlike the other services whose generals generally walked alone or with one aide, admirals were often preceded down the rings and corridors by a "flying wedge' of factotums shouting: "Make way for the admiral!" We plastered ourselves against a wall so as not to be run over.

Mercifully, the Annex was demolished in 2013 to make way for the unfortunate latest expansion of Arlington Cemetery and the construction of the spectacular metal contrails that serve as the U.S. Air Force Memorial.

The Real Enemy

At the Pentagon, to a much greater degree than anywhere else in the vast federal enterprise, it is always budget time. The day after the proposed budget for the coming fiscal year is put to bed, it is time for the thousands of budget analysts wandering its 17.5 miles of floors, basements, rings and connecting corridors to begin work on the next year's budget.

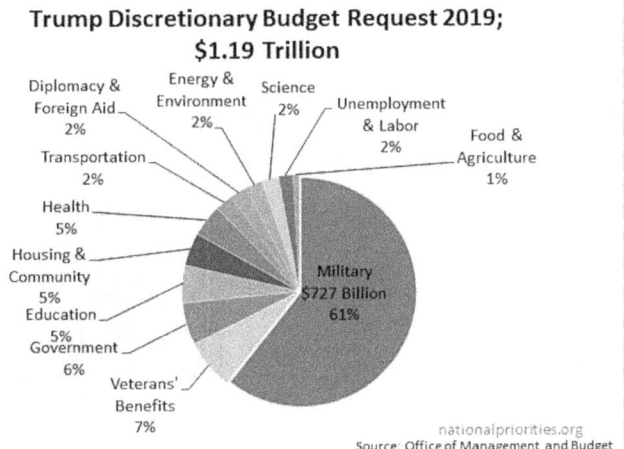

The Military's Favorite Pie
(Nationalpriorities.org –
Source: U.S. Office of Management and Budget)

Nowhere is this taken more seriously than in the Navy and Air Force, the two services with the most dazzling toys, bells and whistles. They are always conscious that the money pie only has so many slices and, if they are going to get what they view as their fair share (which they each deem to be the whole pie), they need to be super-vigilant. Consequently, both services put their best minds to competing against one another at budget time. Their second-best minds were assigned to fight the Cold War. Left unstated was that the fast track was reserved for the budget victors, not the warriors worried about the Soviet Union. I witnessed this many times in meetings over budget matters vs. meetings regarding war fighting. It left me feeling a bit exposed.

Weaponizing

The cobbling together and implementation of contracts for new weapons systems is a dirty business that, like sausage production or lawmaking, is not something anyone wants to observe. I had a very peripheral and modest involvement in two such contracts where I was asked to provide some legal guidance regarding miniscule elements of the contracts.

The DIVAD

By the time I was dragged into this project, it was under siege from multiple critics and in danger of being deep-sixed. The M247 Sergeant York DIVAD (Division Air Defense) was an anti-aircraft weapon based on a platform derived from the Patton Tank. It was intended to be a low-cost weapon that would build on a variety of existing, off-the-shelf technologies. It did not quite

The DIVAD
(Wikimedia - CC BY-SA 3.0)

work out that way and was finally cancelled in the mid-1980s after serious cost overruns, not to mention that it was probably the goofiest-looking weapon in the U.S. arsenal.

Along the way, as the DIVAD program was creaking toward oblivion, one of the attempts to salvage the disaster was to claim that it could serve a dual purpose as an anti-tank weapon. This also became a non-starter after a needless expenditure of additional funds when it was discovered that the range of the guns on the Soviet tanks it was supposed to destroy were greater than that of the DIVAD's guns, meaning that the Russkies could stay out of range and still blow the DIVADs to kingdom come.

Fighting the Bradley

The Bradley Fighting Vehicle was designed as a replacement for the workhorse Armored Personnel Carrier, one of the core infantry weapons that served the U.S. so ably in World War II and beyond. The Bradley, however, came with several limitations that were the result of a combination of cost overruns (a guaranteed malady of every weapons development process) and nit-picking efforts to satisfy the huge number of cooks that wanted so desperately and unwittingly to spoil the stew. In attempting to accommodate every interested party's demands, the contract managers satisfied no one.

The Bradley Fighting Vehicle
(U.S. Army – Public Domain)

Armored Personnel Carriers were able to carry a full infantry squad at the faster-than-walking pace essential to fighting a land war with a mobile force. The Bradley advocates, however, added so many bells and whistles to the inside of the vehicle that it could only carry six squad members when an Army infantry squad numbered nine members. That meant that three squad members had to sprint alongside or behind the vehicle, not easy when it sped along at 41 miles an hour (Usain Bolt ramped up to 28 MPH in a 100-meter dash).

But that was not all that this $5 billion-plus project was supposed to accomplish. The Bradley was not only a land vehicle. Like a duck boat, it was also designed to swim. In its first demonstration test at Camp A.P. Hill about 50 miles south of the Pentagon, while being observed by a collection of military brass, it came flying over a hill and raced down and into the Rappahannock River, where it promptly sank, forcing its riders to escape through the hatch since they did not want to drown. That problem, although a considerable embarrassment, was soon resolved.

The Amphibious Bradley – Passengers Playing It Safe On Top Rather Than Inside
(Wikimedia Commons – Public Domain)

The Bradley is still operational today despite its avoidable limitations.

Martinets

After serving under two absolutely marvelous Assistant Secretaries who comprised two of the finest three bosses I ever had (the other was my battalion commander in Germany), I ended my Pentagon career working for a gentleman who was one of those political appointees who got his job because of a school chum, in his case a cabinet officer. This gentleman happened to be an attorney who had had considerable difficulty negotiating the California Bar examination. But that was not sufficient to deter the President from appointing him to a high government position for which he was hopelessly unfit and unqualified.

Worse, one of his first acts was to circulate a memorandum to the staff demanding that they refer to him as "doctor." Now that appellation does not ever apply to attorneys despite their earning a Juris Doctor degree. It is considered unseemly by the profession.

As one of the other lawyers in the office, I took it upon myself to pass around my own memo (unsigned) to the staff pointing out that the American Bar Association looked askance on attorneys who presumed to call themselves doctor. When the new boss saw my memo, he suspected me immediately and, without further ado, dispensed with my services.

The only other instance I am aware of where a lawyer did something similar was Michelle Bachman, a decidedly loopy, not very bright congresswoman from Minnesota, who by some miracle obtained a law degree and passed a bar exam. "Dr." Bachmann became a laughing stock for this and many other bonehead things she did and said, the most recent one being that Donald Trump was a godly man.

Nine Eleven

While what goes on inside the Pentagon is not always in the best interests of humanity and most certainly not of the U.S. taxpayer, I admit to having a very soft spot and tons of admiration for the building itself. Gen. Leslie Groves, the builder of the Pentagon immediately prior to heading the Manhattan Project, was a genius, as were the structure's designers. If there is a more intelligently put together edifice on the planet, I'd love to hear about it.

I should mention before closing out this section that the Pentagon is actually a 10-story building: five above ground and five below. What goes on below ground is unknown to almost all Americans and, for the most part, rightly so. Not everything demands total transparency.

Some of the people in my office claimed that they could hear American Airlines Flight 77 circling over downtown Washington, DC around 9:30 AM on September 11, 2001. We were located about 200 yards from the White House and three miles from the Pentagon, which Flight 77 slammed into 15 minutes later. Our entire staff had been watching the horror of the Twin Towers on television when we heard the news that the Pentagon had been attacked. I went outside and was able to see the smoke rising from the stricken building. Later I found out that a gentleman I worked with during my years at the Pentagon was among the 125 people in the building who died in the attack, along with the 64 on Flight 77. Charlie had been in his office on the Western side of the building when the plane took it out.

Low Energy

G.A.O., No

After my first Pentagon tour of duty came to an end, I wanted to go somewhere else where I could contribute to solving national problems.

My first attempt at making a difference lasted two days. I accepted a job with the Office of General Counsel at the General Accounting Office (GAO), which is now called the Government Accountability Office. GAO is a legislative branch agency that investigates and writes reports about government activities that fall short of their mission and recommends improvements. Participating in making government better excited me.

Unfortunately, GAO also has some other tasks that lack the same excitement potential, some of them so dull and numbing that lawyers have likely expired while performing them. Despite the assurances I had received at my interviews, it was to them that I was assigned.

It's a Gusher!
(SMU Central University Libraries – Public Domain)

I had also been offered jobs elsewhere, one in the private sector and the other by the Department of Energy, that I had declined in favor of GAO. When I came home following my first day at GAO, my wife, seeing me looking like a dead man walking, urged me to, and then demanded that I, quit and find something else. Having been brought up with the maxim "a quitter never wins and a winner never quits," I resisted. However, after my second day watching my pulse rate plummeting and observing the hopelessness on the faces of my colleagues, my wife's wisdom persuaded me that I needed a drastic change. I walked in on day three and resigned.

I called the gentleman who had offered me the Department of Energy job and discovered that it had not yet been filled. He hired me on the spot.

Energy Maven

Given the oil crisis that erupted when the Saudis turned off their spigot four years before, I thought that the newly established U.S. Department of Energy would be perfect for me. Energy had become a daily "top-of-the-fold" issue and would be in the forefront of U.S. concern for a long time to come. It combined economic, environmental and national security concerns, kind of the "Big Three" obsessions of the 1970s and 1980s. At the time, we were in thrall to the volatile and generally hostile Middle East for our energy supplies. Our Cold War Soviet adversary was doing all it could to undermine that dependency. And burning fossil fuels was emerging as the central environmental threat to our quality of life. It was a perfect storm, so to speak. I found the notion of getting involved at an early stage of tackling these major issues very compelling.

Letting Off Steam

I was assigned to the Office of Leasing Policy Development, lawyering involving primarily antitrust law, which also seemed both interesting and intellectually challenging. It proved not.

My first assignment, however, had nothing to do with any of that. It was to develop a set of regulations to govern the geothermal steam industry, a nascent energy source that was in the earliest stages of development. I was too ashamed to say to my new boss that I had not the slightest idea what geothermal was all about.

I was given a set of books, studies, policy papers and monographs and sent off to a private office in order to familiarize myself with geothermal matters and begin drafting regulations. My boss asked for a first draft within six weeks which, at the outset of the project, seemed like a long time. However, once I trudged through all the materials, I only had three weeks left to come up with something that would not embarrass me.

Having only taken baby steps up the steep slope of the geothermal learning curve, I felt that I needed to speak to someone knowledgeable. In the course of my reading, I came across the existence of a prototype geothermal plant in Menlo Park, California. I picked up the phone and called the facility, whereupon I was immediately put through to the director, who was delighted that someone from the outside world was interested in what he was doing. After an hour or so of conversation, he suggested that if I wanted to drill down into the essence of geothermal energy, I contact

A Geothermal Power Plant
(By Gretar Ívarsson geologist at Nesjavellir, Wikimedia - Public Domain)

his friend who ran Iceland's entire geothermal production regime. He told me that Iceland had figured out how to satisfy more than 50 percent of its energy demand via geothermal. He gave me his friend's number and when I hung up, I immediately put in a call to Reykjavik.

I cannot remember the unpronounceable name of the gentleman with whom I spoke in Iceland, only that he was more than willing to give me as much time as I needed to get my questions answered. Fortunately, he spoke impeccable English.

After I hung up, I felt that now I was prepared to put pen to paper (actually fingers to IBM Selectric typewriter keys—my time at the Energy Department pre-dated desktop computing by a few years) and begin writing. At the end of my six weeks of monkish sequestration, I presented a 30-page set of regulations to my boss. He was quite pleased with my work product and assured me that it would have great value when the price of oil exceeded $100 a barrel, which would surely happen sometime in the next 12 months, thereby making geothermal steam price-competitive with oil. I walked out of his office on cloud nine, convinced that I (1) had made a major contribution to American energy independence and thus to global realignment, and (2) would soon be one of the nation's experts on geothermal regulation, much in demand by presidents and chairs of congressional committees.

There was just one hitch. As, a short time later, I was busily writing away, a man burst into my office one day and began laying into me in a very loud voice about the $400 phone bill I had racked up by calling Iceland. He was not happy with me and when I discovered that he was the Deputy Secretary of Energy, I was sure that this was going to be my last day on the job. That did not turn out to be the case and he also did not charge me for the call. When he pivoted on his heel and walked out of my office, I got to thinking that $400 was less than 1/6-

millionth of the department's $6 billion budget. It seemed a miniscule price to pay for my *magnum opus* that would surely change the world.

Within the next year, the price of oil never went above $15 a barrel. My regulations were put on the shelf and are likely still there today, forty years later, under several inches of dust. When it became clear after several months that oil price predictions were way, way off the mark, I began to become cynical about the direction and mission of the Department of Energy. Nothing that occurred during the remaining eight months I was able to endure working there did anything to diminish my escalating dismay.

No Exit

The first time I ever heard about the Strategic Petroleum Reserve (SPRO) was when I read a biography of President Warren G. Harding of "Teapot Dome" scandal renown. At that time, what became SPRO was called the Naval Oil Reserve. That scandal involved the illegal sale of naval oil reserves to commercial firms by the Secretary of the Interior abetted by the Attorney General. The next time I encountered something like this was during my brief cup of coffee at the Energy Department.

By the late 1970s, the SPRO program had migrated from Wyoming to what are called salt domes just off the Louisiana coast in the Gulf of Mexico. These large, cavernous natural structures were deemed perfect for storing massive amounts of oil to be pumped in and then extracted in the event of a national energy emergency

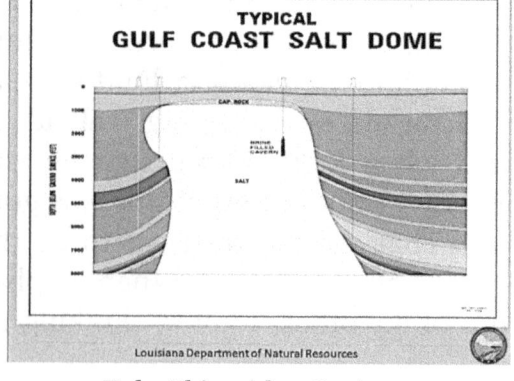

Take This with a Grain . . .

such as another Middle Eastern cut-off of oil exports to the U.S. Little did we know that this scenario was on the cusp of being played out thanks to the Iranian revolution that would erupt within a year.

There was only one problem with this standby approach: it didn't work. Why? Because while our government geniuses had figured out how to get the oil into the salt domes, they had yet to invent a technology to get the oil out.

If I thought my cynicism had subsided after the geothermal fiasco, this absurdity elevated it to stratospheric heights. It occurred to me that this was no way to run a railroad; how could a government so utterly inept ever stand up to an implacable Cold War enemy with nuclear weapons and delivery systems?

And then everything got worse.

Accounting for Royalty

I was given a number of desultory assignments that required little thought and even less action. One of them, however, was the impetus for increasing my contempt for a department that was daily documenting its inability to get anything right.

The directive to me was to draft regulations containing accounting formulas to govern the share of Gulf of Mexico outer continental shelf oil and gas revenues (royalties) owed the government from the production of oil and/or gas on tracts leased to private energy companies. Again, I was being thrown into an arena about which I knew nothing, i.e., accounting. This was destined, I believed, to be yet another instance of garbage in/garbage out. Boy, was I right!

My boss did provide me with a department CPA, a very nice green-eyeshade, pocket-protector type who was the real life avatar of Mel Brooks' Leo Bloom from *The Producers*. We worked well together, mainly because if I was a 50 on the cynicism scale, Mel had worked in government long enough to be off the charts. I was also given a budget to hire a "Big Eight"

CPA firm (now down to the Big Four) to help me understand and develop the regulations. After interviewing partners from three of the Big Eight, Mel and I settled on one of them.

One of our focus firms in drafting the regulations was the biggest of the Seven Sister oil companies (I won't name names, but you can Google it and figure it out easily enough). This firm had recently built an entertainment complex onshore in Texas where its employees stationed on drilling platforms in the Gulf could go for rest and relaxation. It spent a cool $350 million in 1979 dollars (over $800 million in 2019) on its recreation complex. The problem was that, in determining the government's 16.7 percent royalty payment, the company included the cost of this wretched excess in its calculation. Consequently, the government was getting peanuts instead of its rightful royalty share.

So, the first thing we did was itemize the kinds of costs that firms could include before calculating the government royalty, and specifically excluding items like recreational wonderlands. This did not sit well with the energy industry and as soon as they got wind of what we were proposing, they went ballistic. It was not long before an edict came down from on high to eliminate this exclusion from our draft regulations.

Meanwhile, we got nothing out of our CPA firm contractor. I got the strong impression that the firm had decided to give us its bottom-feeding mediocrities rather than its superstars despite the king's ransom they were reaping from the government.

All in all, our regulations were a bunch of *dreck*, unlikely to secure any additional monies to the taxpayer who so generously leased a bonanza to Big Oil. I was now dripping with cynicism.

And then it got worse.

The Third-to-Last Straw

The end of the government fiscal year (September 30) was fast approaching when our boss, an antitrust economist from academia who was about as well-suited to a high Energy

Department position as an uneducated desert sheik surviving on dates and camel steaks, breezed into my section and posed the following question:

"Any of you guys know any professors who might want a government contract? We've got all this money we haven't spent this year and lord knows what Congress will do to our next year's budget if we don't spend it ASAP."

No likely beneficiaries of his largesse immediately came to mind, so he continued his quest to throw away taxpayer money in other sections of his fiefdom.

Despite my surging cynicism, I was nevertheless still naïve enough to be appalled. But it was an object lesson in how our abysmal federal budgeting and contracting system works. Years later I discovered that this kind of shenanigan goes on all over government at every level, but that does not make it right. Contracts for doing nothing of value or nothing at all get tossed around like beach balls on the Jersey Shore. Politicians keep telling us that, if elected, they are going to slash spending by eliminating waste, fraud, mismanagement and abuse. It never happens. Those Four Horsemen of the federal establishment are so firmly embedded that the next time a pol promises to do that, knock him or her on their fat ass.

My only solace was that I had been reading about how the Soviet Union's five-year economic plans actually worked out in practice. This was trickle-down economics writ large. Every Soviet enterprise, no matter how small, had to have such a plan. What that meant in implementation was that everybody in the country spent a good portion of their time crafting what they were going to tell the next higher level *kommissar* about what they intended to accomplish economically by the end of the five-year period. That was good, because it implied a distraction from thinking about how to bury the United States, per Chairman Khrushchev's vow at the UN.

The best anecdote about how the five-year plan worked out concerned a commuter railroad that ran between Sevastopol and Yalta in the Crimea in extreme southern Russia. The five-year plan was rushing to conclusion and the railroad was far from meeting its goal of carrying X number of passengers. Its solution was to round up the local peasants at gunpoint and seal them in train cars under guard so they wouldn't jump off. Then they ran the train back-and-forth between the two towns for a couple of weeks until the five-year plan numbers were reached.

With an adversary like this, who needed to worry about the Cold War?

The Short Straw . . .

If you have ever had the misfortune to have read legislation or regulations, then you know that strict adherence to the accepted rules of grammar, syntax, parallelisms, usage, etc. are not exactly paramount in the minds of the drafters. Except in the mind of my immediate boss at the Department of Energy, an otherwise mild and harmless soul that we worker bees called "Alpha Papa Whiskey" for reasons you don't need to know.

Alpha Papa had an obsession with one—and only one—usage rule: when to use "that" vs. when to use "which." My draft regulations would often be returned to me with no other comment than what he viewed as my misuse of one or the other. It got so bad that he bought me a much-thumbed through, dog-eared copy of a nineteenth century English grammar primer that contained five pages of small, single-spaced type addressing this critical matter. Before presenting me with this tome, Alpha Papa had taken the time to highlight and add marginal notes clarifying the long-and-mercifully-dead knighted and benighted grammarian's exposition.

He was not amused when I added a footnote to an otherwise numbing regulation I wrote concerning the market concentration implications of outer continental shelf oil and gas lease sales in the Gulf of Mexico about the "Wicked That of the West."

The Almost Last Straws . . .

In the dead of a miserable winter, Iranian Ayatollah Khomeini abruptly cut off his country's oil exports to the U.S. in retaliation for our mindless support of the terminally corrupt Shah and his gang of unrepentant thugs. This had the following impacts:

- It spawned the second energy crisis of the 1970s, during which we were reintroduced to long lines and higher prices at gas stations.
- It put the Department of Energy back on the front pages and in lead stories on the nightly news.
- It prompted President Jimmy Carter to make an example to the American people of energy conservation by turning off the hot water at the department, so we could more easily get sick and infect others. It had the collateral effect of terminating my lunch-time runs on the National Mall because I could no longer enjoy a hot shower in the basement dungeon that passed for an ersatz gym.
- It got my outfit a new Deputy Assistant Secretary from the Oklahoma oil industry who rivaled my last DoD boss for rampant cluelessness. His first edict was that he would neither accept nor read any memorandum from his staff (us) that exceeded one page in length. That was not an easy directive for us because the issues we were dealing with were complex and did not necessarily lend themselves to succinct summarization.

We found ourselves spending most of our time on useless, time-consuming exertions aimed at reducing our thoughts down to one page. A great deal was lost in translation. Exasperated, I suggested that the way to comply with his dumb diktat was to simply stop writing when we reached the end of the page. It worked. After some whining about "undermining my authority," he took his protest to his boss who dressed him down for the fool he was.

Again, my reading about the Soviet enemy was reassuring. They were doing stuff like this all the time at every level. We had little to worry about if you discounted megatons and missiles.

. . . And the Straw that Broke the Camel's Back

The legislation that enabled the Department of Energy wrested a whole lot of authorities that had been comfortably housed in the Department of Interior since Eve was just a rib. Bureaucrats do not like to lose any of their turf. Consequently, like the epic annual budget battles between military services at DoD, Interior had it in for Energy and pulled out every imaginable weapon to attempt to do us in. This rapidly evolved from the sublime to the ridiculous.

The ultimate absurdity was a dispute over how to cite the term "Public Law Number" in official legal documents. At Energy, we used the citation preferred by the *Uniform System of Citation*, a.k.a. "The Blue Book," a nasty little tome that attached itself to every law student of the era upon matriculation and stayed so tethered throughout an entire career.

Interior viewed this as a winning wedge issue and when we had to run one of our regulations that had an impact on it by their lawyers, they saw an opportunity to make us look bad.

They did not object to the substance of our regulations, just to the way we cited Public Law Number.

This produced a major wedgie in our second-level boss's undershorts. He decided to throw down his glove and challenge Interior to a fight to the finish over this core issue. The battle quickly escalated. Interior demanded satisfaction in the form of taking the matter all the way up the chain of command to the White House where a meeting was called, chaired by the President's chief domestic policy advisor. Some of my colleagues and I were commandeered by our leader to accompany him as horseholders to the big meeting at the Old Executive Office Building next to the White House, where the President's man did a rain dance on the heads of the two delegations, threatening both with extreme unction.

Recovering from disillusionment is never easy or quick. From the time I joined the department up until immediately following the submission of my geothermal regulations, I thought I might be on my way to becoming the straw that was going to stir the energy drink. Instead, I was so disgusted by this last manifestation of lunacy that I up and resigned my position, giving two weeks' notice.

During which serendipity struck. I was asked to come back to DoD as a senior legal consultant on national security law and policy.

All but one of my colleagues in our little antitrust unit resigned shortly thereafter.

Postscript: Given the anesthetizing nature of our work at Energy, we looked for ways to maintain what passed for sanity. The most rewarding one was the creation of what came to be labeled "the Energy Maven's Football Pool," a sideline we created and managed for fun and profit. In addition to accepting wagers on our weekly list of the point spreads on professional and college games, we always included a special "game of the week" with a pithy accompanying opinion. The one that generated the most action was an entirely fictitious contest between Notre Dame and Yeshiva University, about which we opined: "An epic battle for the soul of America between the Fighting Irish and the Fighting Yiddish."

Chapter 15
Task Force Tasks

National security is the fig leaf against freedom of information.
—Ralph Nader

*A Different Kind of Task Force
(Joint Task Force Bravo, U.S. Southern Command)*
(U.S. Department of Defense – Public Domain)

Both my Army Atomic Demolitions Munitions experience, accompanying security clearance and some of the work I had done as a Pentagon lawyer and subsequently as a legal consultant triggered a request that I manage two successive government-wide task forces dealing with emergency legal authorities available to the U.S. government. I did this a number of years apart in the early-to-mid 1980s while building the business I launched in 1979.

Friendly Data

The first task force was given the mission of aggregating all of the *non-classified emergency legal authorities* of the U.S. government and putting them into a computerized database.

The charge was to identify every such authority that could be invoked in any kind of emergency situation from a limited-in-scope natural disaster all the way to a global thermonuclear war and its aftermath.

Our job entailed meeting with the top lawyers in every government agency and picking their brains about what they believed should be included in the database. That was not quite as forthright as it might appear at first glance. The U.S. government has a great many agencies beyond merely the cabinet departments and independent executive agencies such as the Environmental Protection Agency and the Securities and Exchange Commission. The almost-contemporaneous *Federal Legal Directory* listed 744 U.S. government law offices. If you examine any large U.S. government department or agency, you will discover that there are often numerous subordinate offices that have their own law offices and legal authorities which they may invoke in the event of an emergency. That meant visiting hundreds of organizations and speaking with hundreds of attorneys. While our limited resources did not allow us to visit every one of these law offices, we were able to talk to more than half of them and research the legal authorities of the rest without having to meet face-to-face. I personally went to many of these meetings.

The project took a full year and unearthed many surprises along the way. For example, it was an eye-opener how many general counsels and chief counsels knew very little about their agencies and even less about the emergency legal authorities at their disposal. Another revelation was how brief many of their tenures were at their agencies. On average, those who were political appointees (at that time more than half were still career officials) barely remained with their agencies long enough to enjoy a cup of coffee. Unfortunately, that diminished the value of many of these face-to-face meetings.

Once we compiled the emergency authorities, which amounted to thousands of laws, regulations and executive orders, we had to distill each one of them down into a consistent, readable, summary *precis* with a citation to where the full item could be found in either the *United States Code* or the *Code of Federal Regulations* (which includes presidential executive orders). We completed that Herculean task and turned our finished product over to the technical staff hired for the project for keypunching into a database.

When all of this was complete, a meeting of all interested parties was convened in the large Department of Commerce auditorium in order to explain the database and how it was designed and intended to be used. Hundreds of legal and technical people from around the government attended and witnessed a demonstration.

Since this took place in the early 1980s, when desktop computing was still suffering birth pangs, there were some serious issues that immediately emerged and which became the subject of vigorous and often contentious debate—and not a little contempt—at this two-day assembly. First, the search software was so Neanderthal that it worked less than 50 percent of the time. Second, the database tended to freeze. Third—and this was a mind-blowing revelation to me and my team—if you scrolled down the pages and missed the precise item you were seeking, you had to return to the top and begin to scroll down all over again. The software did not allow scrolling up.

I was on the panel for this meeting and brought up what to me was the most disturbing deficiency of the database by far: it was not secure. If some kind of hacking software existed—at that time we did not use this terminology—then the hacker could monitor what the database searchers were seeking and know in advance what authorities were going to be invoked to deal with whatever emergency loomed or was in progress. There was a very pregnant pause when I raised this point. Then, one of the other panelists—I cannot remember whom, but he was a high-ranking Justice Department official—said we did not have to worry about that.

I then asked if any thought had been given to how the database was going to be updated. Again, this appeared to be an entirely new thought. I guess the answer was "no."

And that was that.

This being the government and my consulting contract having ended, no one ever shared with me whether this database was actually deployed and whether anyone went to it in an emergency. Later, when I was an outside legal advisor to the Federal Emergency Management Agency, I tried to find out about the fate of the database, but no one knew anything . . . or they were too embarrassed to say. I never did find out if this had all been a complete waste of time and resources.

I personally benefited from this project beyond the obvious financial remuneration for tackling it. Learning so much about the inner legal workings of the entire government proved invaluable in the business I and a partner had launched a little earlier, an enterprise that in its early years focused very heavily on those inner workings.

Let's Play Two

The title of this section requires a tip of the hat to the great Chicago Cubs shortstop, Ernie Banks, who always wanted to play a doubleheader on a nice summer day. My doubleheader was getting the call a couple of years after my first foray into task forces to run another one. This time around, the project looked to have both strong legs and a powerful rationale. It was clear from the outset that the work we would be doing would have value.

Superficially, as it was described to me by the overseers, it appeared to be nothing more than "Emergency Authorities, Part Two." However, the more I listened, the more I realized that was not at all the case. Instead, while I was chosen to lead this new task force because I had led the first one, this time around we would be examining some very serious *classified* material and making recommendations for elimination, retention and addition to an extremely important body of work: the classified standby authorities that the government might call on in the event of a national emergency, again including everything up to a nuclear holocaust.

I had no idea that these authorities even existed. I learned that they had been developed in the late 1940s coincident with the enactment of the *National Security Act of 1947*, a major piece of Cold War legislation that dramatically reorganized the U.S. defense, national security and intelligence establishments into an entirely new template that is still largely intact today. The Act renamed the Department of War the Department of the Army, established the Department of Defense and the position and Office of the Secretary of Defense, created the Department of the Air Force as a separate and co-equal military service, separating it from the Army (it was the "Army Air Force" until the end of World War II), protected the U.S. Marine Corps as an independent service under the Department of the Navy, and established the National Security Council in the White House, and the Central Intelligence Agency. It also established the Joint Chiefs of Staff.

In addition, and here is where our task force came into play, the broad language of the Act was used to develop a set of standby legislation, regulations, executive orders, presidential proclamations and other documents, almost all classified, that could be invoked in an emergency. The impetus for the task force was that these standby emergency documents had not been reviewed or updated for almost 40 years.

This task force was much larger than the last one, notwithstanding that the number of legal authorities under review was only a fraction of the thousands we had to examine during the first go-round. However, each one of these required much closer scrutiny because we were not only considering them in light of present-day circumstances, but also for legal sufficiency and for their future value.

To handle this, I was allocated resources to hire and put together an almost 50-person team including attorneys who were detailed to me from around the government as well as outside contractors comprised of two legal research companies and individual attorneys and paralegals. While my role was primarily managing this group of people, giving the final blessing to their findings and recommendations, and writing a final report, I was also privy to all of the documents in the collection.

Some of them were mind-blowing doozies, authorizing governmental actions that probably did not pass constitutional muster. But that was not my call. I was directed to worry only about conflicts with existing law, not whether what the documents authorized was legal in the first place.

We recommended sweeping changes to the canon of dated standby authorities. It was a relatively simple matter to suggest which ones should be excised and which should be amended to conform to present-day circumstances. Much more difficult was determining what needed to be added to cover contingencies that did not exist in 1947, such as cybersecurity threats, a barely emerging concept in the mid-1980s. From my prior task force experience, this was very important to me and I went into it to the very limited extent my technological understanding would allow.

I cannot talk about what we found in the documents other than to say that the powers that government might claim and justify by an emergency go way beyond what you can possibly imagine. Beyond even Donald Trump's wildest authoritarian fantasies of a constitutional set-aside.

Chapter 16
Health Effects

We share the same biology
Regardless of ideology
— Sting, The Dream of the Blue Turtles

Cold War health effects have a double meaning for me:

1. The immediate and long-term macro impacts of nuclear weapons blasts (i.e., Hiroshima and Nagasaki), above and below ground testing, e.g., Novaya Semyla, Semipalatinsk, Bikini Atoll, etc. and reactor accidents; and
2. The micro impact, meaning their personal impact on me, the author, my ADM platoon colleagues, and other "atomic veterans."

The Macro Impact

What Happens When the Bomb Goes "Boom?"

A nuclear detonation creates a huge fireball followed by a mushroom cloud. Together, they suck up everything they touch—soil, water, people, animals, inanimate objects, etc. The cloud rises into the high atmosphere. If the explosion is big enough, it reaches up into the stratosphere and even the ionosphere. Eventually it loses its upward momentum. Some of the radioactive debris it carries can stay aloft for months before it is dispersed by the winds and slowly falls to Earth, not necessarily near ground zero. The U.S. "Castle Bravo" hydrogen bomb test in the remote Marshall Islands, the largest nuclear detonation ever by this country, produced a mushroom cloud that reached 110,000 feet and sailed around the world for 18 months, blanketing much of the Earth with dangerous radioactive fallout.

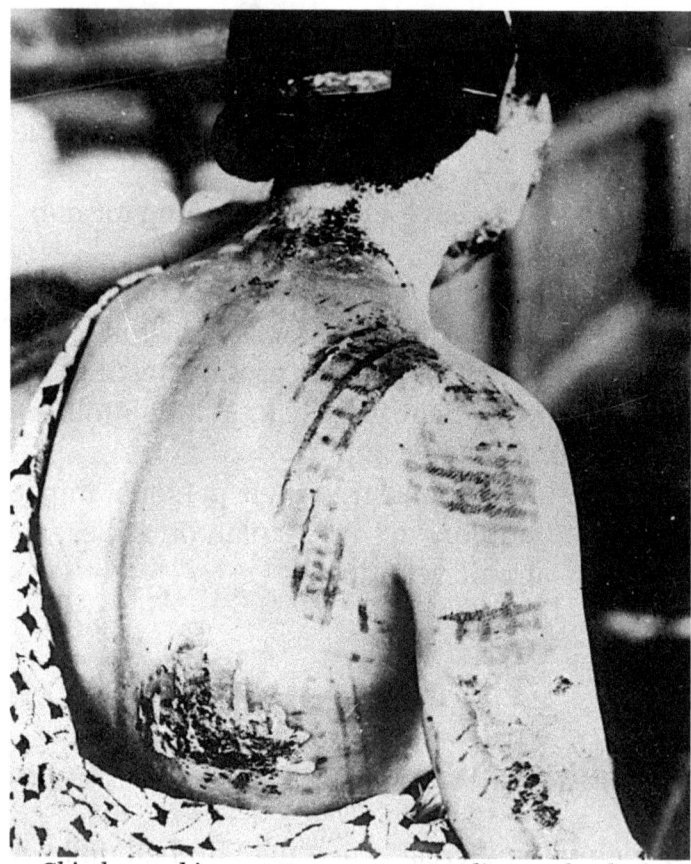

Skin burned in a pattern corresponding to the dark portions of a kimono worn at the time of the Hiroshima explosion. Japan, circa 1945
(National Archives and Records Administration
Public Domain)

A good description of what occurs at a detonation comes from former Secretary of the Air Force Tom Reed who, early in his career, witnessed an atmospheric bomb test in the Pacific, about 30 miles away from the blast:

Even though we were wearing black goggles, and even though the yield was much lower than expected, the sky was filled with light. When all seemed dark, we removed those goggles, only to be blinded all over again. The ball of fire was white, then took on incredible colors—yellows and purples . . .

When the blast arrived, two minutes after the flash, coffee flew everywhere. Several fellows were knocked over. Emotionally, I was too, for there's nothing in the human experience that in any way relates to the detonation of a nuclear device on the distant horizon, no matter how "small" or how far away. I cannot imagine what it would be like to be any closer.

There's the light, a brightness that simply does not stop. People talk about a flash, but a thermonuclear detonation is not a flashbulb event. The sun starts to burn on earth. Darkness seems never to return. There are the colors—purples and other hallucinogenic hues . . . There's the heat. It makes no sense to the brain, because the explosion being observed is almost over the horizon, as far away as Baltimore is from Washington. Yet the first flash gives way to an oppressive, lingering heat whose persistence becomes unnerving. And then there's the all-enveloping roar of the savage beast unleashed . . . It takes a while, several minutes, for sound waves to get from detonation point to observer, assuming the observer is a lucky, peacetime scientist. So much else happened that the senses are numb. The first shock wave is not a crack or a pop, as one hears from a gun fired far away. It is the opening of a roar encompassing the senses, seeming to continue forever.

A Brief Reactor Primer

Uranium fuel is loaded into a reactor, and then bombarded with neutrons to trigger a controlled chain reaction that produces a tremendous amount of heat and transforms some of the uranium into plutonium. This is the same process used to make plutonium for a bomb, except in that case, the plutonium is the desired result; the heat produced is the waste product. When you want to produce energy for industrial and consumer consumption, the heat is the object and the plutonium is the waste product. The heat produces steam that turns turbines that in turn generate electricity.

It sounds pretty simple, but it is anything but because you are dealing with one of the most dangerous and volatile substances imaginable and with processes of incredible complexity. If something goes wrong, several calamitous scenarios can ensue. They did in the three most widely publicized and well-known nuclear reactor accidents: Three-Mile Island, Chernobyl, and Fukushima Daiichi. Together, they serve as object lessons of the huge risks involved in generating power using nuclear fuel. More on each of these disasters below.

Despite careful engineering design and redundancy, stuff happens. Probably the worst thing that can happen is a cooling system failure. Neutron bombardment produces tremendous heat, meaning reactors are designed and constructed so that a steady flow of water will always be available. Absent water to cool the fuel rods (sealed metal tubes containing uranium pellets) and moderate, i.e., slow down, the fission chain reaction, overheating is inevitable. It does not take long for lack of water to allow fuel temperatures to rise so high that the reactor experiences a meltdown that turns the solid fuel to liquid which then burns through the containment vessel, spewing radiation—the invisible danger—far and wide.

Accidents

Three Mile Island

The Three Mile Island Nuclear Power Plant
(Centers for Disease Control and Prevention – Public Domain)

A riveting, albeit entirely fictional, movie about a nuclear reactor meltdown, *The China Syndrome*, was released on March 16, 1979. Twelve days later, the worst American nuclear reactor accident in our atomic history occurred at the Three Mile Island (TMI) power station in the middle of the Susquehanna River a few miles south of Harrisburg, Pennsylvania's state capital. TMI Unit No. 2 experienced a wildcat overheating of its fuel rods that was perceived by the media and public as bringing to life the fictional treatment in the movie. The public perception to this day is that Unit No. 2 either melted down or came very close. The timing of the two events could not have been worse for the nuclear energy industry. The movie seemed to presage the accident.

TMI Unit No. 2 was a pressurized water reactor (PWR). This design is the main nuclear workhorse used throughout the U.S. and abroad and is still the most common type of reactor producing power today. There were few questions raised about the risks involved when TMI was constructed. The level of secrecy surrounding reactors was, and still is, military in nature.

The Calamity

TMI is a long, narrow island in the middle of the Susquehanna. Unit No. 2 had only been in operation for a year. Shortly after midnight on March 28, 1979, the pumps feeding heated water to the heat exchangers stopped working. Pressure in the cooling system's pipes began to increase quickly. A valve designed to relieve the pressure then failed to close completely. The warning light for this was on the *back* of the control panel, so operators did not know about it for 80 minutes, during which cooling water continued to pour out instead of cooling the fuel containers.

The control room engineers shut down the reactor as soon as they became aware of the incident, but the shutdown process takes a long time before the fissionable material inside the reactor stops producing heat. Absent a cooling system, reactor temperatures kept rising. Soon, the cans containing the nuclear fuel began to burst, adding to the already intense heat.

Worse, the zirconium metal in the fuel can casing began to react with the steam, thus producing highly flammable hydrogen. Now the risk of a hydrogen explosion was added to the Murphy's Law ("what can go wrong will go wrong") mix. Had the hydrogen exploded, it would have dispersed huge amounts of radiation across central Pennsylvania.

But that was not all that the now frenzied control room staff had to worry about. The problems kept compounding. Some of the highly radioactive cooling water vented into the air and rained down on nearby Middletown. The press quickly got wind of the situation and the increasingly desperate battle to contain the problem and avoid a China-syndrome-like meltdown and/or a hydrogen explosion. Confusion about the accident and the risks was rampant. Metropolitan Edison, the utility that operated TMI, was no help.

The Response

In that pre-Internet, pre-cellphone era, phone lines quickly became overstretched. Communications between TMI and the U.S. Nuclear Regulatory Commission (NRC) in Washington became difficult. NRC Chairman Joseph Hendrie said he and Pennsylvania Governor Richard Thornburgh were "operating almost totally in the blind. His information is ambiguous, mine is nonexistent." Just what you don't want to hear from your government during a crisis. It did not help that America's reassuring uncle, Walter Cronkite, called the TMI accident "the first step in a nuclear nightmare." The media went wild with speculation about apocalyptic scenarios.

Then . . . nothing happened. The radiation release was negligible, amounting to a miniscule *one ten-millionth* of the subsequent Chernobyl reactor accidental release seven years later. The average individual dose received by nearby residents was the equivalent of a chest X-ray. Ultimately, the safety systems worked, but the psychological damage was enormous. U.S. reactor construction came to a screeching halt and was not (haltingly) resumed for almost 40 years. The sense that incompetence ruled destroyed the industry.

Governor Thornburgh initially advised anyone living within ten miles of the plant to stay indoors. Later, he urged children and pregnant women to "get out of Dodge." 140,000 people had already fled the area without an evacuation order.

The Unit No. 2 cleanup took 14 years. At this writing forty years after the accident, 99 percent of Reactor No. 2's radioactive waste has been removed and the unit is still waiting to be dismantled.

TMI was the U.S. nuclear industry's loss of virginity. The day of the accident, the U.S. had 140 reactors in operation with 92 under construction and 28 more awaiting NRC approval. The accident brought all new construction as well as the approval process to a screeching halt.

My Friend, the First Responder

In 1977, the late Edward Shomaker, one of my closest friends, became the first attorney hired by the NRC who did not also have an engineering degree. He was, however, attractive to the agency because he spoke Russian and had an MA degree in Russian Area Studies. There was a sense in 1977 that the Nixon-Brezhnev "détente" would soon lead to cooperative efforts with respect to exchanges of information about the two countries' nuclear weapons and reactors and that it would be valuable to have someone with knowledge of Russia and Russian language on board. Détente, however, collapsed shortly thereafter when the Soviet Union invaded Afghanistan and U.S.-Soviet relations quickly soured.

At that time, Ed had become somewhat "lost" at the NRC, which quickly forgot about his Russian expertise. Lacking a STEM background, Ed was tasked with being the agency's Freedom of Information Act (FOIA) lawyer, responsible for initial reviews of public requests for agency information and recommending whether documents should be released or withheld.

When the NRC learned of the accident at TMI, it assembled a team of 12 staff members under the leadership of Harold Denton, the agency's Director of the Office of Nuclear Reactor Regulation and the nation's leading authority on nuclear safety, and sent it to TMI to investigate, advise the President and Governor of Pennsylvania, and undertake damage control. Just a week before, Denton had gone to the movies to watch *The China Syndrome*.

Anticipating a barrage of media and public requests for information, Denton took Ed, the agency's FOIA officer, with him to TMI. While the NRC team was at TMI, a special phone line was installed that connected it directly to the White House and President Carter.

The NRC's TMI team walked into a scene of chaotic dysfunction. They found that radiation had been released, although no one could determine then how much had escaped into the atmosphere and the river. A large hydrogen bubble in the reactor building was in danger of exploding. The pumps that forced cooling water into the 36,000 uranium fuel rods had been turned off. A relief valve was locked into the open position, allowing radioactive steam to escape. The fuel rods in the reactor core were overheating, resulting in a partial meltdown. It was mayhem.

Overnight, Denton became a national icon. His calm demeanor during televised news conferences reassured the nation. Within a few days, the hydrogen bubble disintegrated, the reactor began to cool and the danger was over. After three weeks at TMI, Ed and the NRC team returned home.

When I first met Ed several years after the incident, he told me about both the incredibly thoughtless design of the TMI Unit No. 2 control panel (the warning light on the back) and of meetings between the NRC staff on hand and the Pennsylvania Governor and Lt. Governor (William Scranton III) during which the panicked Pennsylvanians had to be talked out of taking unwarranted extreme measures to deal with the crisis.

The minimal TMI radiation release was greatly overblown by media hysteria fueled by *The China Syndrome*. It sold movie tickets, newspapers and ads during nightly news shows, but it set American energy policy back at least a generation. The effect on America was profound, far beyond what was warranted. The illusion of nuclear power safety was dispelled. Public trust in nuclear energy went down the toilet. Not a single new nuclear reactor has come online since the 1979 mishap. At this writing, only one new reactor is under construction, the first since the TMI accident, and it is years behind schedule.

But TMI was hardly the last word in nuclear disillusion. Only seven years later, the TMI accident looked like nothing compared to what happened in the land of the other superpower.

Chernobyl

There are fools who can overcome any foolproof system.
— Frank von Hippel, Princeton University

Ed Strikes Career Gold

In the time between the accidents at TMI and Chernobyl, Ed Shomaker, his background finally being recognized and valued by the NRC, was appointed Director of the Health Effects Program of the agency's International Programs Division. He was finally given the opportunity to use his Russian language skills and cultural knowledge to maximum effect. He quickly became one of the world's leading experts on the macro impact of nuclear accidents. The program he essentially developed and led dealt with exchanges of information with the NRC's Russian and Ukrainian counterparts (Moscow's Kurchatov Institute and Kiev's State Nuclear Regulatory Inspectorate of Ukraine) with respect to what the U.S. and those nations were learning about the health impacts of nuclear reactors and weapons as well as what needed to be done to avoid future calamities.

Ed was the ideal first director of this important program not only because he spoke Russian and understood Russian history, politics and culture, but also because of his prior experience with nuclear accidents, principally Three Mile Island (TMI).

Meltdown

Late on Friday, April 25, 1986, the minimally-trained reactor operators began to power down Chernobyl's Reactor Unit No. 4 for annual maintenance. At the same time, they wanted to use the shutdown procedures to test whether the reactor could provide temporary electrical power to control the plant if it lost outside power. However, the reactor began to lose power before the operators were ready for the test, so they recklessly disabled safety systems in order to keep the reactor operating, including removing almost all of the control rods that controlled the speed of the fission reactions.

The control rods consisted of 1,700 separate tubes surrounded by graphite, which regulates neutron flow. It is the neutrons that generate the chain reaction that produces the superheated steam that turns the turbines, thus producing electric power. The control rods are intended to slow down the neutrons when they are inserted into the reactor core. Protocol mandated that a minimum of 30 control rods must remain in the core at any time. That did not happen here.

The immediate result was that the fuel load went out of control. In less than a second, the power went from close to zero to 50-100 times the plant's maximum-rated capacity. The fuel melted and a runaway nuclear reaction went totally out-of-control.

At 1:23:48 AM on Saturday, Reactor Unit No. 4, 59 miles north of the Ukrainian capital, Kiev (now Kyiv), exploded. It was not only the worst nuclear accident in history, it was also the worst industrial accident of all time.

The blast was so powerful that it blew the 10-foot thick, 2,000-ton lid off the top of the reactor. The lid fell sideways into the uranium core, exposing it to the open air for the next ten days. The first explosion caused the reactor core and surrounding structure to disassemble. However, the core reconfigured itself and formed a critical mass. Ten seconds later, with the reactor surging to 400-500 times its normal maximum power, there was a much more violent second blast that has been labeled "a full-fledged nuclear explosion, like a bomb." The RBMK reactor design was also to blame. It was seriously flawed and never should have been built. Instead of the core being encased in a steel pressure vessel, each fuel assembly was enclosed in an individual, flimsy 8 cm diameter pipe (a "channel").

The red-hot core (burning at 5,000 degrees Fahrenheit) prompted fears of a third explosion. While that did not happen, the core caught fire. The Soviet military sent helicopters to "bomb" the reactor with neutron absorbers. Chopper pilots who flew through the toxic plume died shortly thereafter. Meanwhile, no neutron absorbers made it into the core.

Reactor operator Valery Khodemchuk's body was never found, presumably vaporized by the blast. A second operator, Vladimir Sashonek, was knocked unconscious and quickly died of severe radiation burns. Three other workers died within a few minutes of the explosion. Six firemen rushed to the reactor in their shirtsleeves with no protective gear. They all died within a few days. In total, 30 people who were on site either at the time of the explosion or soon thereafter died. An additional 209 were treated for acute radiation poisoning, their long-term health compromised.

The Remains of Chernobyl Reactor No. 4
(International Atomic Energy Association)

As the operators had powered down from 3,200 to only 30 megawatts for maintenance, they inadvertently turned off the all-important cooling system. The reactor immediately overheated and began a chain reaction. The nuclear control rods were ordered to be lowered to stop the chain reaction, but it was too late and too hot. The channels containing the uranium fuel ruptured, which raised temperatures ever higher, causing the two massive explosions. The blasts released a tremendous amount of radiation into the atmosphere. Some of the airborne uranium elements had half-lives of only a few seconds; others for at least a generation.

The operators did not know what to do next. It was revealed long after the accident that they had never conducted safety drills because they did not want to alarm the local population.

Sixty-nine additional firefighters joined in within a few hours, trying to douse the flames. More than half of them were not wearing protective, lead-lined suits, only gauze face masks. Within weeks, 20 of them died of acute radiation poisoning.

The Kurchatov Institute sent a team to Chernobyl the day after the blasts. Tens of thousands of inhabitants of more than a hundred nearby towns and villages were haphazardly evacuated without any organized plan.

The Pentagon had a satellite passing over Ukraine when the explosion happened, so it knew about the accident within minutes. However, news of the accident did not reach Moscow until 3 AM.

The radiation release was more than hundred times larger than those at Hiroshima and Nagasaki combined.

Initially, the Kremlin said nothing. The outside world first heard about the explosions 30 hours later when a radiation alert alarm went off at a Swedish power station a thousand miles downwind. Reindeer herds in Northern Sweden were put off-limits to hunters, rendered too dangerous to eat by the Chernobyl plume. The first "plume" from the accident traveled over neighboring Byelorussia (today, Belarus), the Baltic states and Scandinavia. On the day of the accident, U.S. interpreter Irene Firsow, a friend of mine, on a visit to the Soviet Union, happened to be in Minsk, Byelorussia a few hundred miles north of Chernobyl and directly in the path of the plume. A man she encountered took off his shirt, only to suffer a severely burnt torso, likely from fallout from the plume. When he tried to obtain medical treatment, he was told he did not meet the definition of a victim.

The Soviets by then had a long history of understating the number of victims of their nuclear accidents. Narrowly defining "victim" was par for the course.

A second plume dropped fallout over France, Italy, Switzerland, the Low Countries, Britain and eventually the U.S. The Ukrainian people were among the last to know. Three days after the incident, a tiny paragraph appeared in the bottom left-hand corner of page three of the principal Kiev newspaper citing an "incident" that was "under control." It was not.

What remained of the reactor roof was full of lethal material. At first, the cleanup involved robots pushing these toxic items off the roof into the opening created by the explosions. When that did not work, Soviet Army soldiers were sent onto the roof. They were called "bio-robots." Each soldier was instructed to carry four blocks of graphite and throw them into the pit, then run away from the danger zone as fast as possible. Each was limited to absorbing 20 Roentgens. Some soldiers arrived at this extremely dangerous level in less than a minute. More than 3,400 men participated in this roof run. This was followed weeks and months later by a rash of bio-robot deaths as the Soviet government denied that the roof runs had anything to do with this carnage.

The U.S. immediately offered its expertise and assistance, but Moscow rejected it. Months later, desperate, the Soviets did ask for our help. Ed was one of the U.S. government officials who received and acted upon the request.

The graphite in the core burned for nine days, continuing the release of radiation into the atmosphere. More than 5,000 tons of boron, dolomite, sand, clay and lead were dropped into the burning core by helicopter in an effort to douse the fire.

Unlike TMI, the Chernobyl accident was an actual meltdown. The catastrophe was exacerbated by the faulty design of the reactor, including the absence of an adequate containment shell.

Consequences

Kiev, the closest big metropolis to Chernobyl, was largely spared any adverse effects of the accident because of its prize pink chestnuts. The city fathers maintain unique watering trucks to tend to the chestnuts and deployed these immediately after learning of the explosions to wash down the city's buildings, the vast majority of which, at no more than six stories high, were well within reach of the water trucks' hoses. This happy accident was also a big psychological boost for Kiev's 2.5 million citizens.

Valery Legasov, the Soviet atomic scientist charged with overseeing the official review of the accident, secretly recorded his concerns about Chernobyl and its portents for the future of Soviet nuclear power based on the RBMK's flawed design. He called Chernobyl "the apotheosis and peak of the economic mismanagement in our country over decades." Legasov fell into a deep clinical depression due to his study of the accident. Unable to live with the lessons he learned, he committed suicide on the second anniversary of the accident.

It was arguably the accident and ensuing cover-up that tolled the bell on the Soviet Union, brought down as much by public outrage as by Party Chairman Mikhail Gorbachev's *glasnost* and *perestroika*. It wasn't just the reactor that exploded that day. It was also the myth of Communism.

Today, it is still too early to know what the ultimate death toll from Chernobyl will be. Some scientists estimate that more than 1 million people exposed to Chernobyl radiation will die before their time. Ten years after the event, researchers noted that there had been a dramatic increase in thyroid cancers in individuals exposed as children. A total of 722 cases are documented, a huge increase in the typical number expected of the population studied. The geographical distribution of those cases is consistent with the Chernobyl radioactive plume and is attributable to fallout from it.

In addition to the physical health impact of the accident, there have been a series of studies of the psychological consequences. The affected populations exhibited significant increases in anxiety, depression and psychosomatic disorders.

Six of the men found responsible for the accident were scapegoated by the Soviet regime and sent to Siberian labor camps following what amounted to the equivalent of a Stalin-era show trial. Scapegoating was the rule following any Soviet misfortune.

The other three RBMK reactors at Chernobyl were not shut down immediately after the accident despite their similar design flaws. Unit No. 2 went offline in 1991 after a turbine fire. Unit No. 1 endured until 1997, and the last of the Chernobyl RBMKs, Unit No. 3, lasted until 2000.

Ed Goes Nuclear

Only a handful of foreigners were invited to visit Chernobyl. Ed and interpreter Irene Firsow were two of them. Ed was even allowed inside the remains of Unit No. 4. His foray into the reactor was a high-risk proposition because radioactive dust was still swirling around the ruined core for years after the accident. A cameraman who filmed a documentary about Chernobyl and who went inside died soon thereafter. Donning a hazmat suit (absent about 16 inches of lead, there is no protection from gamma rays) and surgical cotton mask (respirators were reserved for the Soviet scientists and engineers working at the site), Ed was allowed to enter and tour the destroyed reactor. The protocol for site visit duration was 20 minutes maximum. I don't know how long Ed was in there. (See Appendix B for an explanation of how radioactivity is measured.) When he returned from Chernobyl, Ed gave me a videotape of what he witnessed. The devastation seen up close was far more horrible than what the Western media had been able to show us.

Several years after his Chernobyl trip, Ed hosted a dinner with his Ukrainian counterparts to which my wife and I were invited. The U.S. Department of State provided an interpreter so I was able to speak to the Ukrainians, several of whom had been posted to Chernobyl immediately after the accident. A number of these managers, scientists and engineers had received dangerous doses of radiation far above the level deemed "safe," a vague standard that presupposes that there is, in fact, a measurable safe level. They all had unnatural, beet-red complexions. One of them told me that some of his similarly situated colleagues were already dead from radiation poisoning and that he suspected that he would soon be joining them. That made for quite the somber evening aside from the multiple vodka toasts to the entire Soviet and American chains of command.

Ed Shomaker was instrumental in helping the Soviet Union and its successor Russian and Ukrainian states improve the safety of their reactors, largely through promoting a culture of safety via increased collaboration between his NRC Health Effects program and his Eastern European counterparts. He encouraged visits of Soviet, Russian and Ukrainian nuclear engineers to our power plants as well as other Western nations' plants and launched twinning arrangements between Eastern and Western power plants.

Ed died several years later from a cancer that had gone undetected until it was too late to treat due to an egregious medical error that was later adjudicated to be malpractice. Although the proximate cause/primary site was a tumor on the back of his knee resulting from an earlier injury, I still wonder if either his Chernobyl visit or his years' earlier service as a night security guard at a Florida nuclear power plant (he moonlighted while in the Army monitoring conversations in Russian between Cuban and Soviet officials) might have played a role.

In 1992, Ed received the NRC's Distinguished Service Award, the highest honor the agency can bestow. The citation accompanying the award read as follows:

> *In recognition of his exceptional contribution to the success of cooperative programs between the United States and the nations of the former Soviet Union. As Senior Project Manager for these programs, Mr. Shomaker has played a vital role in the joint effort to prevent a second nuclear catastrophe in Eastern Europe. The*

people of his own country and those of the former Soviet Union are in debt to him for his tireless and dedicated endeavors for public safety and international cooperation. Despite grave illness, Mr. Shomaker has continued to give of himself unstintingly. His selfless and indeed heroic work has been an inspiration to all privileged to work with him. He stands as an example of public service at its very finest.

Ed Shomaker and Friends (Notre Dame Cathedral)
(Michele Shomaker Collection)

Cleanup

The expectation is that Chernobyl Unit No. 4 will remain radioactive for at least 100,000 years. The hastily and shabbily constructed, 24-story steel and concrete tomb that was thrown up to cover its remains, a.k.a., the "sarcophagus," soon began to show cracks and likely leaked radiation. It was intended to last longer than the pyramids of Giza.

The Chernobyl cleanup is considered the most difficult civil engineering feat in modern history. There is considerable evidence that the inside of the sarcophagus was falling down.

However, no one could enter in order to assess the actual damage and the risk, if it collapsed, that the ensuing radioactive dust cloud could cause another catastrophe. It does not help that the sarcophagus was riddled with around 1,600 square meters of holes. Nicolai Steinberg, chief engineer at Chernobyl for the ten months following the accident and later head of Ukraine's atomic energy regulatory agency, put it this way following the construction of the sarcophagus (see below): "From an engineering standpoint, no one can tell you what will happen to the sarcophagus in the next half-hour." He repeated that to me at the Shomaker dinner.

In 2018, a much more solidly constructed dome (a.k.a., the "New Safe Confinement") was built enveloping the sarcophagus. It is designed to prevent radiation leaks for the next 100 years.

Ultimately, 600,000 workers were involved in the Chernobyl cleanup and sarcophagus construction. Many received more than 35 Roentgens of radiation, a dangerously high dose. Some workers actually collected hyper-dangerous fuel rods manually, absorbing lethal doses of radiation.

More than 3 billion people in the Northern Hemisphere received doses of radiation from the accident. Mortality predictions resulting from Chernobyl range anywhere from 5,000 (Soviet authorities) to 20,000 deaths (the scientific community), primarily from thyroid cancer and leukemia.

Andrei Sakharov, the father of the Soviet hydrogen bomb and later the titular leader of the civil rights/civil liberties movement that helped bring an end to the U.S.S.R., called Chernobyl "the nuclear monster that had gone out of control." For the next 25 years, we were told that Chernobyl was the worst case come to life. In 2011, we experienced a nuclear horror that may have exceeded that optimistic prediction.

Fukushima Daiichi

The Geology

Japan sits squarely on the Pacific Rim earthquake zone, a.k.a, the "Ring of Fire." This region experiences more earthquakes, volcanic eruptions and tsunamis than any other place on Earth.

The Ring of Fire engulfs Japan, making it one of the highest risk areas in which to rely on nuclear power for electricity. Building nuclear power plants in Japan should have been a non-starter from the beginning. The extreme risks involved should have precluded opting for nuclear energy, but as is usually the case, money talks loudest and greed prevails.

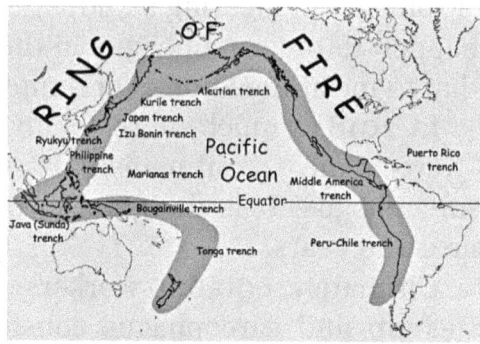

The "Ring of Fire," the Most Unstable Region on Planet Earth
(U.S. Geological Survey – Public Domain)

Mother Nature Objects

At 2:46 PM Japan Standard Time on March 11, 2011, a massive earthquake off Japan's east coast occurred, its epicenter 43 miles east of the Oshika Peninsula of Tohoku at a depth of 18 miles below the Pacific Ocean surface. Its magnitude on the Richter Scale of 9.1 made it the most powerful earthquake ever recorded in Japan and the fourth most powerful ever since recordkeeping of such events began in 1900.

The earthquake was so strong that it shifted the home island of Honshu 8 feet to the east. Honshu's east coast sank a little over three feet (since then, it has risen back up and now exceeds its original height).

Earthquakes are a constant danger to reactors wherever they happen to be located. Building them in high-activity seismic zones borders on the insane. Moreover, positioning them in a coastal area is lunacy because earthquakes often generate tsunamis. The peril increases by several orders of magnitude.

Aerial View of Ishinomaki, Japan after the Tohoku Earthquake
(U.S. Marine Corps photo by Lance Cpl. Ethan Johnson - Public Domain)

That is exactly what happened next. The Tohoku earthquake triggered one of the most powerful tsunamis ever to strike the Pacific. Its waves reached an unheard of height of approximately 133 feet (picture a 13-story building).

Fukushima's four reactors automatically shut down when the earthquake struck. But the tsunami put the emergency generators that powered the pumps that cooled the reactors out of operation. Their heat spiked and led to *three* meltdowns, which resulted in explosions that released radioactive material into the atmosphere.

All of this had been foreseeable, but was dismissed. The risk analysis that the Tokyo Electric Power Company (TEPCO), the plant's owner, was presumed to have done had in fact not been done. Moreover, there were no disaster or evacuation plans in place. The chaos surrounding the emergency evacuation directly and indirectly caused 1,600 deaths, primarily of elderly nursing home residents.

The disaster caused massive disruption to the people in nearby communities. Most of them will never be able to go back to their homes. It also caused Japan to rethink its growing reliance on nuclear power and to shut down 43 of the nation's 54 reactors. Despite 80-percent public opposition to nuclear power post-Fukushima, Japan's obligations under the Paris Climate Change Agreement have prompted it to reverse course. It intends to bring all of its reactors back online by 2030. In contrast, Fukushima caused Germany to decide to move completely away from nuclear power over the next decade. France, which gets 80 percent of its electricity from nuclear, is also rethinking its energy future.

Fukushima prompted a slowdown in U.S. reactor construction as well. Six of the eight new projects approved in recent years by the NRC have now been abandoned, while the only two still moving forward are experiencing massive cost overruns due to the demand for increased safety measures. So much for the revival of the U.S. reactor industry after decades of inactivity due to Three Mile Island.

Fukushima was the worst nuclear incident since Chernobyl. It is also the only such disaster other than Chernobyl to be classified a "Level 7 event" on the International Nuclear Event Scale.

The cleanup and decontamination is estimated to take 30-40 years. The low-end cost estimate is $180 billion.

Bomb Tests

The innocent victims of several U.S. and U.S.S.R. above-ground nuclear weapons tests might successfully argue that Chernobyl was by no stretch the worst nuclear accident in history. Their stories follow:

How to Wax a Wild Bikini

The Castle Bravo H-Bomb Test
(Pexel.com – Public Domain)

At dawn on March 1, 1954, the Japanese trawler *Diago Fukuryu Maru (Lucky Dragon No. 5)* was fishing for tuna in the Marshall Islands. Suddenly, an enormous orange ball brighter than the Sun appeared on the western horizon. All 23 crew members ran on deck to view the phenomenon. Within minutes this new sun disappeared, replaced by a gigantic mushroom cloud.

Two hours later, white ash started to rain down on the boat. It continued for five hours. A number of the crewmen purposely tasted the ash, which was the residue of what had been the coral island of Namu, part of Bikini Atoll, 100 miles distant from the trawler.

The *Lucky Dragon*'s crew decided to haul in its nets and head for home 1,200 miles away. Before they reached their home port, they began vomiting over the side of the boat. Their skins began displaying burns and sores. Their hair started to fall out. Their gums began to bleed. It was a wonder anyone was healthy enough to steer the boat.

Two weeks after the boat docked in southern Japan, the crew members were still sick. Hiroshima and Nagasaki fresh on their minds, local physicians soon diagnosed the problem: Acute Radiation Poisoning. The doctors wrote to the U.S. Atomic

Energy Commission (AEC) asking for treatment advice, but never received an answer. AEC Chairman Lewis Strauss ordered the non-response, believing without any supporting evidence that the fisherman were Communist spies.

One crewman died five months later. The rest recovered, but their lives were altered forever. Japan's unique experience as the only nation to have been the target of nuclear weapons generated several urban legends: that radiation exposure was contagious; that a stigma attached to anyone victimized by radiation. Crew members had to move away and enter into a *de facto* witness protection program in order to lead normal lives.

Daigo Fukuryū Maru in early 1950s, shortly before the incident (Japanese book "ASAHI CHRONICLE" published by Asahi Shimbun Company. Public Domain, Wikimedia)

The *Lucky Dragon*, it turned out, was just one of more than 100 Japanese fishing boats in harm's way that morning. The long-term effects of these other crews' exposure to the Castle Bravo blast are unknown.

The broader impacts of the explosion and resulting exposure were significant:

- Tuna stopped being sold in Japan and the moratorium lasted for years.
- Japan's tuna fishing industry was destroyed.
- "Castle Bravo," at 650 times the yield of two 1946 tests, sent radioactive material around the world and contaminated seawater more than 1,200 miles away, including Japan.
- The 6,000 residents of the atoll were evacuated before the 1946 "Able Baker" A-bomb tests. Following "Castle Bravo," it became clear that they would never be able to return.

- A 2016 study found that radiation levels on Bikini Atoll are more than six times what is considered safe.
- The disaster resulting from the test prompted the making of *Godzilla*, the film about a mutant monster created by atomic tests that goes on to make hash of Tokyo.
- Despite the world's nuclear powers limiting their testing to remote, uninhabited areas, Castle Bravo and its after-effects confirmed that no one on Earth was safe anymore. Fallout from hydrogen bombs was a global threat.

The not-so *Lucky Dragon* was constructed at and launched from Wakayama Prefecture. In one of life's strange coincidences, Ed Shomaker's son, Thomas, married a girl from Wakayama.

Veterans Who Glow in the Dark

Between 1946 and 1962, the U.S. tested more than 200 above-ground and undersea nuclear weapons. A large number of soldiers, sailors, airmen and marines were ordered into known danger zones near where these bombs were detonated, some of them witnessing more than 30 such tests. The government did this in order to assess the effects of radiation on them.

A disproportionate number of these servicemen and women suffered health problems in the years and decades after observing these blasts. The litany of maladies includes rashes, sores, throat illnesses, lung problems and cancers, with prostate cancer at the top of the list. Applications for compensation to the U.S. Department of Veterans Affairs have, in many cases, been summarily rejected on the grounds that the health complaints fall outside the parameters of the list of diseases that qualify for benefits.

When these warriors were sent into harm's way, they were neither forewarned nor told where they were going or why. In essence, this was a government-directed guinea pig program, or a canary-in-the-coal-mine exercise if you prefer.

Beginning in 1946, thousands of sailors were stationed on naval ships in the Marshall Islands for tests that included Castle Bravo. One of these was the late father of a friend of mine. Before he passed away, he described the experience to me. What I came away with was confirmation of everything I had and have since read about the program and the ignorance in which the victims were kept.

U.S. Army Troops Intentionally Positioned Close to an Exploding Atomic Bomb
(Wikipedia – Public Domain)

Thousands of Army troops and Marines stood or hunkered down in trenches adjacent to the Nevada Test Site. Air crews were ordered to fly their planes into mushroom clouds. Submarines and frogmen were sent underwater to be present while nuclear blasts were detonated. Airborne troops were parachuted into blast sites shortly after detonations. The government wanted to know how troops would react to a nuclear explosion on the battlefield and also to see what it did to equipment. Does the term cannon fodder come to mind?

It is difficult to pin down the number of military members so exposed. Estimates vary widely, with the high estimate being around 400,000 troops.

Few studies have been done on the health effects on this population. A 1979 study of 3,000 observers who had been positioned near a 1957 Nevada Test Site detonation found that the leukemia rate among them was more than twice as high as in the civilian population. The only other studies we have to go on are with reference to Hiroshima and Nagasaki survivors.

They have suffered increased cancer rates. Their children had smaller heads than normal and more physical disabilities. There never has been a coordinated attempt to study or track the health effects of radiation on the Atomic Veterans or their children.

That has changed somewhat in the past 25 years. The U.S. government's former consistent attitude toward atomic veterans was altered in their favor by Congress's 1996 repeal of the *Nuclear Radiation Secrecy Agreement Act*, which rescinded the Atomic Veteran "oath-of-secrecy." This permitted Atomic Veterans to discuss publicly their participation in nuclear weapon testing and post-test activities without legal penalty. Sadly, by that time thousands of Atomic Veterans, many of whom suffered radiation-induced health issues such as cancer, were gone. Congress has since enacted legislation to compensate certain Atomic Veterans and their families, but they have to surmount many bureaucratic obstacles in order to receive any compensation.

Tsar Bomba

America was not the only superpower intent on testing nuclear weapons and building bombs that could hold the world in thrall. Its Soviet Cold War rival was doing much the same thing. If there were differences they were as follows:

- The Soviets pushed for bigger bombs; and
- They did not care even as little as the American authorities about causing grievous harm to innocents.

The "Tsar Bomba" blast of October 30, 1961 was the largest explosion in human history. Its 5-mile wide fireball could be seen 620 miles away. Its mushroom cloud reached 40 miles high, seven times the height of Mt. Everest, and its base extended 25 miles wide. Every single building in *Severny*, 34 miles from ground zero, was destroyed. In towns hundreds of miles from ground zero, wooden houses were destroyed and stone structures lost their roofs, windows and doors. This included broken windows in homes in Finland and Norway. The blast's thermal pulse was felt 170 miles away. Heat from the explosion caused third-degree burns 60 miles from ground zero. The energy yield was 8.1 on the Richter earthquake scale.

It is difficult to wrap one's head around these colossal numbers. To make it easier, consider this: *Tsar Bomba's explosive power was more than 17 times the entire power unleashed by all of the explosives detonated during both World War I and World War II.* That included bombs, mines, artillery shells, grenades, ammunition, torpedoes, depth charges, breaching charges, shape charges, rockets and naval artillery, *as well as the* Manhattan Project's Trinity explosion plus Little Boy (Hiroshima) and Fat Man (Nagasaki).

The Tsar Bomba Fireball and Beginning of the Mushroom Cloud
(nationalinterest.org)

If a bomb the size of Tsar Bomba were detonated over New York City, it would destroy not only the city and its five boroughs, but also take out all of Long Island, Westchester and the lower Hudson River counties, New Jersey and Connecticut. More than 25 million people would die from the initial explosion alone, with many more to follow from the residual health effects.

Tsar Bomba was one huge mother.

Nuclear's Dirty Secrets

Rocky Flats

The Soviet Union was not the only superpower to hide what was really going on with its nuclear weapons and reactor programs. The U.S. was as secretive as possible given the constraints of an otherwise open society.

The standout example is the cover-up of what happened at Rocky Flats, Colorado, 15 miles outside of Denver and the site of one of America's premier nuclear weapons production facilities. Plutonium began to leak from barrels of radioactive waste early in Rocky Flats' history, which began in 1952. Being a windy area, airborne contamination spread rapidly, a fact that was not revealed to the public. Then, in 1957 and again in 1969, plutonium waste spontaneously combusted and caught fire, spreading additional radioactive toxins. These accidents were also kept secret. Relatively low levels of radioactive isotopes were released into the atmosphere throughout the 40-year life of the plant through daily operations as well as more minor accidents. The wind carried this contamination into the Denver suburbs.

It took until the 1970s for the public to discover what was going on at Rocky Flats. A 1972 study concluded that the fallout over the Denver area was much higher than "normal" fallout (whatever normal is) and that ground plutonium contamination ranged up to hundreds of times that from bomb tests and had spread off the reservation. By the time of this revelation, the population of the Denver area had been exposed to steady radioactive contamination for 20 years. Undeterred and ignored by the authorities, the pollution went on for another two decades despite years of protests and even an unprecedented joint FBI-EPA raid in 1989.

Rocky Flats then halted weapons production and began to shut down the plant. It was declared a Superfund site the same

Cleaning Up Rocky Flats
(U.S. Environmental Protection Agency - Public Domain)

year (an area is declared a Superfund site if it has been assessed as one that could or has released hazardous substances that may pose a threat to human health or the environment). It took 14 years to clean up the above-ground contamination. The underground contamination, however, remains untouched. Measurable radioactive contamination in and around Rocky Flats will stay the norm for thousands of years.

It is too early to know the long-term health effects of the Rocky Flats fiasco. However, the government claims that the area is now perfectly safe for habitation. To underscore its assertions, portions of the former facility have been declared a national wildlife refuge. Notwithstanding all the assurances, you might want to defer building your dream home there for a few thousand years.

The United States has over 94,000 metric tons of nuclear waste that requires disposal. Our commercial power industry

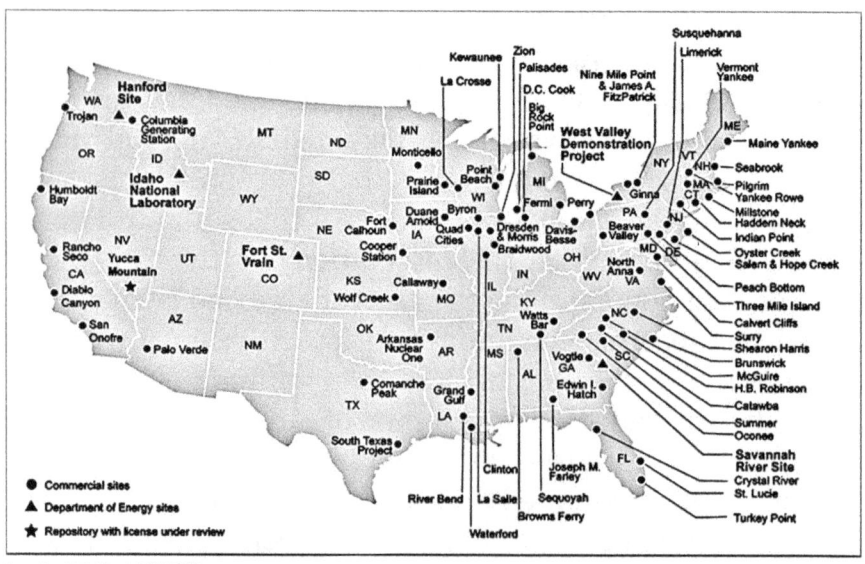

U.S. Nuclear Weapons and Reactor Waste Sites
(Department of Energy)

alone has generated more waste ("spent fuel") than any other country—nearly 80,000 metric tons. This is enough to fill a football field about 66 feet deep.

As we can see from the Rocky Flats example, nuclear waste poses serious risks to human and environmental health. The U.S. government's nuclear weapons program has generated spent nuclear fuel and high-level radioactive waste that accounts for most of the rest of the total at about 14,000 metric tons. The amount of waste is expected to increase to about 140,000 metric tons over the next several decades.

Hanford

Hanford, Washington, along the Columbia River in Southern Washington State, was established as a key component of the Manhattan Project. Three Hanford nuclear reactors produced the plutonium used in "Fat Man," the atomic bomb dropped on Nagasaki on August 9, 1945.

Eventually, Hanford became home to no fewer than nine reactors and five enormous processing plants. For 40 years, it was "radioactive-central," producing more than 63 tons of plutonium that supplied the majority of the 60,000 nuclear weapons in the U.S. arsenal. Today, following its decommissioning, only one reactor remains operational, transformed into a power plant producing electricity.

Storing Nuclear Waste at Hanford
(National Oceanic & Atmospheric Administration)

Almost two-thirds of the nation's radioactive waste is stored at Hanford, most of it in drums like the ones in the photo above. Hanford is by far the most contaminated nuclear site in the U.S. and is the focus of the largest environmental clean-up effort outside of Chernobyl.

Yucca Flats

Yucca Flats, a desolate area 100 miles northwest of Las Vegas, was the scene of 842 nuclear detonations between 1951 and 1992. In addition to its dubious distinction as the most bombed place on Earth, it is also the most irradiated place on the planet. Over its 40-year active existence, thousands of workers were exposed to radiation, prompting some to label it the "national sacrifice zone."

The Yucca Flats Test Site—
The Most Bombed Place on Earth
(National Nuclear Security Administration – Public Domain)

Like Rocky Flats, Hanford, Yucca Flats and 77 other sites in 35 states, nuclear waste is largely stored where it was generated. There is still no U.S. disposal site despite spending decades and billions of dollars researching potential permanent sites, including Yucca Mountain in Nevada (46 miles southwest of Yucca Flats) that has had a license application pending for years to authorize construction of a nuclear waste repository. However, NIMBY ("not in my back yard") invariably wins the day and politicians fear for their survival if they contest that.

The Micro

Tick-Tock

Plutonium is an element that does not occur in nature. Instead, it is the result of the neutron bombardment of uranium in a nuclear reactor. It is one of the most toxic substances on Earth. If only a single microscopic plutonium particle lodges in a lung, it can cause cancer by irradiating only a few cells.

My first Medtronic pacemaker was powered by a small kernel of plutonium-238 with a half-life of 88 years. Three U.S. companies manufactured these devices: Cordis Corporation, Medtronic Inc. and Coratomic Inc. I only discovered that I was carrying plutonium around in my chest years later when I received a replacement pacer, one not powered by plutonium, manufactured by a different company.

The thermoelectric battery in my first pacer contained 2 to 4 curies of plutonium-238. The heat from the decaying plutonium generated the electricity that stimulated my heart. The U.S. government denies that low-dose plutonium is dangerous, claiming that there is a safe level of exposure to the substance. This assertion is very much in government's interest to claim given the vast amounts of this incredibly lethal element lying around places like Hanford and Rocky Flats.

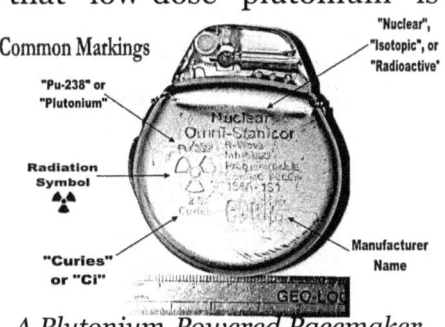

A Plutonium-Powered Pacemaker
(Los Alamos National Laboratory)

If you looked at the back panel of one of these plutonium-powered pacemakers (which is impossible without ripping open your chest), the information you would see imprinted there would scare the pants off you: the designation "Nuclear," "Isotopic" or "Radioactive;" "Pu-238;" the three-triangle radiation symbol; and the number of Curies being put out by the device.

When an individual with one of these plutonium-powered pacers died or required a replacement device, the old pacemaker was supposed to be removed and shipped to Los Alamos, New Mexico where the plutonium was recovered. No, this did not count as organ donation by the deceased despite its contribution to our weapons program.

The U.S. Food and Drug Administration, which approves medical devices, blessed this insanity for years, relying on other government agencies' assertions that plutonium in low doses is not dangerous. That was and is not true. Dismissing the dangers of all this plutonium allowed to run around in human bodies is refuted by the entire nuclear science community as well as the scientific and medical evidence. If you breathe in a microscopic *Pu* particle, that could be all she wrote. Plutonium-powered pacemakers were phased out in the first decade of the twenty-first century.

My pacemaker was only one of my two contacts with the core element that is such a poignant symbol of the Cold War. The other was my two years of service in my ADM unit in Germany, where we handled plutonium nuclear weapons rather often. Although we were assured that there was zero exposure risk, keep in mind that the assurer was the same government that claims that there is a safe level of exposure to plutonium.

We did not always wear dosimeter badges when we entered our bunkers to check our war reserve nukes. When we did, however, their utility in alerting us to dangerous radiation levels was totally useless because we had to turn them off to be read. I don't remember ever receiving a report of the results of any exposure.

For the next almost 40-plus years, I experienced no health problems that I could attribute to two years of working with nuclear weapons. Like many of my ADM co-workers, I took a voluntary sperm test when I returned to the U.S. following my Army service. I "passed" and subsequently fathered two children, so I concluded that particular function had not been affected. In the last decade, however, my immune system has been compromised, a genetic anomaly in my family. I have to wonder if being around atomic bombs and handling them from time-to-time has something to do with my condition, which requires periodic medical tests and bone scan X-rays (sometimes more than 20 during one visit) that make me cringe as I contemplate how much radiation I might have absorbed during my life.

While writing this book, I learned that I have thyroid cancer, one of the cancers most prevalent among Atomic Veterans, Hiroshima and Nagasaki survivors and people exposed to the Chernobyl plume. My doctors believe that this could have been caused by my exposure to nuclear weapons during my Army Atomic Demolition Munitions service.

Chapter 17
The Spy in the 'Hood

You can't be a real spy and have everybody in the world know who you are and what your drink is. That's just hysterically funny.
    −Roger Moore (opining on Bond, James Bond)

I was driving home to Arlington, Virginia from my office just across the Potomac River in downtown Washington, DC on President's Day, 1994, when I turned into my cul-de-sac and screeched to a halt just before almost running over Wolf Blitzer. Blitzer was standing in front of a CNN broadcast truck replete with satellite dish atop a ten-foot pole, fronted by a cameraman and jabbering into his microphone.

My Neighbor, Aldrich Ames
(Federal Bureau of Investigation)

My first thought was that my 16-year old son, a budding computer geek, had done something awful like hacking into the Pentagon's computer system. Instead, what CNN and a host of similar trucks and newsy celebrities on adjoining streets were reporting was the FBI's arrest that day of one of my neighbors—Aldrich "Rick" Ames.

Ames had been arrested a block-and-a-half from his home just around the corner from me; my wife and I passed his house almost every day while walking our dog.

We neighborhood residents had known something strange was going on for at least six months prior to Ames' arrest. For one thing, almost every evening we could hear a small plane buzzing overhead. When we looked skyward, we observed a single-engine, red airplane circling the neighborhood. Post-arrest, we discovered that one of the neighbors had called the Federal Aviation Administration to complain about the noise generated by the plane. He received a phone call several days later requesting that he keep silent about the plane.

A group of the men in the neighborhood got together on Saturday mornings for a brisk walk—our lame excuse for exercise. When we walked down the street past Ames' house, we noticed and remarked on two anomalies: (1) a funny-looking square box affixed to the telephone pole just outside Ames' house and pointing toward it; and (2) a van parked across the street with side signage reading "McLean Rentals." We learned later that both were surveillance devices directed at his home.

The Ames Arrest
(Federal Bureau of Investigation)

Another indicator that something weird was afoot was the suddenly altered rental status of the house on the corner of our street directly kitty-corner from Ames' residence across the street. The house had recently become a rental when our neighbors, a French couple, were abruptly transferred after 18 years in Arlington—P was a diplomat at the French embassy and A was the local reporting talent for a Paris TV station—to Bangkok, Thailand. The new tenants were a group of 30-something, very buff men and women who wore business attire all the time. Not your customary renters.

The most interesting incongruity, however, had to do with our neighborhood Wednesday morning trash pickup which, for years, had been done by energetic Latino men. Suddenly, the trash was being handled either very early or very late by big blond guys with crewcuts.

We talked about these goings-on, but with no suspicion that they had to do with either a neighbor or Cold War espionage.

The Ames family—Rick, his Colombian wife, Rosario, and their little boy, had purchased their home—we found out later that they paid $600,000 in cash—several years before. Rosario and the boy were always friendly when we came by with Baskerville (a.k.a., "Baskie"), our West Highland White Terrier, who captivated both mother and child. Mr. Ames, in contrast, always hung back, misanthropically averse to much in the way of neighborly communication. One of their two vehicles was a top-of-the-line Jaguar that cost somewhere in the neighborhood of $70,000.

It took the CIA almost ten years to figure out that they were harboring a major Soviet spy in their midst, working in, of all places, Soviet counterintelligence. Until I worked on this book, I wondered how someone like Ames, a nondescript, mid-level functionary with a well-known history as an alcoholic (one of my sources told me that, when Ames was in Rome, he was found one evening passed out on a sidewalk) and an undistinguished career at the Agency, could possibly have been entrusted with such a sensitive position. The explanation I received from my anonymous source who worked in the same division with Ames was that his superiors in every position in which he worked were so eager to pass him on, i.e., wash their hands of him, that they often gave him undeserved, glowing evaluations just to get rid of him.

Tragically, this bumbling approach to a problem employee wound up costing the lives of somewhere between 12 and 32 U.S. double agents, people whose names Ames had given up to his Soviet handlers in return for $2.5 million in cash and another $2 million deposited for him in overseas accounts by the KGB.

When you drive around the CIA parking lot (which I was able to do on several occasions), you are confronted with a sea of modestly-priced Hondas, Toyotas, Fords, Chevys, and the like. Seventy-thousand-dollar Jaguars tend to stand out. The

CIA, pathetically, never noticed. The agency's defense was that Ames claimed that the money came from his wife's wealthy family in Colombia, an assertion the CIA never bothered to check.

During the 9-plus years it took the CIA and FBI to determine that Ames was one of the biggest security risks in the history of the United States and finally shut him down, patriots died.

Two months after he was arrested, Ames pled guilty to espionage and plea-bargained a sentence of life in prison without parole. Rosario also pleaded guilty to conspiracy to commit espionage and tax evasion, receiving a five-year sentence despite claiming she had been coerced by her husband—the FBI produced surveillance evidence during sentencing that showed her a willing participant. She served her sentence and subsequently was deported to Colombia, rejoining her son who had been in the care of relatives there.

Reverberations

Twenty-five years later, the hoopla about our neighbor has not really gone away. The neighbors still talk about it from time-to-time.

When things calmed down a little, a number of authors came by and interviewed neighbors about the case with an eye to writing books. At least four books were published in the next several years, some of which were close to accurate. Several authors "upscaled" our neighborhood, undeservedly so.

The Ames "Manse"
(Author's Collection)

We are pretty much an average Arlington middle-class demographic, kind of "Goldilocksian:" not wealthy; not poor.

The Justice Department's Asset Forfeiture Division seized the Ames house and personal property and sold them at auction. Rumor had it that the house purchasers were "Ames groupies" who reveled in the tales of international intrigue associated with the home and the case. They had collected, according to the rumors, some Ames memorabilia which they kept in the house.

For several years, entrepreneurial tour companies made the Ames house a stop on their spy and scandal tours of Washington. Tour buses came by and stopped so that their primarily Japanese clients could get out and snap pictures of the house while listening to tour guides breathlessly describe the drama.

Ames was not the only spy who plied his espionage wares in our neighborhood. Robert Hanssen, the FBI man who followed Ames into Soviet super-spy lore a few years later, used to mark the telephone pole down the street a few blocks below the Ames residence with chalk indicating to his handlers that he had left secret documents for them at a nearby dead-drop.

Both Ames and Hanssen occupy special elite status in the pantheon of U.S. spies. The damage they did to America's national security was immense and is a condemnation of how lax our intelligence agencies can be when it comes to outing moles and protecting us.

Robert Hanssen Mug Shot
(Federal Bureau of Investigation)

Epilogue
Takeaways

Now, I am become Death, the destroyer of worlds.
  —Robert Oppenheimer (quoting the Bhagavad Gita)

At this point, you would be correct to conclude that I view the Cold War with some ambivalence. It was, for all its binary simplicity, a very complicated era, the residue of which leaves us feeling binary ourselves: not exactly good, but rather relieved that we got through it without being killed or killing ourselves; and not exactly bad but remorseful about what we as a country did to the planet and a great many of its inhabitants by lifting the lid on the atomic Pandora's Box.

The Assessment Formula

The lessons we take away from the Cold War may be the most important ones that humanity has ever had to understand and apply. If we ignore them, the future of mankind is likely to be truncated long before anything like climate change causes the Sixth Mass Extinction.

This epilogue aspires to provide that assessment.

Evaluating the pros and cons of any historical era requires: (1) knowledge of how we got there, followed by (2) a cold-blooded after-assessment of what it all meant, and (3) the application of the widely-quoted George Santayana caveat: *"Those who do not remember the past are condemned to repeat it."* God knows, we do *not* want to go there ever again.

Historical Highlights

The Radium Obsession

A hundred years ago, many people believed that radiation was the elixir of life, a magic potion cure-all absent any adverse consequences. That delusion did not last very long.

On November 8, 1895, German engineer/physicist Wilhelm Roentgen detected electromagnetic radiation in a wavelength range known as X-rays, a discovery that won him the first Nobel Prize in Physics in 1901. In 1896, the husband-and-wife team of Pierre and Marie Curie isolated the radioactive element radium from uranium ore and discovered that it could kill cancer cells. Their achievement was not an immediate sensation. That happened seven years later when they, along with Henri Becquerel, won the Nobel Prize in Physics for their work on radioactivity. Newspapers worldwide breathlessly reported on the prize and that Curie was the first woman to win a Nobel Prize, generating a sudden craze for radium that was an extension of the mania that Roentgen's discovery had produced when it was announced.

Marie Curie
(Wikimedia – Public Domain)

The newspaper articles created the radium fad. With no real research, they attributed miraculous powers to the element: cures for cancer and blindness, transforming old age into youth, powering ocean vessels (and blowing them up), a worthy "substitute for gas and electricity," "a positive cure for every disease," and so on.

By 1906, doctors were smearing radium directly on tumors. People began demanding radium from their physicians. It became a popular drink and its healing properties vis-à-vis a whole host of ailments were widely promoted. Even the American Medical Association endorsed it!

Soon, radium went beyond being merely a medical panacea for virtually every disease or ailment. It was now being proclaimed as a health nostrum as well. The enthusiasm was such that adding it to virtually anything and everything was deemed a can't-go-wrong strategy. The world was dazzled by the glow-in-the-dark substance.

Postcard Advertising Radium Baths at the Will Rogers Hotel in Claremore, Oklahoma
(Wikipedia – Public Domain)

Radium-based products proliferated: toothpaste, chocolate, lipstick, face cream, cigarettes, suppositories, condoms, hand cleaners, wool, bread, butter, bottled water and of course, watch dials. It was the latter application that eventually brought down the radium industry and extinguished the hype.

The United States Radium Corporation hired hundreds of young women and girls to apply radium paint to watch dials. The women were told that the paint was harmless. They were instructed to "point" their brushes using their lips to hone them to a fine point. The majority of the workers thus ingested large amounts of toxic radium and contracted severe cases of radiation poisoning, which killed quite a few of them and left many others horribly disfigured.

Public zeal began to wane when a wealthy socialite and former U.S. Amateur golf champion, Eben Byers, died in 1932 of multiple cancers from binge-drinking almost 1,400 bottles of a radium concoction that was sold as a patent medicine. Before he died, he lost his jaw and holes appeared in his head. He had to be buried in a lead-lined coffin to protect mourners and visitors to his gravesite. Two years later, Marie Curie, the discoverer of radium, died of aplastic anemia due to a lifetime of scientific research involving radiation and from carrying radium around constantly in her pockets.

You might think that after living through this kind of human tragedy, mankind would abandon the quest to exploit radioactivity as far too dangerous to contemplate.

Not so. Less than a decade after Marie Curie's tragic death, all was forgotten. We went from luminescent watch dials and the tragedies they caused individuals to finding ways to apply the same elemental properties of radioactivity to devising means to destroy millions of human lives in an instant.

Nuclear Fission

Lise Meitner

It was another woman physicist who first traveled the road that led to the atom bomb. Lise Meitner was a Viennese Jew who, while working in Berlin, discovered nuclear fission by adding an extra neutron to uranium and, along with two colleagues, realized that this process must release a tremendous amount of energy. Shortly thereafter, she was forced to flee Nazi Germany in order to save her life, helped by the great Danish physicist, Niels Bohr. Meitner's two male colleagues were subsequently awarded the Nobel Prize for their work with her on fission despite the fact that she led the project and made the crucial discovery. Her work was so significant that she received 19 nominations for the Nobel Prize in Chemistry between 1924

Lise Meitner around 1906 in Vienna
(Wikipedia)

and 1947 and 29 for the Nobel Prize in Physics between 1937 and 1965. She never won.

The "Mother of the Atomic Bomb" fled to Sweden and eventually became a Swedish citizen and a member of the Royal Swedish Academy. She received many honors both during her lifetime and posthumously, including having element 109-Meitnerium—named after her.

Three other physicists took the crucial next step toward harnessing the atom in order to build a weapon capable of terminating humanity's brief run.

The Einstein Letter

Credit for launching the Manhattan Project that resulted in the A-bomb is accorded the famous letter from Albert Einstein to President Roosevelt in which he warned FDR that the Germans were working on a super weapon that could win them the war if they beat us to its development. However, Einstein did not write the letter. He only signed it and served as the conduit that the actual authors—Hungarian-American physicists Leo Szilard and Edward Teller—needed to get FDR's attention. Whether they were really concerned about the German A-bomb program or were just looking for work is open to question.

U.S. intelligence could have told them that there was little danger from a German bomb program. Among other hurdles, without Lise Meitner's involvement, a German A-bomb program was going to be a very steep

Albert Einstein Official Portrait 1921 Nobel Prize (Wikipedia)

slope. In any event, the program, such as it was under the leadership of renowned physicist Werner Heisenberg of

The Most Important Letter Ever Written
(Wikimedia Commons – Public Domain)

> Albert Einstein
> Old Grove Rd.
> Nassau Point
> Peconic, Long Island
>
> August 2nd, 1939

F.D. Roosevelt,
President of the United States,
White House
Washington, D.C.

Sir:

    Some recent work by E. Fermi and L. Szilard, which has been communicated to me in manuscript, leads me to expect that the element uranium may be turned into a new and important source of energy in the immediate future. Certain aspects of the situation which has arisen seem to call for watchfulness and, if necessary, quick action on the part of the Administration. I believe therefore that it is my duty to bring to your attention the following facts and recommendations:

    In the course of the last four months it has been made probable - through the work of Joliot in France as well as Fermi and Szilard in America - that it may become possible to set up a nuclear chain reaction in a large mass of uranium, by which vast amounts of power and large quantities of new radium-like elements would be generated. Now it appears almost certain that this could be achieved in the immediate future.

    This new phenomenon would also lead to the construction of bombs, and it is conceivable - though much less certain - that extremely powerful bombs of a new type may thus be constructed. A single bomb of this type, carried by boat and exploded in a port, might very well destroy the whole port together with some of the surrounding territory. However, such bombs might very well prove to be too heavy for transportation by air.

-2-

The United States has only very poor ores of uranium in moderate quantities. There is some good ore in Canada and the former Czechoslovakia, while the most important source of uranium is Belgian Congo.

In view of this situation you may think it desirable to have some permanent contact maintained between the Administration and the group of physicists working on chain reactions in America. One possible way of achieving this might be for you to entrust with this task a person who has your confidence and who could perhaps serve in an inofficial capacity. His task might comprise the following:

a) to approach Government Departments, keep them informed of the further development, and put forward recommendations for Government action, giving particular attention to the problem of securing a supply of uranium ore for the United States;

b) to speed up the experimental work, which is at present being carried on within the limits of the budgets of University laboratories, by providing funds, if such funds be required, through his contacts with private persons who are willing to make contributions for this cause, and perhaps also by obtaining the co-operation of industrial laboratories which have the necessary equipment.

I understand that Germany has actually stopped the sale of uranium from the Czechoslovakian mines which she has taken over. That she should have taken such early action might perhaps be understood on the ground that the son of the German Under-Secretary of State, von Weizsäcker, is attached to the Kaiser-Wilhelm-Institut in Berlin where some of the American work on uranium is now being repeated.

Yours very truly,

A. Einstein

(Albert Einstein)

"Uncertainty Principle" fame, was highly uncertain of achieving anything remotely akin to a positive result. Hitler did not have much interest in an A-bomb and consequently did not devote much in the way of resources to something he and his Nazi elite deemed a pipedream.

Across the pond, however, the quest to build the bomb moved forward like no other project in human history. More than 2,000 theoretical and applied physicists and tens of thousands of other Americans were commandeered for the project. Cities and massive production facilities appeared in the mountains of Tennessee and New Mexico, the plateaus of Colorado and the riverine lowlands of Washington State. In a remarkably short time, the Manhattan Project achieved its goal and propelled the planet into the Nuclear Age.

The Japanese Surrender

August 15, 1945. General MacArthur looks on as Japan Surrenders
(U.S. National Archives)

The scene is the deck of the battleship, *U.S.S. Missouri*, docked in Tokyo Bay in August 1945. At a desk on deck, Japan signs the unconditional surrender document that ends World War II with General Douglas MacArthur looming over the signatories. I got chills when I touched the desk during a visit to the *Missouri* now docked at Ford Island across from Pearl Harbor.

Ever since, the planet has debated whether (1) President Truman needed to drop two atomic bombs on Japanese cities in order to avoid an invasion of the home islands in which at least 1 million American troops could potentially have lost their lives, and (2) Japan surrendered because of the A-bomb attacks. Truman apologists have largely won the day, claiming with hubristic conviction that, absent the annihilation of Hiroshima and Nagasaki and the instant vaporization of 130,000 of their residents, Japan would not have surrendered six days after the second bomb was dropped. However, if you read the transcripts of Japan's Supreme War Guidance Council in Tokyo, you cannot help but come to a different and much more disturbing and uncomfortable conclusion: Japan surrendered because the Soviet Union invaded Japan on the same day as the bomb detonated 2,000 feet above Hiroshima. A massive Soviet force of 1.6 million Red Army troops crossed the border into Japanese-occupied Manchuria and quickly defeated the Japanese defense forces.

When the Council was informed of the atomic bomb blast and the devastation it wrought, its members concluded that at least it was not as destructive as the earlier fire-bombing of Tokyo. Until the Soviets so dramatically changed the equation, Japan was still committed to continuing to fight. However, it was only when word of the Soviet invasion was received by the Council that its members went to the Imperial Palace to inform Emperor Hirohito and recommend unconditional surrender.

Atoms for Peace

> *On the one hand ... and on the other*
> —Tevye in *Fiddler on the Roof*

Utter destruction was only one side of the nuclear coin. The flip side was a commendable idea that President Eisenhower pitched when he spoke to the United Nations General Assembly in one of his valedictories after eight years as Commander-in-Chief. To paraphrase: *Let's transition from building bombs to constructing reactors and producing clean, cheap electricity so we can light and warm the world.* The enthusiasm for the notion that there could be some good to come out of splitting the atom instead of just wreaking massive destruction was worldwide. It captured many imaginations, including commercial firms that could not have distinguished between pictures of bombs from bowling balls. In fact, early reactors commissioned by Israel, Pakistan and Iran were actually built by a company that previously was best known for manufacturing bowling equipment.

Atoms for Peace Postage Stamp
(U.S. Postal Service)

Thus began the selling of nuclear power as a clean, safe alternative energy source. That pitch, as this and previous chapters illustrate, was not quite accurate.

Soon, hundreds of nuclear reactors went up all over the world. They even appeared on surface ships and submarines. This plus side to what the U.S. and Soviet Union had initially introduced in an effort to destroy or deter remained a positive until Three Mile Island and especially Chernobyl.

Other Pluses

Something else positive that derived from our nuclear obsession may be the environmental movement. Like all good ideas, environmentalism has more than one parent: we can thank three, one "mother" and two "fathers," for making it part of the societal and political discourse:

- Rachel Carson, who gave birth to the movement with her groundbreaking book, *Silent Spring*;
- Richard Nixon (yes, that Richard Nixon), who was the father and chief promoter of both the original

landmark environmental law, the *National Environmental Policy Act of 1970*, and the Environmental Protection Agency; and
- Mikhail Gorbachev, who attempted but failed to cover up and subsequently minimized the environmental devastation caused by the Chernobyl catastrophe. What he accomplished was to raise global consciousness about environmentalism and the dangers of nuclear power.

Another plus: the binary world created by the atomic bomb actually kept the world reasonably stable and safe for 45 years and arguably for the additional almost 30 years since the fall of the Soviet Union.

Ever-Present Dangers

It Ain't Over

What did we learn?

First, like the Sorcerer's Apprentice in the Goethe poem, mankind should not unleash forces that he does not fully understand how to control.

Second, the Cold War made us realize how truly vulnerable we all are. It stoked existential fear across the globe like nothing before in history. That fear has subsided somewhat in the last 30 years, coincident with the collapse of the Soviet Union and the *de facto* end of the Cold War. It should not have, however, given that the binary world of two nuclear-armed-to-

The Sorcerer's Apprentice
(Ferdinand Barth - *Goethe's Werke*, Public Domain, Wikimedia)

the-teeth superpowers has morphed since then into, at minimum, a "trinary" world of three superpowers—the U.S., Russia and an increasingly robust and assertive China—that among them have more than 13,000 warheads pointed at one another. This alone means that (1) either the Cold War never really ended despite the Soviet Union's collapse, or (2) we are in the grip of a second Cold War, this time one of such complexity that it makes the former binary one look simple. In addition to the massive megatonnage that the contemporary parties can hurl at each other, there are also other members of the global nuclear club: France, the UK, Pakistan, India, Israel and North Korea. Together, they have 900 atomic warheads in their arsenals.

In the aggregate, the world is a much more dangerous place today than it was 30 years ago. The danger escalates when you factor in (1) the lax nuclear weapons security protocols of some of the newest members of the nuclear club, (2) the high risk that unstable regimes may share their weapons and technology with terrorists, and (3) the Russian attacks on our election systems and democracy, which may prove more devastating than the nuclear threat, especially under an administration that welcomes such onslaughts and refuses to defend against them.

We may, in fact, already be in the throes of a Warming War or at least a new Cold War.

We All Get Sick

Between 1954 when the first-ever hydrogen bomb was detonated, and 1963 when the test ban treaty between the U.S. and Soviet Union prohibiting above-ground testing went into effect, every single human being on Earth received some of the fallout from above-ground testing. It is impossible to know how many people actually died as a result over the ensuing decades. Some scientists estimate the number at tens of thousands.

The half-life of the 110,000 plutonium fuel rods constituting nuclear waste sitting in rusted containers at the now-closed Hanford, Washington nuclear production complex site is

24,110 years. It will take almost 50,000 years for this vast area along the Columbia River to become safe for humans to live or even walk around there. Like Rocky Flats (see Chapter 16), Hanford and the beautiful area surrounding it have been destroyed forever.

Ed Shomaker and Irene Firsow's first-hand experience with nuclear energy reflected an honest effort by the U.S. government to make the promise of atoms for peace as close to a working reality as possible. Thus the launching of the NRC's Health Effects Program, a transactional initiative to share knowledge of what did go wrong, what could go wrong, lessons learned, and proposed prophylactic measures that should be taken. Unfortunately, successful transactions require good faith on the part of all parties. Russia and even Ukraine did not join the conversation in good faith. According to Firsow, the blame game played by Moscow and Kiev was solely intended to bleed the West for money. To a great degree, it succeeded. Today, to the extent that there exists a health effects program and information exchange between the U.S. and its Eastern counterparts, it has been downgraded and subsumed so deeply within the NRC that it does not even show up on the agency's organization chart. That is a huge loss for our country and for humanity.

The Nuclear Coffin Springs a Leak

Irresponsible governmental behavior regarding radioactive waste has not ended despite the tragic lessons of Hanford, Rocky Flats and the many other nuclear facilities left to pollute the planet once nations have squeezed them dry of their capabilities. As I put the finishing touches on this book, it was announced that the "Runit Dome" is likely leaking radiation into the ocean around the Marshall Islands.

The dome was constructed two decades after the relatively small (18-kiloton) 1958 U.S. "Cactus" bomb test that left a bomb crater more than 100 meters in diameter and a depth of almost 10 meters. The crater became the repository of radioactive material resulting from 43 atmospheric tests on Enewetak Atoll from 1948 to 1958. A large circular concrete dome capped the crater in order to seal off the radioactive material inside. Among those materials are significant quantities of Plutonium-239, one of the most dangerous substances extant.

Prior to commencement of the test program, the 150 or so residents of Enewetak were relocated about 125 miles away. During the 1960s, Enewetak became a primary target location for testing ICBMs and later for test firings of a rocket motor. These tests also left residues of radioactive substances.

The Runit Dome
(U.S. Department of Defense)

In 1980, Enewetak residents were told it was now safe to move back home. Only it was not.

Around 800 islanders now live about 12 miles from Runit Island. The 18-inch thick Runit Dome has developed ominous cracks. It turns out that the crater was never lined before being capped. Moreover, climate change has caused rising seas that threaten to undermine what little might be left of the dome's structural integrity. Many islanders suffer from health problems likely attributable to radioactive waste.

A 2013 inspection commissioned by the U.S. government and conducted by Lawrence Livermore Laboratory concluded that radioactive fallout in the Enewetak lagoon sediment was already so high that a catastrophic failure of the dome would not necessarily result in locals receiving increased dosages of radiation. (This is where you say: "Are you kidding me?")

What Must Be Done?

Eight calls for action demand practical responses:

1. **Recognize that we're at war.** The first step toward defending ourselves from the threats coming at us in Cold War II is recognizing that we are in fact at war. Russia is as intent today on destroying us as it ever was during Cold War I. Vladimir Putin is no different than any Soviet leader with whom we had to contend during the period from 1945-1991, with one exception: he is smarter and shrewder than his Communist predecessors. Putin is embarked on a sophisticated campaign to return Russia to global supremacy at U.S. expense. If we continue to act as if nothing happened in the 2016 election and that the Russian threat to American democracy is a myth, we will soon find ourselves regretting that we did not take the menace from Moscow seriously.

    Defense is only the first step in countering the Russian threat. We must also find ways to go on offense against Putin's grand plan. We need our own grand strategy designed to preserve our democratic values and undermine the Russian totalitarian push. We cannot simply ignore what is going on or play "by the rules" when our mortal adversary is intent on doing us in.

    We are already locked into another Cold War, this one a new one, with China. China is aggressively moving into areas of the world and arenas where the U.S. has withdrawn or is no longer interested, including major forays into our own hemisphere (Latin America). The Obama administration's attempt to "tilt" America's commercial and strategic interests toward Asia is now a shambles. China is now unquestionably the dominant Pacific power and its influence will only continue to expand in conjunction with the U.S. retreat.

China is on the cusp of being the third power with a "nuclear triad:" the ability to deliver nuclear weapons via land-based ICBMs, heavy bombers and submarine-launched ballistic missiles (SSBMs). The majority of its 300 nuclear warheads (soon to double) are aimed at the United States. In addition, its stockpile of tactical nukes is growing rapidly, as is its military presence throughout Asia and beyond.

We need to recognize this threat and act accordingly to defuse or minimize it. The longer we wait, the more difficult it will be to re-engage.

2. **Seek arms reduction.** The steady series of talks aimed at reducing the threat that resulted in atomic weapons reductions by the U.S. and Soviet Union must continue and must, at a minimum, expand to include China and in due course the other members of the nuclear club. The ultimate goal should be the elimination of all nuclear weapons by all nations that have them along with a strong inspection and verification program. The interruption and partial reversal of this process by the Trump administration is a dangerous mistake that cannot be allowed to continue.

3. **Work toward non-proliferation.** We must do everything we can through a combination of "carrots and sticks" to limit the nuclear club to its current membership and dissuade aspirants from seeking to join it. The United States needs to rejoin the *Joint Comprehensive Plan of Action* (a.k.a., Iran nuclear deal) and resume

negotiations with that country to achieve a more lasting and comprehensive agreement. Abandoning the JCPOA was a huge mistake as it could enable Iran to proceed full-speed-ahead to develop nuclear weapons.
4. **Strengthen security at nuclear facilities (weapons storage sites and reactors).** The lax national systems and procedures historically and still currently in place for securing nuclear weapons and facilities must be strengthened both domestically and through the development of international standards. The U.S. can provide considerable technical expertise toward this goal.
5. **Plan for nuclear waste.** The nations of the world that have accumulated dangerous levels of toxic nuclear pollutants must shore up their storage and disposal regimes for dealing with this major risk to human health and the environment. It is a lot cheaper to plan this up front than to defer dealing with it until a facility is operational.

    This particular can has been kicked down the road for entirely too long. In the U.S., nuclear waste disposal has been politicized to an unacceptable extent. The problem of accumulating waste has reached a level that might already be beyond the point of no return. With every passing year, the dilemma of where to permanently dispose of nuclear waste grows larger and more complex.
6. **Be realistic about nuclear energy.** We should not give up on what could be a major interim contributor to the switch from fossil fuels to renewables. Nuclear energy does not come with a guarantee of safety despite the bromides issued continuously since the early 1950s by the U.S.

government, specifically by the Atomic Energy Commission and subsequently by its successor agency, the NRC. Both agencies have a long history of suppressing information about the real risks of nuclear power. The problem with the NRC, as with several other federal agencies with conflicting missions, is that the Commission has dual, antithetical missions: (1) to promote nuclear energy; and (2) to assure nuclear reactor safety.

Fossil fuels are also highly dangerous. Over their history, they have resulted in far more deaths and illness than has nuclear power. However, the difference is that a potential nuclear catastrophe could kill a massive number of people at once, as well as over time, than a fossil fuel-related accident such as a mine explosion or an oil well blowout.

As reactors evolved from the early modest-size ones to today's much bigger ones, they became riskier. The paramount public interest in nuclear safety means that we need to think in terms of smaller, more manageable reactors. That means we should look to the U.S. Navy for guidance, given its impressive, 65-year history of building safe small reactors with an unblemished track record of (perhaps) zero accidents.*

There is no reason land-based reactors cannot adopt and adapt the same technology and their operators undergo the same rigorous training as their surface ship and submarine counterparts.

Note: Two U.S. atomic-powered submarines have gone down: The USS Thresher in 1963 during a deep-diving test 200 miles off of Cape Cod, killing all 129 officers, crewmen and military and civilian technicians aboard. The USS Scorpion in 1968 went down 400 miles southwest of the Azores, with the loss of all 99 crewmen aboard. Neither went down as a result of a nuclear reactor problem.

Irene Firsow visited numerous nuclear power plants during her career as a Russian-English interpreter for talks between representatives of the two superpowers. She observed that both Russians and Americans were meticulous followers of the many detailed rules contained in their operator manuals, with one exception: Russian operators did not pay as close attention to safety procedures. Russians were rule followers because they lived in a society governed by granular rules that drilled down into virtually every aspect of societal and human behavior. However, they obeyed rules by rote, prompted by fear, causing much to be overlooked. Firsow performed a lot of Chernobyl-related interpreting and translating in Russia and Ukraine, but also in the U.S. When the NRC (one of her clients) brought people over from Russia and Ukraine to advise and assist them in developing power plant manuals, she found them to be very detailed. But that did not mean that, once back home, they bothered to follow them.

American power plant operators, in contrast, are painstaking rule observers because so many of them in fact come from the nuclear Navy where they became accustomed to doing everything by the book. This is another argument for incorporating naval safety and security procedures into civilian reactor operations.

We also need to (1) perform exhaustive risk assessments with respect to power plant location,* (2) build in the best, most up-to-date

---

Note: At the beginning of the nuclear power era, the protocol was to locate reactors far away from metropolitan areas. However, as time went on, reactors began to be located closer to cities. Today, five reactors each surround Chicago and Philadelphia and seven ring New York City.

safety and security protocols plus redundancy, and (3) mandate detailed, worst case scenario collateral damage prevention and evacuation planning.

Andrei Sakharov, who knew a thing or two about nuclear power, advocated an international law that would prohibit building nuclear reactors on the Earth's surface. He said that we could only approach complete safety if reactors were located underground. This is a proposal that should not be allowed to be swept aside by governments and private power companies.

We also need to continue to pursue non-nuclear and non-fossil, renewable alternatives as the eventual cornerstone of our energy policy. As wind, solar and other renewable energy prices come down, we must move away from both fossil fuels and nuclear.

7. **Commit to nuclear transparency.** National governments and the atomic science and construction engineering communities must finally come clean about the hazards inherent in a nuclearized world and be brutally honest in their statements and releases about the safety of local facilities (reactors, waste disposal sites and weapons storage sites) and of radiation exposure. Seventy years of dissembling, denying and denigrating the dangers and of cover-up must stop.

All of the member nations of the nuclear club are complicit in this with the two Cold War superpowers being the most culpable. Until Three Mile Island and Chernobyl, peaceful atomic energy was promoted as a panacea, the apogee of safety, environmental sensitivity and reliability. The public in both countries bought into this

Pollyannaish propaganda to such an extent that communities often welcomed with enthusiasm word that a nuclear power plant was going to be constructed in their neighborhood. News of power plant glitches was suppressed. Our government still downplays the dangers of nuclear waste seeping into our fields and waterways from abandoned sites like Hanford.

It took two decades for word about the Soviet nuclear accident at *Chelyabinsk* in the Urals to reach the west (to this day neither Russia nor the CIA, which knew about the disaster from U-2 overflights, has revealed its cause), and 32 years for the Soviet Union to grudgingly admit that a deadly nuclear accident occurred at its primary nuclear weapons test site (116 above-ground and 340 underground explosions) at *Semipalatinsk*, Kazakhstan on September 29, 1957. A chemical explosion scattered highly radioactive fission products and waste into the atmosphere that eventually fell to the ground over three provinces. The radioactivity released, said the Russians a generation later, was a massive two million Curies. There is, however, reason to believe that the actual amount was ten times what was admitted by the Russians. One Curie can fry a human. Not only was the soil contaminated, rendering the huge farm population in the affected area destitute; people were also irradiated by contaminated food and drinking water and by objects in their homes, including their own clothing. Mass evacuations ensued, but these were too late for many victims.

The Russians have a consistent history of pretending that nuclear power is safe and that there have been minimal adverse health impacts from 75 years of uranium mining, testing, radiation leaks and accidents that they have for the most part effectively concealed. After Semipalatinsk, the Kremlin directed that all information about increases in leukemia deaths be wiped from official records.

Nuclear transparency demands much more than just being truthful about the bad stuff. State regulators almost always approve power industry demands for subsidies when their predicted costs exceed the consumer and business rates that have been previously approved. This is often done *sub rosa* and the only notice consumers receive are cryptic fine-print announcements on their utility bills. This too must stop. The paying public has the right to know the true cost of nuclear power.

The NRC has always operated under a guiding principle of "an acceptable level of radiological risk to the public." Moving forward, that too is unacceptable. While risk is inherent in every human endeavor, some risks are so great that they need to be scrutinized every which way from Adam before the cause of the risk is allowed to proceed. That has not been the case with NRC certifications of new reactors. There have to be many additional safety redundancies incorporated into reactor licensing applications before builders are allowed to proceed. In addition, existing reactors must be retrofitted with the same level of safety redundancies.

It is a sad commentary on the bumbling steps toward safety and security that the NRC does not even have anyone on its staff with the title, "Risk Manager," let alone a whole department or section devoted to risk management.

8. **Boost education**. We must undo the downgrading and, in some instances, the complete disappearance of history education from our K-12 schools and from university core curriculum requirements. Studying the Cold War and its lessons is essential to our future. At the same time, the public needs to learn that nuclear energy is a reasonably safe form of energy for the interim (see above) and that orders of magnitude more people have been killed and had their health adversely affected by hundreds of years of fossil fuel extraction and use than by nuclear reactor radiation releases. Mining coal is the most dangerous occupation in the world. More than 15,000 miners worldwide are killed every year, and this is an undercount because nations do not want to reveal the real numbers. Several hundred thousand miners suffer injuries and illnesses each year that threaten their life expectancy and quality of life.

Public confidence in nuclear power dropped to zero after Three Mile Island. Chernobyl only underscored public fears and hysteria generated by activists who knew very little about the pros and cons of this energy option. In the 25 years after Chernobyl, nuclear gained a modicum of acceptance due to concerns about the devastating effect of fossil fuels on climate change. Then along came the Fukushima accident and public anxiety about nuclear energy escalated once again.

Little has been done to restore public confidence in nuclear energy in the last 40 years. The public has no idea that reactor safeguards and design upgrades have, by themselves, made nuclear reactors, power plants and energy much safer than they were before Three Mile Island. The public also did not understand that the lunacy that prompted the Soviet Union to design, build and operate unsafe RBMK reactors and then man them with poorly-trained operators is far removed from U.S. safety protocols. Our citizens are also uninformed about the differences between Japan's high-risk geography and geology that made a Fukushima accident virtually inevitable and the revised U.S. policy of situating our power plants in much more stable locations (only one nuclear power plant remains operational in earthquake-prone California, for example).

Finally, our politicians and influencers need to develop and educate the public about a grand strategy to transition from fossil fuels to renewables that includes a transitional role for nuclear energy.

The bottom line: we need to do what is necessary to make certain that we are not all extinguished by the *critical mess* we have created and that we can apply the lessons of Cold War I to prevail in Cold War II.

As I was putting the finishing touches on this book, two things happened that heightened, if possible, the concerns expressed in these pages about both a resumption of the Cold War and the inability of world leaders to realize or care about the devastation that nuclear weapons can unleash:

1. *Russia grudgingly released information about an August 8, 2019 accident in which seven senior nuclear scientists died when an advanced "Skyfall" cruise missile powered by a nuclear reactor exploded on launch and spread radiation throughout the region. The accident happened near the port of Severodvinsk where Russian nuclear submarines are serviced.*

The insanity of using a reactor to fire a missile demonstrates that Cold War II is hurtling toward the same lunacy so prevalent during the first go-round. Professor Angela Stent, director of the Georgetown University Center for Eurasian Russian and Eastern European Studies and an expert on nuclear non-proliferation, calls the new Russian cruise missile a "flying Chernobyl."

Initially, the Russian government lied about the accident, claiming that there was no radiation release. Moscow was forced to change its story when increased radiation levels were measured outside Russia. Radiation levels in the Severodvinsk region skyrocketed to 16-20 times the normal background level.

Last year, when President Putin proudly announced the existence of this new super weapon, he said the new missile will have unlimited range because of its nuclear-fueled engine, calling it "invincible."

It is clear that, despite the passage of a generation since Chernobyl, Russia has learned nothing about either nuclear safety, transparency or the risks to world peace that should have been core Cold War lessons.

While what the Russians are up to is horrific enough, President Trump's reaction only served to intensify the horror: "We have similar, though more advanced, technology."

The Russian cruise missile and the Trump administration's reaction makes it unlikely that either side will want to extend the 2010 New START nuclear arms reduction treaty when it expires in 2021.

2. *In late August 2019, Axios reported that "'President Trump has suggested multiple times to senior Homeland Security and national security officials that they explore using nuclear bombs to stop hurricanes from hitting the United States,' according to sources who have heard the president's private remarks and been briefed on a National Security Council memorandum that recorded those comments."*

The Axios report goes into detail about Trump's exact words during these sessions. The stunning ignorance and abysmal judgment expressed by the leader of the free world is mind-boggling. Fortunately for humanity and Americans specifically, this dangerous and ridiculous notion never eventuated in a formal policy process.

That both atomic and atmospheric scientists universally agree that this idea cannot possibly work—hurricanes generate energy equivalents of 10-megaton nuclear bombs without benefit of being nuked, and thus would be undeterred—is beside the point. Detonating a nuclear weapon inside the eye of a hurricane would not only kill all of the sea life below for hundreds of miles; it would also turn part of the Atlantic Ocean into a dead zone while carrying toxic fallout directly into the United States. It should also be noted that pursuing this insane idea would be banned under the Peaceful Nuclear Explosions Treaty between the U.S. and the former Soviet Union.

God help us.

Richard Hermann
December, 2019

Appendix A
Chilling with the Coldest Warriors

I am not afraid of an Army of lions led by a sheep; I am afraid of sheep led by a lion.
–Alexander the Great

It is hard to lead a cavalry charge if you think you look funny on a horse.
–Adlai Stephenson

The story of my personal Cold War encounters would not be complete without some cameos about some of the more interesting cold warriors I encountered along the way who were charged with defending the "American Way of Life" during those turbulent and uncertain times. It was a colorful era. I'll put my cold warriors—cranks included—up against anyone when it comes to a collection of fascinating folks.

For the most part, I've just used initials or nicknames to describe these warriors.

Boot Camp

"The General"

S was a doomed soul who had no business being anywhere near the U.S. Army or basic training. His company colleagues accorded him the *nom de guerre* of "The General," a commentary on his being anything but.

His entire physical presence, affect and demeanor shouted "victim." He was a seriously compromised individual in every sense—physically, mentally and emotionally—and the kind of person men in a group situation zero in on and pick at like vultures on roadkill. Think *Lord of the Flies*.

S was drafted into the Army despite enough health issues to have made him the poster child for the highly prized Selective Service designation "4-F." The term was conferred on someone indicating that he was "not acceptable for service in the Armed Forces" due to medical, dental, or other reasons. It originated in the Civil War, where it disqualified potential recruits who did not have four front teeth with which to tear open gunpowder packages.

S had a speech impediment, a fused spine, an inability to run more than a few steps before collapsing, seriously decayed teeth, the acme of acne, a tremor, an ineradicable rank odor, a perspiration problem that would have made him the prime catch by Frank Herbert's "Fremen" (*Dune* cultists will understand) and, to top it off, was a little slow on the uptake. He was a chain smoker, ornery as all get-out, and invited abuse at every occasion. Overlaying all of his problems was that he was also Jewish. He stood about 5'6" but weighed only about 105 lbs. He was so sickly that, on marches to distant places like the rifle range, I carried his backpack while someone else toted his rifle.

To make matters worse, S simply could not remain silent when verbally assaulted. This was the case not only when his attackers were other soldiers, but also when the abuse spewed out of the mouths of the cadre. This did not sit well with the drill sergeants, so they retaliated against him at every opportunity. When the company received a 24-hour pass to travel to Philadelphia, S stayed behind on KP.

When he collapsed at the beginning of a double-time run (double-time is about as fast as a sprint by a snail on steroids), he was immediately set upon by his own platoon mates. I offered to his platoon sergeant (nickname "Catfish") to take him into my platoon. Catfish denied my request on the grounds that "one Jew is enough in any platoon."

When I was in the midst of the involuntary Soldier of the Cycle competition, the First Sergeant insisted that I go on sick call one morning to see if the medical staff could divest me of the U.R.I. I (and everyone else) had been afflicted with for most of basic training. They wanted me as healthy as possible for the rest of the competition, a 180-degree turnabout from their customary negative attitude about sick call. S asked to go with me and this time the drill sergeants did not say no. However, this perennial victim still was harassed, this time by the physician who, after scrutinizing S, told him he should donate his body to a medical school. He then added that if he ever saw him on sick call again, he would recommend that the Army immediately ship him to Vietnam. I could not see what S did or said to deserve that.

The last evening of boot camp, S came to say goodbye. He was wrapped in two soaking blankets by his erstwhile comrades who had dumped him into a hot shower. When he warned them that he intended to report them to the Army Inspector General, they wrapped him in the blankets and this time dumped him into a cold shower.

S was recycled at the end of boot camp. When I returned to Fort Dix to await my flight to Germany, I heard that he had died of a heart attack during his second basic training go-round.

Cyclops

Cyclops, whom we met in Chapter 10, was to slow learning what a sloth that does *Tai Chi* every morning is to slow movement. He could not grasp what the Army tried to teach him no matter how hard he tried. I found that out because I spent many evenings after hours reviewing the day's lessons with him. Nothing helped.

He also came loaded down with fears and phobias. In 5th grade, he told me, his gym teacher forced him to climb a rope. He got halfway to the top and could not descend. The fire department had to be called. Cyclops was also afraid of water, so much so that the thought of showering evoked a level of terror most people associate with snakes and public speaking.

Like S, Cyclops suffered more than a battalion's share of verbal and physical abuse from both fellow trainees and drill sergeants. No matter that, in contrast to S, he never talked back. He also was denied a pass to Philadelphia and had to remain behind on KP while the rest of the company cavorted in the City of Brotherly (and assorted other varieties of) Love. This was especially agonizing for Cyclops because he was from South Jersey, just across the Delaware River from Philly, and had a girlfriend there. I offered to let him have my pass and substitute for him on KP, but when Sgt. A-M found out, it was a no go accompanied by profuse bi-lingual profanity.

Fort Leonard Wood

Sergeant 'Spoon

Foxtrot Company's two NCOs were a pair of gentle giants, Sergeants 'Spoon and D. Both treated us more like humans than what we were accustomed to at Fort Dix. They seemed to understand that intimidation did not work as well with "seasoned" trainees as it did with "newbies." They were the models of what drill sergeants should be.

Sgt. 'Spoon spewed a series of military maxims during our formations, a few of which imprinted as life-long lasting memories. Before we went out to the Big Piney Swamp for a week of what was called "RVN" (for Republic of Vietnam) training, he warned us about the assortment of poisonous snakes—Copperheads, Cottonmouths—that populated the area:

The Big Piney River of the Missouri Ozarks
(www.rollanet.org)

"Beware of the snake, men . . . because the snake
will definitely bite you."

That's a hard one to forget. 'Spoon had a way of getting his point across.

The other "Spoonism" that stuck with me had to do with the blank rounds that our M-16s were supplied with when we had to run around doing rifle and "cover me, bravo" drills and, again, in preparation for our week on the Big Piney:

"Attention, all you men!
Note what I have in my hand—a paper bag.
Note that in my other hand I have a rifle
loaded with blank rounds.
Note what I do with the rifle . . ."

. . . whereupon 'Spoon fired it directly at the paper bag, and continued:

"Note what the blank round does to the paper bag."
The blank put a nasty hole, edges badly singed, in
the side of the paper bag.
"Think what the blank round can do to your face!"

I never forgot what the blank round can do to a face.

L.L.

L.L. was an African-American soldier "straight outta Compton" (in his case straight out of South Central Los Angeles). He came armed with an obsession for fires, starting them to be more precise.

Every night we had to take turns standing what was called "fire watch." In other words, someone had to be awake at all times while everyone else was sleeping in case our tinder box of a World War II wooden barracks caught on fire. Once it was discovered that L.L. was an aspiring arsonist, he was excused from fire watch. Moreover, it became vital for whoever served on fire watch to keep a close eye on L.L. in case he could no longer bear a night without a conflagration.

L.L. was so fascinated with flames that, when we were practicing firing bazookas, he positioned himself directly behind one of those big, unwieldy weapons so that he could "experience" the heat from the fire that emerged from the back of the bazooka when it live-fired. One time he experienced it a little too intensely and had to make a trip to the post infirmary in order to get his singed face treated.

When he returned to the company, he was undeterred. We often caught him staring wide-eyed at his Bic lighter flame. Somehow we graduated from AIT unsinged.

ADM

Scuttlebutt had it that ADM soldiers were selected on the basis of the Army's version of an IQ test given to all new troops shortly after they enlist (or, in my case, got drafted). I always suspected that this was not a consistent selection process because there were some real bozos in my ADM platoon. The admin guy who gave out the special weapons storage site phone number to my caller from the Soviet Union for one; "Tuna" James who always took the bait and never learned from experience; Hogan Littlefield who kept a detailed count and quality analysis of his bowel movements—you get the drift. Nevertheless, there were also a bunch of smart guys who impressed. And a good number of them qualified as

268' wide by 53' deep SADM Crater
(U.S. Army – Public Domain)

"characters." I suppose that was logical given the Catch 22 absurdity of our mission and the consummate creative means of diverting and distracting from the harsh reality of perhaps having to launch World War III, which if it involved us and our "special" weapons, was likely to be a war of total annihilation.

LDF

LDF was the second sharpest knife in the ADM drawer or any other drawer for that matter. He was a creative genius and got in a great deal of trouble as a result. He claimed he was an honor graduate of "Webster Handy College," which if you thought about it was a reference to a dictionary. He built a giant loom in his barracks room and taught himself to spin and weave like an early seventeenth century cottage industrialist. When ordered to paint our rooms in preparation for an inspection, he asked our platoon leaders if they had a color preference. When they said they didn't, he painted the entire room—walls, floors and ceiling—glossy black, then secured high-gloss, luminescent white paint that he used to create a planetarium. When the inspector opened LDF's door and stepped into the room, he emitted a primal scream because he thought he was falling through deep space. LDF went unpunished because he had been told that the paint color was up to him. For his riskiest endeavor, he purchased a general officer's dress blue uniform and shoulder stars, commandeered a staff car and driver, and took a trip to Munich.

The capstone of his military career was when we were asked to submit designs for an ADM unit patch. LDF's design (as you can tell from his antics, he had an artistic streak) won going away. It consisted of a mushroom cloud looming over a small building with the words "This We'll Defend" arcing around the cloud's perimeter. You had to look very closely to see that the building was our post snack bar.

Scrawny Body

Scrawny came to ADM directly from the hollows of West Virginia coal country. One of the gentlest and most generous people you would ever want to meet, his quiet demeanor hid quite a talent. He played a mean guitar and accompanied himself on the harmonica à la Bob Dylan (he and I wrote a song together). He was country-music obsessed and snuck off from work many afternoons to go up to his room and tune into the *1505 from Nashville* on Armed Forces Radio. He took leave and went home, got married, and brought a 15-year old bride back to Germany. He claimed that he lost his virginity at age eleven to a set of late-teen twins.

SB was a member of my ADM Team Two and, despite being several years younger than me, took me under his wing as soon as I arrived. A week into my tour of duty, he bought me a bicycle that served me ably for half-a-year until I was able to purchase a car (see below).

Spidey

PP (a.k.a., "Spiderman") served as our platoon's supply sergeant. He was tall, wiry and laconic with a wry sense of humor that could always be counted on for creative contrarianism. He was also quietly willing to test the ethical boundaries of virtually any kind of behavior, undergirding his leaps of faith beyond the strictures of conventional morality with arguably sound justifications.

For example, while he took his job as supply sergeant very seriously, especially where M-16 rifles, .45 caliber pistols and ammunition were involved, he had a decidedly different attitude when it came to more mundane items like Army-issue clothing and non-lethal equipment. When I was about to leave Germany and fly back home, he made sure that I had two new field jackets and liners, plus a pair of spanking new combat boots to ship back to the world. Sadly, my illicit Army clothing and boot stash was stolen somewhere between Bremerhaven, the German port of departure for servicemen's personal effects and household goods, and Bayonne, New Jersey, the arrival point.

Spidey was also into other in-demand products. The Turkish *gastarbeiter* (1 million strong guest-workers) imported by the German *Wirtschaftswunder* (economic miracle) then in full swing to do the jobs that Germans no longer would, brought with them a literal ocean of hashish and opium far superior in quality to the low-rent cannabis available on post. Hatchick, the Turkish towel boy at the Warner Kaserne gymnasium who was also the local purveyor of this top-of-the-line drug array, found a willing, high-volume customer in Spiderman. Spidey himself did not use. Instead, he periodically shipped his stash home to his brother via the Army Post Office (APO) system. The proceeds enabled him to launder them into a high-end Mercedes, a Harley, and some sophisticated sound equipment that he was then able to ship home as household goods, free of charge.

I lost contact with Spidey once I left the ADM platoon. He resurfaced again several years later when one of the broadcast networks did an in-depth news piece on conditions in Mexican prisons where American drug dealers were incarcerated. One of the interviewees was Spidey who was doing time for transporting drugs over the Southern border into the U.S. via burro. Apparently, he had been doing this for several years and had amassed a considerable fortune. Despite violating a host of U.S. laws, he was extradited to Mexico.

Hostileman

The smartest person I ever met did not graduate from high school. We bonded immediately upon his arrival at the ADM platoon and his placement on Team Two. He came accompanied by a young wife and they lived in an apartment in nearby *Litzendorf*, a village with stucco houses and *hausfrauen* (homemakers) who came out every evening and swept the streets and sidewalks in front of their houses. I spent a lot of time in their apartment, a welcome home away from my barracks home.

I urged Hostileman (the nickname conferred by me, derived from the suddenness with which he could fly off the handle and do serious damage—example below) to get his high school diploma via the General Education Development (GED) test. He did, acing the exam despite never studying a minute for it.

Hostile's ability to sprint up the learning curve manifested itself in how rapidly he absorbed all of the quirks, nuances and local idiosyncrasies of our unit. Within weeks, he could perform our routine functions better and more efficiently than any of us.

Unfortunately, his nickname suited him perfectly. His temper was legendary. The worst display of Hostile going ballistic occurred when another soldier engaged in some light flirting with H-man's wife at one of our parties, only to find himself dragged outside the bar and in danger of having his lips torn off before we were able to pull Hostile off him.

We maintained our friendship after the Army. I even flew out to Chicago at his and his wife's behest in a futile attempt to save their marriage. By then, their family had expanded with the arrival of a lovely little girl.

Following the divorce, I heard from Hostile two more times:

- First, when he was arrested in Illinois for allegedly driving the getaway car after a bank robbery. He claimed that he bought his way out of jail by bribing the judge, the prosecutor and his own attorney, who had a conspiracy going where they conspired to shake down defendants. This being Illinois, Hostileman's story was plausible.
- Second, a few years later when I received a middle-of-the-night phone call from the local jail in Hilo, Hawaii. He had been arrested, this time for, shall we say, a rather creative criminal enterprise. He had received a contract from the University of

Hawaii to attempt to grow an indigenous tomato. Hawaii imported all of its tomatoes and the shipping costs made them very expensive. The university gave Hostile a substantial amount of acreage on the Big Island on which to conduct his experiments. He decided that it would be highly profitable to devote some of this acreage to growing other, higher-value plants, namely *cannabis*. When the local constabulary discovered this, he was arrested.

There was little I could do for him from 6,000 miles away. He was eventually indicted, convicted and served significant jail time. Then we lost touch.

The Owl

"The Owl" was a member of our platoon whose nickname came not only from his owlish visage, affect and quiet, patient personality, but also from the fact that he could rotate his head around his neck at least 270 degrees. If ever a nickname fit, this one did. I've included him here not only for himself, but as a representative of a phenomenon I frequently ran across—a soldier who married a local German girl and brought her back to "the world." I personally knew of three soldiers who fell into a "honey trap" where the bride was mainly interested in getting to America.

The Owl fell in love (or something) with a German woman at least five years his senior. She had four children by four different men, comprising a rainbow family within which each child was a different ethnicity, color or national origin. She also was alleged to have had a questionable history if some of the old-timers in the platoon were to be believed. They were convinced that they had encountered her on many occasions hanging out in some of the more dubious bars that catered to American soldiers who were seeking fee-based companionship.

Nevertheless, The Owl was hooked and a wedding date was set. Unfortunately, The Owl was slated to depart the reception early in order to report to a NATO conventional demolitions school several hours south of Bamberg.

The wedding went off without a hitch and the invitees repaired to a local restaurant overlooking the Regnitz River just out of town. The reception quickly turned into a raucous celebration during which far too much alcohol as well as a variety of banned substances were consumed. Almost everyone was roaring drunk, the bride and groom included. The bride disappeared for about thirty minutes, presumably because she was going to be sick. It turned out later that, instead of seeking out the *Damen* toilette, she found her way into a coat closet with the best man in tow.

Despite a blood-alcohol level that topped the charts, The Owl left the reception at the appointed time and drove to his school. After he in-processed, he ate dinner and went to bed. He woke up with a monumental hangover in the middle of the night and decided to phone his bride. A sleep-besotted male voice answered the phone.

When he returned to our platoon following two weeks at the demolition school, several of us tried to suggest to him that his wife likely married him merely to get her ticket punched to the U.S. To no avail. When he left us and went back to the world, he took her and the children with him. Word got back to us six months later that she had abandoned the children and run off with an Air Force guy.

This sad story was hardly unique. It was to repeat itself several times over before I arrived at my discharge date.

Shape Charge

The Staff Sergeant in charge of Team Two was a kindly, 30-something, low-key, mild-mannered fellow saddled with a shrew of a German wife and two unruly kids, as well as Team Two's five creative disrupters. He was intimidated by us and thus cut us more slack than we deserved. Punishment for our frequent misbehaving and questioning of orders was non-existent.

We nicknamed him "Shape Charge" because, physically, he resembled the Army explosive of the same name. His physique looked something like an overweight bowling pin.

Shape Charge took our mission very seriously. He was committed to making certain that Team Two would function at peak performance in the event anything as insane as a war reserve mission came our way. The Army was fortunate to have someone so dedicated.

Preparing a Shape Charge for Detonation
(Buckley Air Force Base – Public Domain)

The tension arose because the rest of us thought that only a lunatic could possibly have devised such a loony-tune set of missions that were surely destined to fail. Consequently, our attitude was a compromise between "why bother?" and "what-me-worry?"

Becoming an Army lifer, however, might have been the best thing that ever happened to Shape Charge. Before enlisting, his career was likely ordained to dead-end at the Midwestern city airport where he parked airplanes. You know, the fellow with the flashlight standing in front of a taxi-ing plane as it arrives seeking the proper gate.

Coiny

Coiny (not his real name, of course) was the permanent party gopher assigned to our nuclear weapons site headquarters shack. Most of his day was spent answering the phone, which rarely rang, and running errands for the Sergeant-in-Charge, a martinet of mythic proportions.

To stave off the stultifying boredom of his job, Coiny developed a unique skill that I have never encountered anywhere else: if you dropped a coin onto a desktop, he could tell you its value (penny, nickel, dime, quarter or half-dollar). Moreover, he was "bi-coinial," i.e., he was able to perform the same feat for German currency as well.

During my brief stints in the headquarters shack, I passed the time by testing his prowess and taking bets with soldiers on temporary assignments at the site. All my meager funds were, of course, bet on Coiny. He never let me down.

Cable

Cable's tale of woe was one for the ages.

He was drafted into the U.S. Marine Corps in 1967. As the Vietnam War heated up and Lyndon Johnson was rapidly running out of men interested in signing up for the privilege of being blown up by a landmine in a rice paddy in Southeast Asia, it became necessary to draft individuals not only into the Army, but also the Marine Corps. When I reported to the Armed Forces Entrance Station for induction into the Army in December 1968, the first thing the sergeant there had us do was count off by sevens. He then directed each number seven to step forward and said: "Congratulations, gentlemen. You are about to become United States Marines." I was a number six, a much-relieved number six. No matter how dismal and oppressive Fort Dix was going to be, I suspected that Parris Island was probably orders-of-magnitude worse.

Cable did his three years in the Marines, including a year in Vietnam, and was honorably discharged at the end of his obligation . . . only to find himself drafted into the Army a few months later! Despite his protestations, he went through basic training for the second time, then was shipped off to Germany and Headquarters Company, 82nd Engineer Battalion, the unit to which my ADM platoon was attached.

Cable argued his prior service at every stop along the way. No matter. He was in the Army and that was that. He once asked me if this could arguably be deemed double jeopardy. Sadly, since this had nothing to do with criminality, it could not.

So, Cable decided on a scorched-earth strategy. If jumping through all of the available legal hoops was futile, he resorted to doing what he could to sabotage basic, day-to-day missions in hopes of getting thrown out of the Army. Nothing worked:

Initially, Cable tried cantankerousness. He simply refused to do anything he was ordered to do. This included things like showing up for morning formation, keeping his attire clean and his boots spit-shined, or maintaining a regulation length haircut. The powers-that-be kept punishing him with KP and all-night guard duty. But he was undeterred.

When none of that worked, he escalated to DefCon 4 and began pouring water on his bed during the night so that it appeared that he was a bed wetter. Even that did not get him any consideration for a possible discharge, or even a referral for a psychiatric examination. He then took to hysterical shouting and feigning Tourette-like tics. Again, he got nowhere.

While all this was going on, Cable kept getting reassigned from one job to another until he finally was tasked with being the barracks Permanent Latrine Orderly, a thankless and disgusting task customarily reserved for the soldier who could not do anything else or who was the biggest fuck-up in the company. Cable purposely botched that assignment, leaving the toilets in the barracks even more disgusting than normal. The complaints from the rest of us were so vigorous that the company commander, at his wit's end, pulled him off that duty and made him . . . a cook, the last way-station in which every Army neer-do-well ultimately wound up.

I could have predicted that putting Cable in the mess hall was not going to end well. Within a week, the already abysmal quality of our meals declined to the point of inedibility. They were already terrible regardless of any Cable sabotage because our Mess Sergeant, it was later revealed, was selling our company food allotment to the Germans while stealing C-rations, mixing them up, and feeding us a concoction that he labeled different names of marginally acceptable fare. The way his scam came to light revealed his essential stupidity: he and his wife began to openly drive their new, expensive Mercedes vehicles and park them outside the mess hall. The cars had to have cost them multiple years' salary absent the illegal supplement earned from diverting our victuals to the locals. Once he and his *frau* were apprehended—and Cable's sabotage operation finally earned him a court martial—our meals improved significantly and it was no longer necessary to spend our meager remuneration at the base snack bar.

Cable's denouement came at the court martial. Until his mess hall defiance, Cable's tactics designed to force a discharge had never gone beyond minor offenses that did not rise to the level of violations of the *Uniform Code of Military Justice*. He never went AWOL, for example, which would have put him squarely in the cross-hairs of the legal authorities. Unfortunately, he eventually did something egregious enough: a fellow cook saw him climb up on the counter and lean over a vat of soup, unzipping his fly. To this day, I cringe when I visualize this scenario. If an army marches on its stomach, we were in deep trouble.

I can't remember the charges that were brought against him at his Summary Court Martial, the lowest level military judicial proceeding, geared toward minor offenses. I went to see his JAG lawyer before the trial and told him about Cable's being drafted after being honorably discharged from the Marines. He already knew the tale from his client, but was skeptical about its veracity. However, he was a young attorney on the make and agreed to contact the Marine Corps and determine whether this could possibly be true. When he entered a duplicate original of Cable's discharge documents and a letter from the Marine Corps Commandant into evidence, Cable was out of the Army and on his way home by the end of the week—after 18 months of involuntary servitude for which pain and suffering he was never compensated. FTA (look it up).

"Ridgely"

The closer I got to my separation date ("the shorter I got" in Armyspeak), the more I kept getting rousted out of my ADM platoon for "special" assignments. One of these was to escort a soldier, who was separating and going home, to Rhein-Main Air Force Base for his flight to The World. I was instructed to make sure he got on the plane and was buckled into his seat. I was to wait until I could visually confirm that the plane had taken off before returning the 130 miles to Bamberg. I was assigned a driver and a jeep.

The reason for all of this hoopla was that Private First Class "Ridgely" did not want to go home to the U.S. He much preferred to remain in Germany where he had acquired a girlfriend.

When I received this assignment, Ridgely was more than a month beyond his separation date. His initial trip to Rhein-Main was never completed. Instead, he made for his girlfriend's apartment, which was where the military police found him several weeks after he went AWOL. They escorted him back to base and confined him under guard to a third-floor room in our battalion headquarters building.

A day later, he jumped out a window and fell directly into a roll of triple-concertina barbed wire, cutting himself in multiple places. That escape attempt having failed, he was first treated for his wounds at the base infirmary, then confined under closer guard in the MP barracks, where there were iron bars on the windows.

This is the point where I entered the mix.

We started our journey to Rhein-Main with Ridgely in the back of the jeep while I rode shotgun. That was my first mistake. We accessed the *Autobahn* and headed west. About halfway there, Ridgely said he needed to make a "pit stop" to relieve himself, so we pulled off the highway and entered the small city of *Wertheim-am-Main*, stopping at a *gasthaus*. Over Ridgely's objections, I accompanied him into the men's room. I had my back turned (mistake no. 2) to give him some privacy. When it seemed that he was taking an inordinately long time to do his business, I turned around and saw him squeezing out of a window. I grabbed his legs and pulled him back in. He begged me to let him go, but I would have none of it, although I sympathized with his desire to stay in Germany with his girlfriend.

That's when I made my third and last mistake. I foolishly kept the same seating arrangement in the jeep when we resumed our journey. On our way out of town, we stopped at a stop light for about 30 seconds before getting back on the autobahn. As we moved along at 70 miles an hour, I turned back to say something to Ridgely and was confronted with an empty seat. Ridgely was gone, having likely escaped when we stopped at the light.

I ordered my driver to get off the autobahn at the next exit, then get back on and return to Wertheim. We did, but Ridgely was nowhere to be found.

I dreaded returning to base and having to report to my battalion commander that I had lost my "prisoner." When I did, Col. Allaire was forgiving, thanks to the strong bond I had formed with him when he and I were teammates on the U.S. Army Europe volleyball team the previous year, competing in Germany and France (we lost in the quarter-finals to the Italian Army team whose 6'8" spikers stomped all over us).

However, Ridgely was quickly rounded up once again at his girlfriend's apartment. This time, he was escorted to his airplane under armed guard.

I assume that, had something similar occurred in the Red Army, the Soviet Ridgely would have been shot along with me.

Rosi

"Rosinante" was my amazing P.O.V. ("privately-owned vehicle," Armyspeak for a car). When I was promoted to grade E-5 six months after arriving in Germany, I was eligible to buy a car. I went with a friend who was knowledgeable about things mechanical to Opel Kowalski in downtown Bamberg, where I shelled out $100 for a much-used, previously-owned-by-multitudes, 1952 "Racing" Taunus, a Ford product manufactured in Germany. Rosi was a small, 26-horsepower (not a typo), Carolina-blue machine that looked like an oversized aspirin tin on wheels. It had a five-on-the-column manual shift and an odometer that surely had to have turned over countless times. It got more than 60 miles to the gallon on the Autobahn and, with Army-subsidized gas at 18 cents a gallon, cost next to nothing to drive.

Rosinante's Sister
(Wikimedia - MartinHansV - Public Domain)

Rosi needed a great deal of work to enable me to pass the German inspection, a three-step ordeal designed to make life difficult for the occupation army. One of those steps was a rigorous vehicle inspection. It was my good fortune to have a friend in the motor pool who took care of everything. Once she was road-worthy, Rosi and I had many adventures together.

She had a top speed of only 65 miles an hour going downhill and about 50 on level ground. Going uphill was another matter altogether. We suffered several major breakdowns traversing Alpine mountain passes, the worst being on the 7,000-foot St. Gotthard Pass that connects German-speaking Switzerland with the *Ticino*, where the primary language is Italian. Road construction restricted travel to only one lane as we approached the top of the pass. Rosi collapsed about a quarter-mile from the top, blocking summer holiday traffic in both directions. Panicked, I ran up to the top of the pass—no mean feat at that altitude—and got on the emergency telephone at the side of the road. Whoever answered did so in Italian, so I was linguistically challenged. Neither "my car broke down near the summit," "*Mein Wagen geht nicht,*" nor "*ma voiture ne partira pas*" evoked a response. Desperation, however, can work wonders even when it is language at issue rather than lifting a vehicle off someone pinned underneath. "*Mia automobile non fonctionnare*" did the trick, despite my complete ignorance of Italian.

A half-hour later, a Ticino mechanic appeared at the summit, walked back to Rosi with me, and got her going. I'm sure that, given Rosi's distinctive, green U.S. Army license plates, we did little to advance the American cause in Europe.

Rosi was also victimized by real Italians when we made two of our periodic crossings of the Brenner Pass from Austria into Italy. That era was marked by two phenomena that were not conducive to easy border crossings into Italy: (1) the suspicion rampant throughout Europe that U.S. servicemen were all drug dealers; and (2) the Irredentists.

During one foray over the pass, Rosi and I were stopped by the Italian border guards who sent a drug-sniffing dog into the car. When they found nothing, they demanded that I open the trunk. The latch was stuck, so they disengaged Rosi's back seat and sent the dog into the trunk from inside. They put the seat back after finding no contraband, but it could never be fastened down again. This proved problematic when I met my parents later that summer and my poor mother had to bounce around in the back, hitting her head on the interior roof whenever I went over the slightest bump (Rosi's shocks were shocking).

The Irredentists had nothing to do with pulling or cleaning teeth. They were, in fact, a terrorist group that never got over Austria's loss of the South Tyrol after World War I. Fifty-plus years later, their grandchildren were still at it, blowing up the occasional border post, taking down signs in Italian and replacing them with German ones, protesting the "Italianization" of this former German-speaking territory and causing general, low-level annoyance to the Italian authorities.

Towns like Bolzano and Trento were filled with *Carabinieri* and *Alpini*, elite Italian troops, looking to tamp down the irritating Irredentists. My indirect encounter with this fringe group occurred when I had to wait hours at the Brenner Pass frontier to go back-and-forth between Italy and Austria due to some mini-mayhem perpetrated by them.

Rosi was patient and overall a wonderful companion during my travels around Europe. When I left, I sold her to another soldier for $125. I teared up when we parted for the last time.

The Pentagon

This is a supplement to my Defense Department character portraits earlier in this book.

J.B.

J.B. was the best of the three Assistant Secretaries of Defense for Reserve Affairs for whom I worked directly. In fact, he is the best boss I ever had, a touch superior to Col. Allaire, my terrific battalion commander in Germany. He was dynamic, visionary and overflowing with positive energy and enthusiasm. He was a master of measured discipline, carried out in private, and knew when to give a pat on the head for a job well done.

He constantly picked my brains for legal and policy advice and actually listened to what I had to say, no matter how stupid or ignorant I must have sometimes come across. Working for a person like J.B. was a joy.

Unfortunately, J.B. had one classic flaw, very similar to the one that sank my first Pentagon boss. He made every issue into Armageddon. He simply did not know when to hold 'em and when to fold 'em. As a result, he was taken less and less seriously by the Secretary and Deputy Secretary as time went by until he was no longer invited to meetings and was consigned to irrelevancy.

J.B. also never appeared to grasp the clout of the National Guard and Reserve brass. Either that or he simply did not care how powerful they were. General officers in both components had a great deal of influence over their organizations and also cultivated very close ties with members of Congress who served on the Senate and House Armed Services Committees. When J.B., their putative boss, tried to rein them in or engineer their behavior, he got slapped down very quickly.

The final straw that ended his office tenure happened when he decided to swoop into a local reserve unit by helicopter one Saturday in order to see what, in fact, the "weekend warriors" were doing. As he suspected, they were playing cards, sitting around watching television, eating and drinking, having a grand old time earning their pay and retirement points on the taxpayer's dime.

J.B. was not amused and let not only the local unit officers and NCOs, but the entire Guard and Reserve chain of command, know it. When he came into work the next Monday morning, he was summoned to the Secretary's mammoth office and relieved of his position. The complaint from the victimized reserve unit had made it all the way to the congressional committee chairs' ears at light speed.

"Peppermint Patty"

Peppermint Patty was a Marine Lieutenant Colonel assigned to the Employer Support Committee. I first encountered her during my initial stint at DoD when she occupied the office across the hall from mine. I was struck by what a good-looking woman she was, easily the best-looking Marine I had even seen. I discovered much later that, during one of her assignments, she had modeled Marine uniform designs.

Patty, however, lugged around considerable baggage. She was a religious fanatic. One day when my boss arrived at the office, she dragged him into her office and closed the door. Both he and I thought that, in her own way, she was making a play for him. Instead, she pushed him down on his knees, assumed the same position, and announced: "Let us pray!" My naval commander boss was not exactly a fervent believer and so was at a total loss for words. This disappointed Patty, so she let him up and hustled him out.

One day she announced that she would be appearing on Pat Robertson's *700 Club* television show and urged us all to tune in. What we saw and heard was jaw-dropping. Patty described, very matter-of-fact, how she wandered into her bedroom one day and watched her husband shoot himself. Robertson asked if that traumatized her. She replied that she was able to quickly recover from the shock thanks to God's intervention in her life. Then the two of them bent their heads in vehement prayer.

With the Marine Corps Marathon imminent, Patty announced that she intended to run the race. I suggested to her that it was important to train diligently for it, 26 miles and 385 yards being something of a major challenge for someone who had never run before. With a month to go, she still had not put in any training time, her standard response whenever the subject came up being: "God will provide."

God did in fact provide, but only for the first four miles of the marathon. When Patty collapsed, an ambulance took over for the deity.

Task Force II

Lazy Boy

The second U.S. government task force I headed (see Chapter 15) was comprised of about 30 attorneys who were detailed to it from around the government, plus two outside legal research contracting firms that, between them, provided us with an additional 40 attorneys and paralegals.

The detailees were, for the most part, diligent and committed attorneys; the outside contractor staffs not so much, hence they got paid for doing nothing much. I ran into problems with only one of the detailees, a Navy JAG lieutenant commander who often showed up late for work if he showed up at all, groused about his assignments and whose quality of work was mediocre.

After putting up with him for a couple of months, I had had enough and returned him to the Navy accompanied by a scathing letter criticizing his work ethic and commitment to the project. The Navy, perhaps embarrassed, quickly reassigned him to a dead-end job. His reaction was to file a lawsuit in the U.S. District Court naming the Navy, the Executive Office of the President and the Department of Justice (the latter two being joint sponsors of the task force) as defendants.

During the discovery phase of the lawsuit, I was deposed by his attorneys who asked me if I believed that the Navy was justified in transferring him out of his regular job. My response was that if it were up to me, I would have drummed him out of the service. Following my appearance at the deposition, I worried about what I had said. Fortunately, his suit was dismissed by the court several months later.

General Counsel

A major research component of the task force consisted of interviews, many conducted by me, of many of the "higher-ups" of virtually every government department and agency. These were, with few exceptions, very informative and extremely helpful to our project. However, the most glaring exception was one I did with the general counsel of a major cabinet department.

She was a prime example of the "Peter Principle" in operation. The Peter Principle was devised by Laurence J. Peter, who observed that people in a corporate hierarchy tend to rise to their "level of incompetence." That was absolutely the case with this individual. She had no idea of the organizational structure of her department, its enabling legislation, the laws it administered and enforced or much of anything else. Never again did I assume that just because someone was appointed to a top government job by the President, it necessarily followed that they were qualified or had a remote notion of what they were doing. And, mind you, this pre-dated Donald Trump's cabinet appointments.

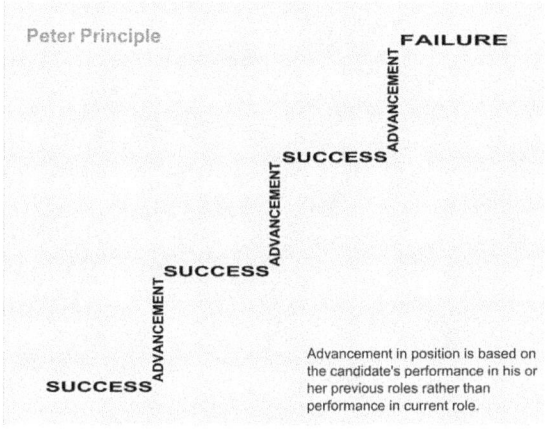

(Wikimedia - Nevit Dilmen – Public Domain)

Appendix B

Measuring Radiation Exposure

This gets confusing. There are four different but interrelated units for measuring exposure to radiation: radioactivity, exposure, absorbed dose, and dose equivalent (mnemonic: R-E-A-D).

1. **Radioactivity** is the amount of ionizing radiation released by a material. This could be alpha or beta particles, gamma rays, x-rays or neutrons and is expressed in terms of how many atoms in the material decay in a given time period (akin to "half-life"). Radioactivity is measured by the Curie (Ci) and Becquerel (Bq).
2. **Exposure** describes the amount of radiation traveling through the air. The measurement units for exposure are the Roentgen (R) and Coulomb/kilogram (C/kg). Geiger counters and dosimeters are the most common devices for measuring exposure.
3. **Absorbed dose** is the amount of radiation absorbed by an object or person. The measurement units for absorbed dose are the Radiation Absorbed Dose (rad) and Gray (Gy).
4. **Dose equivalent** combines the amount of radiation absorbed and its medical effects. For beta and gamma radiation, the dose equivalent is the same as the absorbed dose. In contrast, the dose equivalent is larger than the absorbed dose

for alpha and neutron radiation because these types of radiation are more damaging to the human body. Units for dose equivalent are the "Roentgen Equivalent Man" (rem) and Sievert (Sv). Biological dose equivalents are commonly measured in 1/1000th of a rem (known as a millirem or mrem).

It simplifies the calculation to know that 1 Roentgen (exposure) = 1 rad (absorbed dose) = 1 rem (dose equivalent). The alleged maximum safe level for the average human is 5 R/rad/rem per year. A person would receive a dose equivalent of 1 mrem from any one of the following activities:

- 3 days of living in Atlanta
- 2 days of living in Denver
- 1 year of watching television (on average)
- 1 year of wearing a watch with a luminous dial
- 1 coast-to-coast airline flight
- 1 year living next door to a normally operating nuclear power plant

Acknowledgements

Like all my books, this one traveled from incoherence to coherence through the close editing work of my wife, Anne Marie Canali Hermann, who always gives of herself wholly to my literary projects and does not allow our relationship to get in the way of incisive advice and withering criticism. I would not have it any other way. She makes every book not only readable, but much better.

Others I would like to acknowledge:

David Manuel, my professional editor at Persimmon Alley Press, who did for *Close Encounters with the Cold War* what he has so ably done for my other two books he has tackled: questioned my assertions and cleaned up my language, often knowing what I intend to say better than I do.

Ed Shomaker, one of my dearest friends, with whom I exchanged hundreds of hours of back-and-forth discussion and debate about the great issues of our time, focusing intensively on whether our world was going to survive in the face of the tens of thousands of weapons of mass destruction we have unleashed on the planet. Ed was one of the few people who was in a position to do something about that and he performed his mission with great integrity, enthusiasm and passion for world peace and the health of humanity while he himself went through one of the worst health misfortunes a person can suffer. Why is it that the truly great often die young?

Ed's wife, Michele Shomaker, who tirelessly combed through her home archives to uncover materials that did much to inform my research and writing and contribute to some of the insights in this book. She is a wonderful friend and supporter. Her marriage to Ed is a testimony to her husband's unerringly good judgment.

Russian-English interpreter *par excellence* for numerous heads of state (I can say this because I have seen videos of her prowess), Irene Firsow, who graciously gave of her time to provide context and observations about the Soviet, Russian and Ukrainian nuclear programs and their interactions with their U.S. counterparts.

Finally, the staff of the Cold War Museum in Vint Hill Farm, Virginia, whose drill-down into the sweat-and-stress-inducing details of the Cold War provided some flesh and plenty of nuance to my project.

Bibliography

Books

Anderson, Christopher. *Jack and Jackie: Portrait of an American Marriage.* New York: William Morrow and Company, Inc., 1996.

Arbatov, Georgi. *The System: An Insider's Life in Soviet Politics.* New York: Random House, Inc, 1992.

Bird, Kai and Martin J. Sherwin. *American Prometheus: The Triumph and Tragedy of J. Robert Oppenheimer.* New York: Vintage Books, 2006.

Boyer, Paul. *By the Bomb's Early Light.* New York: Pantheon Books, 1985.

Brown, Kate. *Plutopia: Nuclear Families, Atomic Cities, and the Great Soviet and American Plutonium Disasters.* Oxford, UK: Oxford University Press, 2013.

Burns, James MacGregor. *The Crosswinds of Freedom: From Roosevelt to Reagan—America in the Last Half-Century.* New York: Vintage Books, 1990.

Cockburn, Andrew. *The Threat: Inside the Soviet Military Machine.* New York: Vintage Books, 1984.

Fall, Bernard B. *Hell in a Very Small Place: The Siege of Dien Bien Phu.* Cambridge, MA: Da Capo Press, 1985.

Fasick, Erik V. *Three Mile Island.* Charleston, SC: Arcadia Publishing, 2018.

Fitzgerald, Frances. *Fire in the Lake: The Vietnamese and the Americans in Vietnam.* Boston: Little, Brown and Company, 1972.

Gable, Walter and Carolyn Zogg. *The Seneca Army Depot: Fighting Wars from the New York Home Front.* Charleston, SC: History Press, 2012.

Gerstell, Richard. *How to Survive an Atomic Bomb.* Washington, DC: Combat Forces Press, 1950.

Gray, Mike and Ira Rosen. *The Warning: Accident at Three Mile Island.* New York: W.W. Norton & Co., 1982.

Haŝek, Jaroslav. *The Good Soldier Schweik.* Translated by Paul Selver. New York: Dead Authors Society, 2018.

Hermann, Richard L. *Basic Training Journal.* Fort Dix, New Jersey, 1969.

_____. *Encounters: Ten Appointments with History.* Arlington, VA: Persimmon Alley Press, 2017.

_____. *Mother's Century: A Survivor, Her People and Her Times.* Arlington, VA: Persimmon Alley Press, 2018.

_____ and Linda P. Sutherland, eds. *The Federal Legal Directory: A Guide to the Legal Offices and Key Legal Personnel of the U.S. Government.* Phoenix: Oryx Press, 1990.

Hersey, John. *Hiroshima.* London: Penguin Books, 1946.

Hersh, Seymour M. *The Dark Side of Camelot.* Boston: Little, Brown and Company, 1997.

Hodge, Nathan and Sharon Weinberger. *A Nuclear Family Vacation: Travels in the World of Atomic Weaponry.* London: Bloomsbury, 2008.

Johnson, Paul. *Modern Times: The World from the Twenties to the Nineties.* New York: HarperCollins Publishers, 1991.

Jungk, Robert. *Brighter Than a Thousand Suns.* London: Penguin Special, 1960.

Karnow, Stanley. *Vietnam: A History.* New York: The Viking Press,, 1983.

Klose, Kevin. *Russia and the Russians: Inside the Closed Society.* New York & London: W.W. Norton & Company, 1984.

Kennedy, Robert F. *Thirteen Days: A Memoir of the Cuban Missile Crisis.* New York: W.W. Norton & Co., Inc., 1968.

Khrushchev, Nikita S. *Khrushchev Remembers.* Strobe Talbott, Translator and Editor. New York: Little, Brown, 1970.

Lertzman, Richard A. and William J. Birnes. *Dr. Feelgood: The Story of the Doctor Who Influenced History By Treating and Drugging Prominent Figures Including President Kennedy, Marilyn Monroe, and Elvis Presley*. New York: Skyhorse Publishing, 2013.

McEnaney, Laura. *Civil Defense Begins at Home: Militarization Meets Everyday Life in the Fifties*. Princeton: Princeton University Press, 2000.

McNamara, Robert S. with Brian VanDeMark. *In Retrospect: The Tragedy and Lessons of Vietnam*. New York: Times Books, a division of Random House, 1995.

Moore, Kate. *Radium Girls: The Dark Story of America's Shining Women*. Naperville, IL: Sourcebooks, Inc., 2017.

Monk, Ray. *Robert Oppenheimer: A Life Inside the Center*. New York: Doubleday, 2012.

Oakes, Guy. *The Imaginary War*. New York: Oxford University Press, 1994.

Pearce, Fred. *Fallout: Disasters, Lies, and the Legacy of the Nuclear Age*. Boston: Beacon Press, 2018.

Pringle, Peter and James Spigelman. *The Nuclear Barons*. New York: Holt, Rinehart & Winston, 1981.

Reed, Thomas C. *At the Abyss: An Insider's History of the Cold War*. New York: Ballantine Books, 2004.

Reeves, Richard. *President Kennedy: Profile of Power*. New York: Simon & Schuster, 1993.

Reeves, Thomas C. *A Question of Character: A Life of John F. Kennedy*. Rocklin, CA: Prima Publishing, 1992.

_____. *Twentieth Century America: A Brief History*. New York & Oxford, UK: Oxford University Press, 2000.

Shute, Nevil. *On the Beach*. London: Book Club, 1957.

Suvorov, Viktor. *Inside the Soviet Army*. New York: Berkley Publishing Group, 1984.

Toffler, Alvin and Heidi Toffler. *War and Anti-War: Survival at the Dawn of the 21st Century*. Boston: Little, Brown and Company, 1993.

Tyler May, Elaine. *Homeward Bound! American Families in the Cold War Era.* New York: Basic Books, 1988.

United States Army Training Center Infantry. *Combat Training.* Fort Dix, New Jersey, 1969.

Walker, J. Samuel. *Three Mile Island: A Nuclear Crisis in Historical Perspective.* Berkeley and Los Angeles: University of California Press, 2004.

Wise, David. *Nightmover: How Aldrich Ames Sold the CIA to the KGB for $4.6 Million.* New York: HarperCollins Publishers, 1996.

_____. *Spy: The Inside Story of How the FBI's Robert Hanssen Betrayed America.* New York: Random House Trade Paperbacks, 2003.

Articles and Essays

Anspaugh, Lynn R., Robert J. Catlin and Marvin Goldman. "The Global Impact of the Chernobyl Reactor Accident." *Science*, Vol 242, pp. 1513-1518 (December 16, 1988).

Buford, Talia. "New Jersey's $300 Million Nuclear Power Bailout Is Facing a Court Challenge. Does It Have a Chance?" *Pro Publica* (May 16, 2019). https://www.propublica.org/article/new-jerseys-300-million-nuclear-power-bailout-is-facing-a-court-challenge-does-it-have-a-chance. Accessed May 19, 2019.

Cardis, Elizabeth. "Estimated Long Term Health Effects of the Chernobyl Accident." *International Agency for Research on Cancer* (April 1996).

Eberhardt, Ann Angel. "Plane Spotting in the 1950s." *Small Town Memories* (January 28, 2015). https://bissella9.wordpress.com/2015/01/28/plane-spotting-in-the-1950s/. Accessed June 12, 2019.

Freeland, Chrystia. "Waiting for the Next Chernobyl." *Financial Times* (April 21, 1993).

Ganzel, Bill. "Duck & Cover." *Living History Farm.org* (2007). https://livinghistoryfarm.org/farminginthe50s/life_04.html. Accessed April 17, 2019.

Gonzalves, Kelly. "America's era of duck-and-cover: Images from a bygone era of nuclear panic." *The Week*. https://theweek.com/captured/722874/americas-era-duckandcover. Accessed April 16, 2019.

Greenberg, David. "Fallout Can Be Fun: How the Cold War civil-defense programs became farce." *Slate* (February 20, 2003). https://slate.com/news-and-politics/2003/02/the-ridiculous-history-of-cold-war-civil-defense.html. Accessed June 4, 2019.

Jaczko, Gregory. "Atomic power can't save us." *Washington Post*, section B-1 (May 19, 2019).

Lavine, Matthew. "The Two Faces of Radium in Early American Nuclear Culture." *39 Bulletin of the History of Chemistry 1* (2014).

"Less Than Half Spotter Time Filled In Week." *The Gettysburg Times* (April 5, 1954). Accessed June 12, 2019.

Medvedev, Grigoriy. "Chernobyl Notebook." *Novy Mir*, pp. 3-108 (June 1989).

Olsen, Jack. "The Doves and Gongs of Tokyo. *Sports Illustrated* (Oct. 19, 1964). https://www.si.com/vault/1964/10/19/606284/the-doves-and-gongs-of-tokyo. Accessed June 7, 2019.

Orci, Taylor. "How We Realized Putting Radium in Everything Was Not the Answer." *The Atlantic* (Mar 7, 2013).

Editors. "First nationwide civil defense drill held." *History.com*. https://www.history.com/this-day-in-history/first-nationwide-civil-defense-drill-held. Accessed April 1, 2019.

Pruitt, Sarah. "How 'Duck-and-Cover' Drills Channeled America's Cold War Anxiety." *History.com*. www.History.com (March 26, 2019). Accessed May 15, 2019.

"Summary of the Conference Results." *International Conference: One Decade after Chernobyl* (1996).

Strauss, Mark. "Nuking Hurricanes: The Surprising History of a Really Bad Idea." *National Geographic* (November 30, 2016).

Swan, Jonathan and Margaret Talev. "Scoop: Trump suggested nuking hurricanes to stop them from hitting U.S." *Axios* (August 25, 2019). https://www.axios.com/trump-nuclear-bombs-hurricanes-97231f38-2394-4120-a3fa-8c9cf0e3f51c.html. Accessed August 27, 2019.

Sweet, William. "Chernobyl: What Really Happened." *Technology Review*, Vol. 92, No. 5, pp. 42-52 (July 1989).

"The Legasov Memoirs. Special to the Readers of Nucleonics Week and Inside N.R.C." *Nucleonics Week* (November 3, 1988) and *Inside N.R.C.* (November 7, 1988).

The Uranium Institute. *Chernobyl Accident*. Information Paper #7 (March 2001).

_____. *Annex J*: "Exposures and Effects of the Chernobyl Accident." *Sources and Effects of Ionizing Radiation*. United Nations Scientific Committee on the Effects of Atomic Radiation (2000).

"Under the dome: Fears Pacific Nuclear 'Coffin' is Leaking." *MSN News* (May 26, 2019). http://www.msn.com/en-us/news/world/under-the-dome-fears-pacific-nuclear-coffin-is-leaking/. Accessed May 26, 2019.

Interviews

CIA Counterintelligence Officer (Anonymous), "Aldrich Ames," May 25, 2019.

D. Michele Côté Shomaker. "Edward Shomaker, Three Mile Island and Chernobyl," May 21-22, 2019.

Edward Shomaker. "A Series of Interviews with Edward Shomaker," 1984-1992.

Irene Firsow. "Chernobyl et al.," June 13, 2019.

U.S. Government Documents

Eisenhower, Dwight D. "Memorandum to Federal Agencies Directing Participation in a National Civil Defense Exercise," *Public Papers of the President*. Washington, DC: US Government Printing Office, 1961, 519.

Federal Civil Defense Administration, *A Family Action: Home Protection Exercises* (Washington, D.C.: U.S. Government Printing Office, 1955), 32.

———————————————, *Civil Defense Glossary*. Washington, DC: U.S. Government Printing Office, 1956.

———————————————, *This is Civil Defense: The Official U.S. Government Booklet*. Washington, DC: U.S. Government Printing Office, 1951.

Goldenberg, Stan and Hugh Willoughby. *Why don't we try to destroy tropical cyclones by nuking them?* National Oceanic and Atmospheric Administration, June 1, 2018.

Government Accountability Office. *Resuming Licensing of the Yucca Mountain Repository Would Require Rebuilding Capacity at DOE and NRC, Among Other Key Steps*. GAO-17-340 (April 26, 2017).

Hamilton, Terry. *A Visual Description of the Concrete Exterior of the Cactus Crater Containment Structure*. Lawrence Livermore National Laboratory. Report No. LLNL-TR-648143 (October 2013). https://marshallislands.llnl.gov/ccc/Hamilton_LLNL-TR-648143_final.pdf. Accessed May 26, 2019.

Neufield, Jacob. *The Development of Ballistic Missiles in the United States Air Force 1945-1960*. Office of Air Force History, United States Air Force (1990).

Nikipelov, B.V., G.N. Romanov, L.A. Buldakov, N.S. Babaev, Yu. B. Kholina and E.I. Mikerin. *Accident in the Southern Urals on 29 September 1957*. International Atomic Energy Agency (1989).

Office of Civil and Defense Mobilization. *The Family Fallout Shelter* (1959).

Rowland, R.E. *Radium in Humans: A Review of U.S. Studies.* Argonne National Laboratory, Environmental Research Division, September 1994.

Truman, Harry S. "Statement by the President Upon Signing the Federal Civil Defense Act of 1950," *Public Papers of the President*. Washington, D.C.: US Government Printing Office, 1965, 26-27.

U.S. Nuclear Regulatory Commission. *Backgrounder on Plutonium* (March 2017). https://www.nrc.gov/reading-rm/doc-collections/fact-sheets/plutonium.html. Accessed on April 16, 2019.

_____. *Implications of the Accident at Chernobyl for Safety Regulation of Commercial Nuclear Power Plants in the United States, Vols. 1 & 2* (April 1989).

_____. *Management Directive 10.72: Awards and Recognition* (July 2011). https://www.nrc.gov/docs/ML1009/ML100920199.pdf. Accessed on May 25, 2019.

_____. *Measuring Radiation* (October 2017). https://www.nrc.gov/about-nrc/radiation/health-effects/measuring-radiation.html. Accessed on May 27, 2019.

Speeches

Abagyan, A.A. "Status and Trends in Nuclear Power Development in the USSR." International Atomic Energy Agency and Argonne National Laboratory International Workshop on "Safety of Nuclear Installations of the Next Generation and Beyond." Chicago (August 29, 1989).

Ahearne, John F. "The Case for More Stringent Safety Criteria." International Atomic Energy Agency and Argonne National Laboratory International Workshop on "Safety of Nuclear Installations of the Next Generation and Beyond." Chicago (August 29, 1989).

Rogers, Kenneth. "A Process for Resolving Safety and Institutional Issues of advanced Reactors: Replacing Public Concern with Confidence." International Atomic Energy Agency and Argonne National Laboratory International Workshop on "Safety of Nuclear Installations of the Next Generation and Beyond." Chicago (August 29, 1989).

Rosen, Morris. "Safety Objectives for an Unsure Public." International Atomic Energy Agency and Argonne National Laboratory International Workshop on "Safety of Nuclear Installations of the Next Generation and Beyond." Chicago (August 29, 1989).

Films and Television

Briffa, Edward. "Suicide Mission to Chernobyl." *NOVA* (PBS) (Nov 22, 1991).

Curtis, Bill and Molly Bedell. "Back to Chernobyl." *NOVA* (PBS) (March 1989).

Shomaker, Edward. "Chernobyl: Inside the Reactor" (1992).

Donaldson, Roger. *Thirteen Days*. New Line Cinema, 2000.

Knebel, Fletcher. *Seven Days in May*. John Frankenheimer, Director (1964).

Joffé, Roland. *Fat Man and Little Boy*. Paramount Pictures, 1989.

Kubrick, Stanley. *Dr. Strangelove: How I Learned to Stop Worrying and Learn to Love the Bomb*. Hawk Films, 1964.

Lumet, Sidney. *Fail Safe*. Columbia Pictures, 1964.

Sturges, John. *Ice Station Zebra*. MGM, 1968.

About the Author

Richard Hermann is the author of thirteen books. He is a former law professor and entrepreneur, and the founder and president of Federal Reports, Inc., a legal information and consulting firm that was sold in 2007. He writes a weekly op-ed column (The Rant) and a legal blog (legalcareerview.com). He has degrees from Yale University, the New School University, Cornell Law School and the U.S. Army Judge Advocate General's School. *Close Encounters with the Cold War* is his third book in the history genre. He lives with his wife, Anne, and extraordinary dog, Barkley, in Arlington, Virginia and Canandaigua, New York.

www.ingramcontent.com/pod-product-compliance
Lightning Source LLC
Chambersburg PA
CBHW060338170426
43202CB00014B/2814